The Gospel of the Working Class

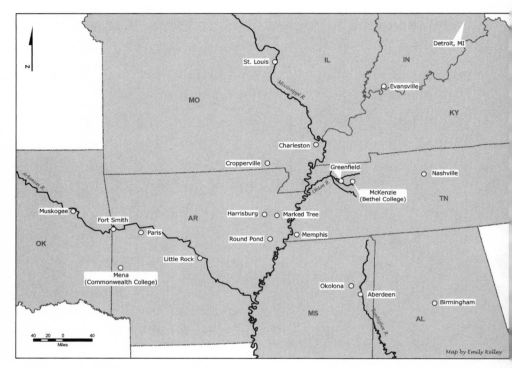

Map: The World of Whitfield and Williams

The Gospel of the Working Class

Labor's Southern Prophets in New Deal America

ERIK S. GELLMAN

JAROD ROLL

University of Illinois Press

URBANA, CHICAGO, AND SPRINGFIELD

© 2011 by the Board of Trustees
of the University of Illinois
All rights reserved
Manufactured in the United States of America
1 2 3 4 5 C P 5 4 3 2 1
∞ This book is printed on acid-free paper.

Library of Congress Cataloging-in-Publication Data
Gellman, Erik S.
The gospel of the working class : labor's Southern prophets
in New Deal America / Erik S. Gellman, Jarod Roll.
p.   cm.
Includes bibliographical references and index.
1. Labor—Religious aspects—Southern States—
Christianity—History—20th century.
2. United States—Social conditions—1933–1945.
3. Williams, Claude Clossey, 1895–1979.
4. Whitfield, Owen H., 1892–
I. Roll, Jarod. II. Title.
HD6338.2.U5S62   2011
331.6'3960730750922—dc22   2011008561
ISBN 978-0-252-03630-9 (cloth)
ISBN 978-0-252-07840-8 (paper)

Contents

Illustrations

Acknowledgments

This book has been a collaborative effort. During graduate school at Northwestern University, our research interests and conversations with our shared advisor and mentor, Nancy MacLean, encouraged us as scholars to challenge the political, geographic, and racial boundaries that so often rule the writing of modern American history. In these conversations, we swapped information (usually over beers) about an obscure sharecropper named Owen Whitfield. Whitfield's life traversed our respective 1930s urban and rural research projects and seemed to call out for a different framework to understand the New Deal and World War II era of protest politics. After coauthoring an article about Whitfield for the *Journal of Southern History*, we decided that the story we wanted to tell was not complete, and could not be complete without also telling the story of Claude Williams, as well as the stories of Zella Whitfield, Joyce Williams, and a diverse "cast of characters" who sought to foment a religious-based labor and civil rights movement in New Deal America. Throughout this process, colleagues have consistently wanted to know how we collaborated on a book together, especially when one author lives in Chicago and the other in Brighton, England. While piecing together this history has been both difficult and fascinating, our work together (truly a fifty-fifty collaboration) and not infrequent debates over interpretation have provided profound motivations and rewards, and we can only encourage more historians to do likewise.

We could not have completed this book without our own cast of indispensable characters. Martha Biondi and Liz McCabe read a draft of the book proposal and provided us with important early criticism and encouragement. Ken Fones-Wolf and Elizabeth Fones-Wolf have supported and challenged our work, in their own scholarship on religion and by sharing the podium with us at several conferences. Meeting in the Bronx with Mark Naison, who knew

Claude Williams well, inspired us to continue and broaden our research. Ron Cohen provided us with key research leads about the musicians in this story, as well as lots of wry humor. Ron encouraged us to write to Pete Seeger, who generously shared stories about both Claude Williams and Owen Whitfield. Abram Van Engen, Robert Cook, and Simon Balto read the manuscript in full and suggested crucial changes, small and large. Emily Kelley provided a great map right when we needed it. We are especially thankful to Rhiannon Stephens, who not only read the entire manuscript (several times) but also provided key ideas that freed the narrative structure of the book. An anonymous reader, Michael Honey, and Nan Woodruff all read the manuscript for the press and provided detailed and cogent reports that shaped the final version.

Piecing together a history that stretches from Detroit to Mississippi was made possible by the generous assistance of archivists, librarians, and other scholars who all went beyond the call of duty to help us. Multiple visits and conversations with William LeFevre at the Reuther Library at Wayne State University helped us frame the project and discover new manuscripts and images, and Mary Wallace assisted us with the reproduction of those images. Both Erika Gottfried and Gail Malmgreen at the Tamiment Library in New York helped us track down oral histories and navigate the Cedric Belfrage papers. At the University of Tennessee, Jennifer Beals and especially Justin Eastwood unearthed new archival materials, including applied religion charts that were assumed lost, as well as important reel-to-reel recordings by Claude Williams that they generously converted to compact disc. Simon Balto provided timely research at the Wisconsin State Historical Society, Matt Nichter gave us several important research leads, while Barry Kernfield and James Quigel directed a precision strike into the voluminous United Mine Workers collection at Pennsylvania State University. Nancy Calhoun at the Muskogee Public Library, Jill Whitfill at Bethel College, and Susan Knight Gore at the Cumberland Presbyterian Church archives provided specific and essential pieces of information. At short notice Jeff Place threw open the doors of the Ralph Rinzler Folklife Archives and Collections at the Smithsonian. And although their employer does not come off too well in this book, the archivists in the Records Management Division of the Federal Bureau of Investigation were always helpful and generous.

Last, we offer our sincere thanks to the Williams and Whitfield families. We are especially grateful to Shirley Whitfield Farmer, who has been so generous helping us to understand her parents' lives and careers and is doing great work to keep their legacies living. We also offer gratitude to two fighters of fascism in our own families, Jack Gellman and Dorothy Bardwell Roll. Their voices were part of the gospel chorus of the working class in New Deal America.

Abbreviations

AAA	Agricultural Adjustment Act
ACLU	American Civil Liberties Union
AFL	American Federation of Labor
CIO	Congress of Industrial Organizations
CP	Communist Party
CRS	Committee for the Rehabilitation of the Sharecroppers
FBI	Federal Bureau of Investigation
FERA	Federal Emergency Relief Administration
FSA	Farm Security Administration
HUAC	House Un-American Activities Committee
MAWC	Missouri Agricultural Workers' Council
NAACP	National Association for the Advancement of Colored People
NLRB	National Labor Relations Board
NNC	National Negro Congress
NRA	National Industrial Recovery Act
NRLF	National Religion and Labor Foundation
NWLB	National War Labor Board
OIBAPMW	Original Independent Benevolent Afro-Pacific Movement of the World
PIAR	People's Institute of Applied Religion
RA	Resettlement Administration
SCHW	Southern Conference for Human Welfare
SNYC	Southern Negro Youth Congress
SSCC	Southern States Cotton Council
STFU	Southern Tenant Farmers' Union

UAW	United Auto Workers
UCAPAWA	United Cannery, Agricultural, Packing and Allied Workers of America
UMW	United Mine Workers
UNIA	Universal Negro Improvement Association

Principal Characters

In order of appearance:

Owen Whitfield, born 1892 or 1894, Mississippi: farmer, preacher, theologian, union officer

Zella Glass Whitfield, born 1900, Mississippi: farmer, union activist

Wallace A. Battle, born 1873, Alabama: educator, college president

Claude Williams, born 1895, Tennessee: theologian, preacher, educator, union officer, candidate for the Senate

Joyce King Williams, born 1897, Missouri: preacher, educator, union activist

Alva Taylor, born 1871, Iowa: theologian, educator

Don West, born 1906, Georgia: farmer, poet, preacher, union activist, educator

Howard Kester, born 1904, Virginia: preacher, union activist, educator

David Fowler, born 1878, Wales: Spanish–American War veteran, politician, union officer

Lucien Koch, born 1907, Oregon: educator, college director

Ward Rodgers, born 1910, Texas: preacher, union activist, political candidate

Willard Uphaus, born 1890, Indiana: preacher, educator, director of the National Religion and Labor Foundation

Myles Horton, born 1905, Tennessee: educator, cofounder of Highlander Folk School

Norman Thomas, born 1884, Ohio: preacher, Socialist Party leader, presidential candidate

H. L. Mitchell, born 1906, Tennessee: farmer, union officer

J. R. Butler, born 1905, Arkansas: lumber sawyer, farmer, union officer

Zilphia Mae Johnson Horton, born 1910, Arkansas: educator, union activist, artist

Lee Hays, born 1914, Arkansas: union activist, musician, songwriter, cofounder of the Almanac Singers

Harry F. Ward, born 1873, England: theologian, educator

Winifred Chappell, born 1880, Iowa: theologian, educator, journalist

W. L. Blackstone, born 1885, Arkansas: preacher, union activist

Leon Turner, born 1907, Arkansas: farmer, union activist

E. B. McKinney, born 1872, Tennessee: farmer, preacher, union officer

John Handcox, born 1904, Arkansas: farmer, songwriter, union activist

Donald J. Henderson, born 1902, New York: economist, educator, union officer

Harry Koger, born 1893, Texas: farmer, union activist

Cedric Belfrage, born 1904, England: novelist, journalist

A. L. Campbell, born 1904, Arkansas: farmer, preacher, union activist

William DeBerry, born 1906, Tennessee: machinist, union activist

Henry D. Jones, born 1889, Wales: preacher, social activist, machinist

Gerald L. K. Smith, born 1898, Wisconsin: preacher, America First Party leader, presidential candidate

Charles Hill, born 1895, Michigan: preacher, union activist, political candidate

John Miles, born 1900, Georgia: preacher, union activist

Robert Hill, born 1906, Virginia: auto worker, preacher, union activist

The Gospel of the Working Class

Introduction
Brothers in the Fight for Freedom

In late 1934 Claude Williams, a white preacher in Paris, Arkansas, was asked by his neighbors to preside over the funeral of a ten-month-old baby. Williams, who was struggling to raise three small children with his wife, Joyce, agreed to perform the hardest task required of any preacher or of any father. But rather than quote a few words from scripture to calm the grieved souls in the pews, Williams said this tragic event was "not the will of God." Instead, he charged that the baby's unnecessary death from malnourishment was "an outright case of murder by our economic system."[1]

Although Williams had not yet met Owen Whitfield, an African American preacher who also hailed from the Southland, he might as well have been speaking about Whitfield's son, John Marshall, who had died of pneumonia just a few years before. Or, he could have been eulogizing the senseless death of John Marshall's brother, Excel Whitfield. Excel, whose name reflected his mother Zella's hopefulness for their family when he was born in 1923, died of malaria at the age of eleven during the height of the Great Depression. Owen Whitfield shared the sorrow song of Claude Williams. He often told his congregants a story about one day in the field when he heard the hungry cry of his daughter come from the house and got angry. "I done worked, behaved myself, kept Your precepts," he cried out to the Lord, "and those that haven't is getting along much better." And Whitfield heard God reply: "I bless you with enough product to fill many barns. Somebody's gettin' it. If you ain't, that's your fault, not Mine." Lesson learned: religion was not about waiting for blessings to occur; it was about crying out against injustice, and challenging people to make their world anew.[2]

What course should a righteous person take in an unjust society? Compromise with it, withdraw from it, or try to overturn it? This book is about two southerners who held a prophetic vision for a more democratic America. Although Owen Whitfield and Claude Williams embarked on their journeys from opposite sides of the Jim Crow color line, they came to an interpretation of Christianity that served as a compass to orient all aspects of their lives. That compass, carried through a variety of natural and manmade disasters in the 1920s and early 1930s, brought them together in the depths of the Great Depression. As their initial skepticism about one another faded—Williams previously feared even touching a black person, while Whitfield wanted only to get away from whites—they came to recognize each other as "brothers in the fight for freedom."[3] What constituted the shape of their common belief was a confidence in the power of meek men and women, black and white, to use their God-given talents to reject and then remove unholy restrictions in their lives. Their story challenges students of the history of the southern working class to take seriously the dynamic power and centrality of religious ideas in social and political movements, which then raises new questions about the assumptions scholars have made about race, respectability, politics, and even gender in the Depression and World War II era.[4]

The work of Whitfield and Williams among cotton pickers, coal miners, and factory hands propelled them to the forefront of national debates about work, race, and democracy in the 1930s and 1940s. Williams first made international news when a group of Arkansas thugs captured and beat him as retribution for encouraging the poorest southern workers to stand up for themselves. Whitfield became well known as the preacher who plotted a demonstration where 1,500 sharecroppers sat down in protest at the crossroads of two major highways in Missouri. Everywhere they went, whether plantation districts, mining camps, or urban working-class neighborhoods, North and South, the pair excited ordinary people and worried those in positions of power. In time their sustained work helped create a poor people's movement culture that carried their ideas further, whether via word of mouth, through the lyrics of artists such as Woody Guthrie and Pete Seeger, or from the pen of novelist Ralph Ellison. The mission of the two preachers to tap the roots of American democracy also vaulted them into high places. For Whitfield, this meant two trips inside the White House, once to debate the President of the United States, and later to confer with the First Lady, and for Williams, it led to a job as the "Labor Minister" of wartime Detroit, the very heart of the "Arsenal of Democracy."[5]

Both Whitfield and Williams attacked the inequalities that prevented Americans from experiencing the full promise of their religious belief. Their faith in God's assurance to the righteous, that Jesus had come so "that they might have life, and that they might have it more abundantly" (John 10:10), informed and compelled their attacks on economic injustice.[6] Historians of labor have traditionally seen religion, and especially religious discontent, as a manifestation of some more tangible set of class relationships.[7] For Whitfield and Williams, the certainties of their Christian belief, particularly their quest to realize the kingdom of God on earth, provided the moral conviction and courage necessary to confront the physical degradation of God's children in poverty, what they considered the most fundamental of southern and American evils.

Their struggle to unlock God's abundance for all led these two preachers to challenge racial divisions in the United States. Southern history, even American history generally, is too often told in white stories and black stories that seldom connect. Although both grew up in a culture defined by racial difference, the pair came to recognize that they, as sons of the southern soil, shared far more than what divided them through a process of reconciliation that began with common religious understanding.[8] Both came from faith traditions (for Williams the Cumberland Presbyterians and for Whitfield the black Baptists) that prized the autonomy of individual believers and congregations in their relationship with God. Both sought to enrich that relationship by pushing at the boundaries of their denominational homes and by steeping themselves in the theology of new breakaway groups, such as the Pentecostal and Holiness churches that attracted poor whites and blacks alike. Their mutual search for a more fulfilling personal relationship with God revealed that southern African Americans and whites shared many of the same hopes, fears, and joys whether in the church, their homes, or at work in the fields. Their careers, in part, tell the story of the recovery of a southern common ground strong enough to support a working-class social movement for greater democracy in Depression-era America.

Whitfield and Williams fashioned a radical version of the Christian gospel that challenged the authority and even the legitimacy of organized religion. Although both were believers and preachers first and union activists second, the pair came to understand that labor organizations often had more to offer as vehicles for God's justice than the denominational Christian church. Their quest to realize the kingdom of God on earth meant that they were willing to work with any ally that promised help, an openness that began with their decision to work with each other. The religious vision that Williams and Whitfield fashioned was an ecumenical one that combined strands of fundamentalism, liberalism, and Marxism in a potent mix catalyzed by the symbols, language, and folk traditions that already existed in American working-class communities. As a result, it often outstripped the capacity of even the most left-wing labor unions to promote what Williams and Whitfield considered true demo-cratic equality.[9] Despite great odds, both preachers remained faithful to the promises they read in the Bible, even though their fidelity often led them to reject earthly institutions, whether church, party, or union.

As theologians of experience and activists of necessity, Williams and Whit-field often fumbled in front of overwhelming earthly exercises of power. They fought a culture of working-class exploitation and racial degradation that was so habitual to their fellow Americans that it seemed as normal and unchangeable as waking up each morning. Their idealism in the face of this unyielding challenge often appeared as fanaticism. Whitfield and Williams sometimes behaved like the right-wing demagogues they preached against. Stubbornly adhering to the purity of their convictions amid the political sectarianism and petty squabbles of their allies, the pair at times acted by blind faith rather than pragmatic discretion. As a consequence, these two preachers often sacrificed short-term gains in exchange for long-term goals that were difficult to achieve. What they always returned to, however, was a vision of the world that empowered working-class people with an abiding faith in the Christian promise of making heaven on earth.

Why write a biography or, more to the point, why read a biography? This book, unlike others in the genre, does not probe the psychological makeup of Williams and Whitfield to explain what made them tick. Instead, the narrative of their lives, individually and together, illuminates an unstable world of social protest that entangles and blurs neat conventional historical categories: white, black, rural, urban, secular, religious, North, South. It is precisely the shifting contexts of the lives of Whitfield and Williams that challenge us to rethink the dominant narratives of American history in the 1930s and 1940s.[10] By looking at this world as they saw and experienced it, we can punch through the partitions erected by historians working in more thematic ways. The complicated lives and careers of these two men provide a clear picture of the messy history experienced by racially, culturally, and regionally diverse groups of American workers in the 1930s and 1940s.[11]

Claude Williams and Owen Whitfield were idealists, leaders, preachers, and visionaries, talented and flawed. Both born to impoverished rural families during the depression of the 1890s, they worked hard, got married, and started families. They had advantages along the way: Claude Williams attended col-lege for a time; Owen Whitfield graduated from high school when most black southerners did not. Despite the earnestness of their mission, both remained rooted in the ordinariness of life and possessed sharp senses of humor. They also worked with the unstinting support of women, their wives Zella Glass

Whitfield and Joyce King Williams, who shared Owen's and Claude's mission by taking to the frontlines themselves as activists and leaders and by caring for families while their husbands traveled and preached. These human traits, in love, in anger, and in humor, were also great forces that made other people listen to and follow Owen Whitfield and Claude Williams. What they achieved with these resources was nothing short of remarkable.

From humble origins, Whitfield and Williams drew on their shared experience of southern hardship to articulate ideas that cut to the heart of America's problems. The way their activism used the past to confront the present makes their story significant for historians of the United States in the twentieth century. If we define intellectual history broadly as the story of men and women thinking, acting, reformulating ideas, and acting again, the intellectual history of these two preachers illuminates a durable but neglected tradition of southern radical thought born in the nineteenth century. As children, Whitfield and Williams inherited the broken promises of Reconstruction, the defeat of Populism by corporate monopolies, the nation's sickening embrace of white supremacy and racial violence, and the disregard of the rural and the poor by a nation enthralled by wealth and modernity. They were both original and important thinkers, but their true impact derived from an uncanny ability to articulate the collective sense of dispossession and injustice shared by southern workers, white and black. While the Great Depression baffled Americans in the mainstream, the people who still toiled in cotton fields, who watched their children die from malaria, who dug coal from the earth—they knew that the nation's troubles stemmed from old sins once forgotten but now returned to demand penance. To use a traditional southern phrase, they understood that sins die hard, like snakes. These people made up the congregations that rallied to Williams and Whitfield, whether they lived in a cotton patch or had moved on to cities like Memphis or Detroit. The story of Whitfield and Williams, and the people they inspired, looks back, before 1900, and forward, beyond 1950 when a new generation called for civil rights in America, but, above all, it testifies to the decisiveness of the working-class struggle in the years of depression and war.

Both preachers fashioned their southern folk inheritance into an oppositional consciousness geared for action in the chaotic social, political, and cultural circumstances of an era defined by economic catastrophe and the worldwide spread of fascism. The following analysis of their lives, therefore, moves the lens of inquiry across geographic and institutional boundaries, and ranges widely across American history to show how these southern activists attempted to challenge the powerful determinism of their day in order to transform their world.

1. Southern Strivings

This story begins in Egypt, a tiny trading town in northeast Mississippi. There, in the heart of Dixie, Owen Whitfield often spent his summer nights in 1910. Sitting at a makeshift poker table in the back room of a pool hall, Whitfield, although not yet twenty years old, possessed a sharp mind, quick wit, and cockiness beyond his racial station. Like other African Americans in the South in the early twentieth century, he felt the influence of Jim Crow in nearly every aspect of his life.[1] What Whitfield, the son of sharecroppers, remembered most from these years was his parents' bid, through their labor, to achieve some independence from the white Mississippians who employed them. The Whitfields wanted their own farm. Yet even such seemingly modest aims provoked the rage of whites, who preferred to keep blacks desperate and dependent as growers of other people's cotton. For thousands of African Americans like Whitfield, this system of Jim Crow was like playing a hand of poker dealt from a stacked deck, but with even less chance of winning.[2]

Owen Whitfield had ambitions beyond a subservient existence. He was like a lot of country boys who came to towns like Egypt to drink corn liquor, smoke cheap cigars, and gamble for coins. There was a place in Jim Crow society for these excitements, so long as African Americans did not contest their lack of citizenship rights. Whitfield, however, grew restless with such rudimentary privileges. He was keen for the kind of autonomy that might create a bit of space for him to apply his talents, particularly his gift for powerful speech. The young Whitfield worked variously as a farmer, a gravedigger, a coal heaver, a lumber sawyer, and a tap dancer. His search both confirmed and tested the boundaries of Jim Crow. Despite the stacked deck, Owen Whitfield continued to gamble against the fate that white people prescribed, because to accept a losing hand was to accept day-to-day survival, bare and raw.

I

We do not know the year of Owen Whitfield's birth. The reason for this absence is as simple as it is evocative. The state of Mississippi did not care much about the births or deaths of African Americans. It issued no birth certificate for Owen Whitfield, nor did it add his name to any register of births. Relegated to second-class citizenship, at best, African Americans lived, worked, and died in 1890s Mississippi without official recognition of their humanity. Since he could not say for sure what year he was born, Whitfield and others guessed: his registration for the World War I draft cited 1892; the Federal Bureau of Investigation (FBI) later claimed 1894; his obituaries listed both.[3]

If the year slipped the family memory, the day of October 14 stuck.[4] Whitfield arrived on the Eagle Nest plantation near the town of Aberdeen in Monroe County in the middle of the cotton-picking season—a mixed blessing for his parents. His mother, Jane, must have been doubly relieved to have a healthy baby boy after carrying the child through a Mississippi summer. The addition was to be celebrated, for this new mouth to feed would in time provide additional field labor for their family. They named the boy Owen after his paternal grandfather, who was born enslaved in South Carolina in the early 1840s.[5] But his birth also complicated the immediate work of bringing in the year's crop, upon which hung the family's survival. Few sharecropping women could escape field labor, even when pregnant, especially at harvest time. To make matters worse, whether it was 1892 or 1894, the economic depression of the early 1890s deflated the price of cotton. The Whitfields needed to pick all of the cotton they could, as fast as they could, in order to get the best price possible. A pregnancy in these circumstances was dangerous. Given the lack of adequate medical care for sharecroppers, any complication during the birth threatened the lives of both mother and baby. At best, Jane Whitfield would have had only a few days to recover from the delivery before she had to hoist her cotton sack and go back into the fields.[6]

That Jane Whitfield's maiden name has been forgotten offers poignant testimony to the particular difficulties black women endured in the rural South. However much black families prized the Victorian ideal of the home as the woman's sphere, few could afford the privilege. The labor of black women was double; they had to work in the field to produce crops and work to fulfill their duties as wives and mothers. Such constant work took a terrible toll. By 1907 Owen's mother was dead.[7]

Thomas and Jane Whitfield had not always worked as sharecroppers; both had been born in the 1860s to freedpeople in Monroe County at the beginning of Reconstruction. After the Civil War, the federal government passed, and the states ratified, the Fourteenth and Fifteenth Amendments to the U.S. Constitution, which provided African Americans with civil rights, including voting rights for men. At the local level, blacks painstakingly secured these rights in practice through political mobilization. Between 1868 and 1874, African Americans in Monroe County elected freedpeople to as many as two-thirds of all county offices. One legacy of that representation was a proliferation of black schools for children like Owen Whitfield's parents.[8]

Yet, by the 1890s Mississippi had become one of the most pernicious places for African Americans. White Democrats across the South reclaimed political dominance in the 1870s through coercion, fraud, and terror. The violence of these attacks marked the earliest memories of the new, postslavery generation. The Ku Klux Klan, at the forefront of white resistance, burned twenty-six black schools in Monroe County in the first half of 1871 alone.[9] These violent acts increasingly limited opportunities for an independent economic and social existence for young African Americans like Whitfield's parents and portended bleaker conditions to come. The white counterrevolution culminated in Mississippi's 1890 state constitution, which established the legal framework for the disenfranchisement and segregation of African Americans and enshrined white supremacy as the governing rationale of the state. "Mississippi's constitutional convention of 1890," future Governor James K. Vardaman admitted in 1900, "was held for no other purpose than to eliminate the nigger from politics."[10]

With their dreams of political freedom crushed by state repression, sharecroppers like Thomas and Jane Whitfield, who had married in 1885, hoped to secure a modicum of economic independence as farmers. Many African Americans did not see a contradiction between their hopes for full freedom and a future life defined by living and working on the land, so long as they owned that land. Owen Whitfield was thus born into a family who worked hard on a plantation in order to escape it to a farm of their own.[11]

The hills of eastern Monroe County offered a decent opportunity for aspiring black farmers. Thousands of black Mississippians acquired small plots on the wooded, marginal soils in the state's eastern and central hill country. Although not rich, these farms afforded limited autonomy. Black owners could raise their own food, largely escape credit and debt, and avoid being supervised by whites. By 1900, 360 black families had acquired land in Monroe County. Owen Whitfield's family desired their own "little piece of land on Nigger Hill," he later recalled, which referenced the common name affixed to these isolated pockets of black settlement.[12]

The Whitfields aimed to raise the capital to make a land purchase by sharecropping on white-owned plantations in the fecund Black Prairie of western Monroe County. There, fifteen miles and a world away from the hills, sharecropping families contracted annually a plot of land, usually forty acres, and in return received housing and half of the crop from the owner. Croppers bought their provisions from local merchants—often on credit, since cash was scarce except at harvest time. They usually had to give their creditor a lien on the next year's harvest, which gave whites control over the planting, cultivation, marketing, and sale of the crop. Sharecropping was certainly never a lucrative arrangement, because bad crops or unscrupulous merchants or landlords could lead to deep debt. But if a family got lucky with the weather, with their health, and with an honest landlord, they could come out ahead when accounts were settled in the autumn. If they did that and supplemented these earnings by working for wages on other farms in the peak weeding and picking seasons, they could accumulate a little cash from year to year.[13]

As the depression of the 1890s waned, the Whitfields found new opportunities in Monroe County. The recent development of the Yazoo Delta in western Mississippi had attracted workers statewide, leaving many places with labor shortages. The Whitfields took advantage and earned supplemental wages in Aberdeen, the county's main town. Thomas Whitfield cut logs for fence posts, performed garden and yard work for white families, and, on weekends, sold fish that he had caught in the Tombigbee River. Jane Whitfield, meanwhile, washed and ironed white peoples' clothes. As with work in the fields, Owen Whitfield and his siblings regularly joined in these labors to support the family's effort to earn their way to independence.[14]

All the while the Whitfields conscientiously avoided doing anything that might discomfit their white employers. The 1890s was a decade of intense racial violence directed particularly at those blacks who defied Jim Crow, whether economically or socially. Between 1888 and 1904 more than 230 black Mississippians died at the hands of white lynch mobs, who routinely tortured their victims in spectacle-style killings.[15] Lynching had wide political support. "If it is necessary," Governor Vardaman declared in 1907, "every Negro in the state will be lynched; it will be done to maintain white supremacy."[16] Given this context, the Whitfields masked their anger at the daily humiliations of Jim Crow. If the "white man give you any of his shit," Thomas Whitfield told his sons, "you humors him." "Never act like you knows anything or got any sense," he told them, "and you'll come out intack."[17]

Yet, behind the veil of obedience, Whitfield's parents offered different explanations for their fundamental lack of physical security.[18] Owen's mother drew her understanding and endurance from Christian teaching that recognized the Devil in the injustices of white supremacy. As the "main pillars" of their churches, rural women like her also served as "spiritual mothers" for their families and communities. Although men dominated in the pulpits, they were a minority in the pews. Thomas, like other black men, was sure that the unfairness of Jim Crow society came down to simple human viciousness. While Jane prayed for divine protection, Thomas looked for ways to outsmart his white neighbors.[19]

Because of their deference and industriousness, the Whitfields gained a reputation among local whites for being "good working niggers." "Nobody," Owen Whitfield recalled, "could say nothing against old Tom and his boys." Such understandings, however degrading, not only kept black families relatively safe but could also help facilitate buying and, more importantly, keeping property. The Whitfields used part of their earnings to purchase a mule and a wagon, important acquisitions that represented a substantial investment for sharecroppers. A team and wagon could enhance a family's immediate earning potential and would certainly be vital to the long-term success of any independent farm.[20]

Thomas Whitfield's fishing prowess exemplified the family's careful balancing act between ambition and caution. Each day after working in the fields, he would load his wagon with tackle, poles, and trotlines and venture to his favorite fishing holes along the banks of the Tombigbee, where he would store the crappie, largemouth bass, and catfish that he caught in a hidden live box. Every Saturday, Thomas and Jane would take the wagon to fetch out the week's catch. In order to ensure that these privileges continued, however, they would first stop at the constable's house to offer him the best fish and then proceed to their usual street corner in Aberdeen to sell the rest. At the end of the day, Thomas would make a final stop at Ike Puckett's to buy a jug of moonshine and then retire to the nearby woods. He would then often make a drunken appearance in town to the general entertainment of Aberdeen's whites. Southern whites were more likely to accept blacks making money if they spent it on liquor, or other harmless amusements, and played the stereotypical black fool. Thomas was by all accounts liberal with drink, but his public displays were, as his son later reckoned, also carefully designed to disarm white unease about his profitable fish mongering.[21]

Sometimes, however, the actor could stumble. In late 1903, after making his usual Saturday trip into the woods, Thomas Whitfield lost control of his mules on his way back into Aberdeen. His wagon scraped the side of a local planter's new buggy. While such an offense could lead to death at the hands of a mob, the constable who enjoyed the Whitfields' fish noted Thomas's usual "friendly" behavior to calm gathering tempers. Thomas Whitfield still faced a fine and the payment of damages, and local white opinion of him soured in the weeks that followed. In the new century, Mississippi whites became less and less willing to tolerate petty entrepreneurs like the Whitfields. To reflect this, the state passed a new Vagrancy Act in 1904 that required African Americans to prove their employment, which in practice required the good word of a white person, or face imprisonment. This law gave white employers another powerful instrument to control black workers.[22]

In the wake of the mishap, Thomas convinced Jane that it was time to leave Aberdeen. Having heard rumors in early 1904 of new farming opportunities across the Mississippi River, the Whitfields left the county of their kin since slavery and moved to a farm outside Harrisburg in Poinsett County, Arkansas.[23] There in the Arkansas lowlands, the Whitfields entered a rough and chaotic agricultural frontier. The counties that bordered the Mississippi River across from Memphis and the Yazoo Delta remained swamped woodlands until the end of the nineteenth century, when the rapid expansion of timber cutting, railroad building, and drainage work opened a burgeoning plantation economy. Life in the lowlands was rife with disease, the work was dangerous, and white violence there was as bad as in Mississippi, but the area appealed to many blacks because it promised plenty of wage work and new farming opportunities.[24]

Now cropping Arkansas cotton, the Whitfields renewed their quest to buy a farm. Although they did well on their first two crops, the availability of land in the wooded hills on nearby Crowley's Ridge stoked their desire to get away from sharecropping. Lying awake one night in late 1905, Owen overheard his parents discussing the family's future—such eavesdropping was hard to avoid, since most sharecropper cabins had only two rooms. They were especially worried about getting old without a place to call their own, and Thomas and Jane vowed that night to do all they could to buy some land. Early in 1906 they left the lowlands to rent a small shack on the ridge and focus their efforts on wage work. Thomas Whitfield quit farming altogether to take a job in a local axe handle mill that paid $1.50 a day and an additional 40 cents for bringing young Owen along to work at his side. Owen and his older brother James also earned cash by digging graves at the white cemetery in Harrisburg for $1 a plot. Jane Whitfield washed white folks' clothes, with Owen often transporting the loads to and from the customers. Over the course of the year, the

Whitfields saved enough money to purchase four acres of land. Life in the woods was not easy, but the family rejoiced in their newfound liberty. The Whitfields grew their own food, made their own clothes, and earned enough wages to buy what they needed from the store. Although the family still had to deal with white supremacy in Jim Crow Arkansas, they felt sheltered from its vagaries in their rugged hillside home.[25]

This moment of self-sufficiency marked the memory of young Owen Whitfield, as did its abrupt end when his mother Jane died in late 1907. No one knew exactly what killed her; Owen noticed she was tired, "just plain wore out." Childbearing and unending labor undoubtedly took a toll. Her funeral was at home, in the small shack she had so lovingly tended. Thomas and the boys built her coffin. But her death was too much for Thomas to take. Recoiling from the loss of his pious and hard-working wife, he turned to drink and gambling, and increasingly went hunting in the woods instead of sweating it out at the mill. Alone, Thomas now failed to meet the difficult challenges that he and Jane had taken up together. Worse still, the emotional and economic fallout from her death strained the relationship between father and children. The homestead became dilapidated, dirty, and overgrown. Although the Whitfields retained their land, the fragile yet resilient family bonds frayed, and as a result, the teenage children contemplated their own independence.[26]

Owen Whitfield left Arkansas in early 1909 and went back to eastern Mississippi to live with his uncle, Chuck Whitfield, a sharecropper on the Black Prairie near the town of Egypt. Chuck Whitfield knew how to farm white-owned land, usually coming out ahead on his crops despite the unpredictability of yields and Mississippi landlords. Although Jim Crow reigned in law and social custom, particularly in towns like Aberdeen, race relations in rural Mississippi were still highly personal. Some landlords, like Chuck's, were content to leave good farmers alone. This particular landlord gave simple instructions: "You know better than I do what to do—just go ahead and do it." This was unusual; others ruled over their tenants like tyrants. Chuck Whitfield recalled another landlord who owed him $3,000 for his crop but doled out only $300 after the deduction of expenses, which included being billed twice for the funeral of his child. Owen's uncle adopted a pragmatic approach to the inconsistencies of this life. He worked quietly, relied on his farming expertise, and when he enjoyed a little success, he never displayed it. Owen learned much working alongside his uncle Chuck: about farming cotton, about avoiding debt, and, most importantly, about balancing ambition and dignity with the perilous realities of life in a white supremacist society.[27]

Still, Owen Whitfield struggled to come to terms with a world that tormented hard-working people. The destinies of black people seemed intimately attached to the South's rich soil but utterly determined by whites who lived better. Like other black teenagers, Owen's passage into adulthood had been both shortened and stalled by his parents' tireless quest for land and his continued dependence on family members to survive. The constraints of Jim Crow made coming of age even more excruciating. A wayward glance misinterpreted, either by a white woman or a police officer, could lead to a beating, jail, or worse. At the very best, a young black man eager to get married, have children, and provide for his family could expect a lifetime of toil with little assurance of security.[28]

Given such prospects, Owen "established a reputation" as a "veteran sinner" in the underworld of Egypt's juke joints. He played dice, womanized, and lashed out in back-alley brawls. Although these experiences made him less naïve about the dark side of life, Whitfield also started to wonder whether his "veteran" status confirmed his tough manhood or doomed him to a life of misery. Whatever the answer, he was not satisfied and worried that he might become like those with whom he caroused: young men who continually neglected their families in favor of the pool cue and the bottle.[29]

It was in the search for something more meaningful that Owen Whitfield stumbled into a revival tent sometime in 1910. His mother had been religious; her sermons about righteousness and sin never left Owen's thoughts. This night, as he listened to the preacher spit hellfire and brimstone, Whitfield wondered about the purpose of a life based on subservience to whites. Did the Lord determine this life for him? Owen demanded an answer in prayer, but God did not speak. Confused, Whitfield drifted out of the revival tent.[30]

Chuck Whitfield provided something of a remedy for his nephew's angst by sending him to high school. Although he needed help on the farm, Chuck took great pride in sponsoring Owen's education. Such power had helped to define southern black conceptions of independence since Reconstruction, because white landlords often dictated when the children of sharecroppers could and could not go to school. Chuck's ability to send Owen to school also spoke to his economic status. State funding for black education was miserly in the South, and no state spent less on black schools than Mississippi. "It will be readily admitted," stated the Superintendent of Education in 1899, "that our public school system is designed primarily for the welfare of the white children." If African Americans wanted to send their children to school, they had to pay for it themselves. Owen Whitfield was lucky that his uncle valued education, and doubly lucky that he lived near Okolona Industrial School—a rare, shining example of black education in Mississippi—where he enrolled. At $15 a year, tuition was not cheap, but Chuck was proud to pay it.[31]

Wallace A. Battle, a black educator trained at Kentucky's interracial Berea

College, founded Okolona in 1902. By the time Whitfield attended, the school served over 250 students on a four-hundred-acre campus featuring a five-story dormitory; a trade shop; an assembly hall; a barn housing pigs, cattle, and mules; and extensive fields for agricultural experiments. The broad sweep of the Okolona curriculum resembled Booker T. Washington's Tuskegee Institute in Alabama. At Okolona, boys learned scientific agriculture and mechanical industries; girls trained in sewing, laundry, and cooking; and aspiring teachers of both sexes studied pedagogy.[32]

Okolona also deviated from the Tuskegee approach by encouraging an academic education. Tuskegee was the most influential model for black education in the South because it accommodated to Jim Crow standards—its all-black student body learned vocations and agricultural skills, which in turn garnered sustained financial support from white donors. Battle, however, believed black children should learn more than good farming and housekeeping.[33] Okolona students took classes in grammar, nursing, chemistry, music, and English literature. The goal was to make sure that the children learned "literature, industry, and morals." Above all, Battle aspired for Okolona's students to learn the power of ideas, dignity of labor, and "spirit" of civic service.[34]

The continued existence of Okolona, however, depended on the favor of whites. Battle's academic aims made keeping "sweet" with locals and attracting northern liberal philanthropy difficult because many whites believed that anything but physical education encouraged unsuitable desires that blacks could never realize. Governor Vardaman, for one, believed that schooling "spoils a good field hand." To mollify potential enemies, Battle invited prominent local whites to join the Board of Directors and emphasized Okolona's goal to train responsible rural leaders. The strategy worked. Whites served on the board, donated money, and lobbied others for further support. Even Mississippi senator LeRoy Percy wrote letters in support of the school's funding drives. He lauded Okolona for providing the "kind of education which will enable [African Americans] to protect themselves from the avaricious and the unscrupulous" and "become producers, practical, experienced, and self-supporting farmers."[35]

The "spirit of service" philosophy that Battle peddled to whites had greater implications when instilled in students like Owen Whitfield. Battle never stopped reminding his charges that their education at Okolona bestowed rare privileges. It was not enough for them to learn. Battle called his students to be leaders, of their communities and of the race. He wanted them to become teachers, to learn industrial trades, and to master the arts of scientific agriculture so that they could "make farm life remunerative" for the masses.[36] To be a self-supporting farmer no doubt meant very different things to Senator

Percy and the children of black sharecroppers. While whites interpreted this as a progressive means of social control, Okolona's students recognized it as a pragmatic route to autonomy. Battle taught his students that if African Americans were to be independent, then it was up to them to lead the way. The Lord, he said, would "help them who help themselves." It was this message, practical yet transcendent, that altered the course of Whitfield's life.[37]

After graduation in 1913, however, Whitfield struggled to fulfill the Okolona mission. He drifted in and out of jobs, first as a dancer in a minstrel troupe and then as a sawyer in the ramshackle lumber town of Derma, Mississippi. But Derma had one silver lining: it was there that he met and fell in love with Zella Glass.[38]

Born in 1900, Zella had a tumultuous childhood. Her mother abandoned the family when she was a baby. Her father remarried an abusive woman, and they hired Zella out at a young age to white households as a domestic laborer. Whether her father did this out of economic necessity or ambition, it was an unusual step because most black men preferred that their wives and daughters not work in white homes where they were vulnerable to lecherous men and their suspicious wives. Zella's father prized her earning potential over her safety, however, and even sent her to work in white-owned fields when she was not cleaning, laundering, and cooking. Life with her family was not much better in their makeshift shack surrounded by timber scraps, mud, and open sewers.[39] Eager to escape her lot, Zella responded enthusiastically to Whitfield's romantic advances. After lying about her age to obtain a marriage license, Zella and Owen wed that November and took jobs on a nearby farm. Their first child, Owen Whitfield Junior, was born in August 1914.[40]

Bringing a child into a world dominated by white supremacy was not easy. Dr. Hardin, a white doctor who also employed both Owen and Zella at odd jobs, delivered their first-born with haunting malice. Their boss was "as mean as he could be," Owen said. When he noticed that Zella was pregnant, Hardin told the young couple that he wanted to deliver the child. This was a strange request since white doctors usually did not deliver black babies, midwives did. When the Whitfields asked why, he replied: "because I want to kill you." Despite Owen's efforts to find another doctor or a midwife, Hardin forced himself to Zella's bedside when she went into labor. Hardin's assertion of control reflected his combined sense of masculine power, racial prerogative, and medical authority. He was drunk and reminded Zella, who was only fourteen years old, about his desire to see her dead. As she began to struggle under Hardin's grasp, he punched her legs until she submitted. "Get your legs up there," Hardin shouted. In the midst of this torment, Zella gave birth to a healthy child. "I decided to spare you this time," Hardin told her after it was over, "but I'll get you next time." The couple agreed that Hardin would not have another chance to fulfill his threat. Soon after the birth of their son, the Whitfields decided to leave Mississippi for good. Owen vowed to never let Zella again work for a white man. In later life he explained that she was too temperamental and likely to get herself into trouble with wayward words. But that explanation also obscured their fear of her physical insecurity at the hands of men like Hardin.[41]

With nowhere else to go, the young family reluctantly relocated to the Whitfield homestead in eastern Arkansas. Thomas's compound remained a mess of garbage, wood, and metal scraps, as well as the comings and goings of his twenty-odd dogs. But he still had the wherewithal to make money. Thomas rented out shacks on his property for $1 a month to local black wageworkers, whom Owen and Zella befriended. Owen joined their ranks by cleaning a nearby white church, taking odd shifts at the axe handle mill, and working the peak cotton seasons. In March 1916 one of their tenant-friends acted as a midwife to welcome Cora, their second child, into the world. Although poor, the family enjoyed some real autonomy in the hills. They could, for example, choose a black midwife to deliver their child. But old Thomas's squalor became unbearable; Owen and Zella soon left for a sharecropping arrangement near the town of Marked Tree in Poinsett County. The Whitfields did not make much money there, around $50 in both 1917 and 1918, but they avoided debt.[42]

The Great War did little to alter their lives. Although he registered for the draft, Owen was not selected to serve. County draft boards in the lowlands, dominated by white planters, often shielded their agricultural laborers from service if they were considered "productive" workers. Independent black farmers often got drafted, while sharecroppers on white-owned plantations got deferments. As a father of three—the couple's third child was born in November 1917—and a responsible cropper, Owen Whitfield found favor with the Poinsett County draft board. The way to avoid the trenches of the Western Front was to keep local whites happy; it was "work or fight."[43]

The promise and peril of 1919 rekindled the Whitfields' determination to seize their own independence. That year they had moved to a farm near Round Pond in Saint Francis County, Arkansas, about thirty-five miles south of Marked Tree. They raised fifteen bales of cotton on fifteen acres. In a normal year that would have been good production, but in 1919, with cotton at a record-high 37 cents per lint pound, the couple cleared $800 on their crop, the most they had ever earned in a year. Thrilled over their unprecedented success, they, like thousands of other prosperous cotton farmers that year, bought a car.[44]

Car ownership offered mobility for rural people long inured to the mule and wagon, but its prestige proved dangerous. Planters abhorred the idea of sharecroppers being able to go anywhere they pleased. "I don't want any niggers driving a car around here," Whitfield's landlord declared. The image of a black man driving his own car could not have been more offensive to the white supremacist mind.[45] That autumn, similar complaints about economically proud blacks led Arkansas whites to massacre hundreds of African Americans seventy miles south of where the Whitfields resided. In what became known as the Elaine Massacre, armed whites roamed like "a rolling killing machine." The Whitfields had seen enough. They pocketed their money and drove back to Marked Tree.[46]

The Whitfields sharecropped for the next two years on land rented by a prosperous black farmer. Although uncommon, African Americans who paid cash rent on land could employ other blacks. In order to obtain such an arrangement, a farmer needed to have significant leverage in negotiations with the landowner, usually in the form of property, whether tools, equipment, or animal teams. Often, as was the case with the Whitfields' tenant landlord, cash renters took on more land than they could possibly work for themselves in order to subcontract the rest to sharecroppers. "Black landlords considered themselves the communities' parents," observed one historian. Bound by a definition of paternal obligation that did not imply the childlike dependence demanded by many whites, black landlords were more likely to allow their croppers certain liberties, such as garden space and some livestock. Unlike most of their white counterparts, black landlords valued the connection between the tiller and the soil, often treating sharecroppers with respect in exchange for productive farming. After years of struggle with white landlords, the Whitfields now looked to steep themselves in this rural black world.[47]

II

Like Whitfield, Claude Williams experienced the frustrations of growing up as an ambitious, talented young man in the rural South. His youth was also defined by the tensions between family survival and an individual sense of calling, between agricultural labor and adventure, and between physical hunger and the thirst for deeper meaning in life. Yet as a white boy, Williams played these games of chance under a very different set of rules. He would have considered it beneath him or, at best, an exotic titillation to sit down at Whitfield's poker table in Egypt, Mississippi. The laws and culture of the Jim Crow South made Williams's youth at once very similar to, yet completely separate from, Whitfield's experience.

Claude Clossie Williams was born on June 16, 1895, in the western Tennessee county of Weakley, where feelings about the Civil War still ran strong thirty years after it ended. Although the state was home to large numbers of Unionists, Claude's father, Jess, like most of his white neighbors, believed foremost in the Democratic Party, where political loyalty meant strident white supremacy, even if his own visage revealed his part-Cherokee bloodlines. Born in Obion County in 1851, Jess Williams had come of age during the war, which in the western theater was largely fought on the farmlands of Tennessee.[48]

Although the war officially ended in 1865, violence continued as former Confederates lashed out at Union supporters and freedpeople. The Williams family surely heard about the violence that broke out in Memphis in early 1866 after black soldiers had protested the arrest of a black wagon driver who had crashed into a white-owned carriage. Over the course of three days, white mobs killed and raped African Americans and burned hundreds of black-owned properties. This was only the beginning. The Ku Klux Klan was founded in the state that same year.[49] All of this bloodshed, Jess Williams recalled bitterly, stemmed from a fight over "damnniggers." To him, the violent overthrow of Reconstruction in the 1870s seemed necessary to right the unnatural wrong of giving black people political rights. "Damnniggers," he explained, now "had to be killed once in a while to show them their place."[50] Yet, in 1891 Jess married Minnie Bell Galey, the daughter of a Republican family whose ancestors had been among the first to settle in Weakley County. Her family embraced Lincoln and abolition. While Minnie did not share her husband's politics, she was, according to Jess, "handsome" and had just inherited a fourteen-acre farm. "She's got right smart of sense," he liked to joke, "but it's Republican sense."[51]

Claude imbibed this volatile political mixture from an early age. From Jess he learned to hate black people, northerners, and Republicans, although this must have been confusing since his mother's family supported the Republican Party. From his mother's brother Andrew he learned to sing "Yankee Doodle." And from Minnie he learned that it did not matter whether one was a Democrat or a Republican as long as you were "for the man that's for the poor folks." She was also the one, like Jane Whitfield, who kept religion alive in the home.[52]

The Williams and Galey families belonged to the Cumberland Presbyterian Church, a rebellious denomination that rejected the Calvinist idea that God had predetermined the fate of individuals. This small but devout band of believers descended from a theological uprising hatched during the Great Revival of 1800 in the Cumberland River Valley of Kentucky and Tennessee. The fight broke out over the doctrine of predestination as stated in the Westminster Confession (the guiding article of American Presbyterianism) and the power of the church synod to police the education of ministers. Predestination, as explained in the Confession, meant that God knew who would go to heaven and who would go to hell, and humans had no power to alter this decree. The Great Revival embodied a democratic evangelical impulse for mass salvation that clashed with the rigidity of predestination, as the founders of Cumberland Presbyterianism declared in 1810: "We do not believe in the doctrine of eternal reprobation. We do not believe that Christ died for a part of mankind only." Their faith stemmed from the belief that "redemption is offered conditionally to all men." It was up to people to accept it.[53]

Theologically, all Cumberland Presbyterians shared a belief in the strictness of biblical commandments and the harsh retribution that faced unrepentant sinners. But Williams and other Cumberlanders also grew up with the belief that God would reward those who remained humble in material life but rich in spirit. The Cumberlanders placed faith in human choice. If the church ever obstructed the personal struggle to earn God's favor, Cumberlanders believed that the individual had the obligation to rebel. "If a Church is so impolitic as to refuse to adopt her creed to the progress of the age," one church leader advised in 1878, "revolution will be the consequence."[54]

Guided by this conservative yet cantankerous faith, the Williamses toiled on their fourteen-acre plot nestled in the hills between the forks of the Obion River. That homestead provided enough fertile soil to raise food and livestock to feed the family but not enough of a surplus to sell for cash. The Williamses were poor, but not unusually so. Claude would later recall that in his youth he wore patched shirts and denim overalls, and so frequently went without shoes that he developed calluses on his feet. In order to raise enough cash to pay taxes, tithe to the church, and buy necessities, the Williamses also share-cropped. This extra work never made them much money, but it was enough to earn them more freedom than the black sharecroppers of the county.[55]

Williams's childhood experience traversed the boundary that separated modern commercial agriculture from an older form of subsistence farming. The family's journey from their hillside homestead to sharecrop on the rich bottomland plantations crossed between the two worlds. Setting out well before the break of day, the family nudged its way by mule and wagon down the crooked dirt roads leading out of the hills. When they reached the sweeping expanse of the Obion River Valley, everyone who was old enough chopped or picked the cotton in groups, while babies lay stashed at the end of the crop row. After the Williamses had harvested the crop, they would take it to the gins along the two railroads that cut across the county. There, landowners and merchants weighed and graded the cotton, and informed the croppers of their pay. The cotton-loaded trains then rumbled away toward the city and markets beyond. In this way the landowners of Weakley and Obion counties—blessed as they were with fertile bottomland soil, good transportation networks, and cheap, abundant labor—became the richest in Tennessee by 1900. That year their cotton and tobacco crops earned well over $1 million. Families like the Williamses, meanwhile, went back into the hills with just a few hundred dollars in their pockets.[56]

But working on commercial agricultural lands gave rise to frustration and fear in people like the Williamses. The power of large landowners in the lowlands foreclosed the opportunities once open to small landowners like Jess and Minnie Williams. Dependency, whether as tenants or wageworkers, stalked the futures of people whose dignity often came from self-sufficiency. The proximity of plantation counties where African Americans made up the majority of tenant farmers only compounded the sense of danger. "There is not as much difference between white and black as is supposed," reckoned one neighboring planter. Such a statement was especially provocative at a time when the southern states erected the legal codes that would underpin Jim Crow society. Jess Williams surely had this frightening zero-sum vision in mind when he told Claude that violence, even murder, was acceptable to keep African Americans in "their place." Although Claude had little famil-iarity with African Americans during his childhood—only 10 percent of the Weakley County population was black—he grew up dreading any kind of contact with them. As a curious youngster, he remembered touching the hair of an African American; immediately thereafter, he washed his hands and spit to rid himself of the disease that he was sure accompanied black skin.[57]

Economic and racial unease fueled popular discontent among western Tennessee's white smallholders. Farmers in the region mounted a succes-sion of political protest movements in the thirty years from 1885 to 1915 that defined the years of Claude's youth as much as did his own family's struggle to survive on their hillside homestead. Tennessee's Ninth Congressional Dis-trict, which included Weakley and Obion counties, supplied the state's most robust and enduring electoral support for the People's Party in the 1890s. Like their counterparts elsewhere, Tennessee Populists protested the deleterious effect of modernization on ordinary people and called for federal interven-tion to protect the interests of small farmers and laborers from the power of monopolistic national corporations. Jess Williams never recorded an affinity for Populism, but the majority of members of the People's Party resembled his profile: owners of land of between ten and a hundred acres who normally supported the Democratic Party. After the demise of Populism in the late 1890s, Weakley's agrarian rebels organized strong local units of the Farmers' Union in the first decade of the new century. These groups also aimed to use their ballots and cooperative power to protect their way of life against encroaching plantation agribusiness.[58]

Despite his youth, Claude Williams would have known about the infamous episodes when these electoral bids gave way to violence. The Williams homestead lay on the southern edge of the Black Patch region of Kentucky and Tennessee where farmers waged a bloody struggle from 1905 to 1911 against the control of the tobacco trust, a monopoly headed by James B. Duke's American Tobacco Company. The Night Riders, as they were known, seemed to be everywhere, clubbing company employees and collaborators with impunity. Much of the conflict took place across the state line in Kentucky, but often very close to Weakley County, as was the case in 1908, when vigilantes threatened to burn the town of Murray, Kentucky.[59] Similar violence erupted that year around Reelfoot Lake, Tennessee, west of Obion County, where vigilantes burned property and murdered outsiders, some of them black, to protect squatters' rights on public land. Tales of armed vigilantes on horseback who defended community autonomy against more powerful external foes must have set fire to the imagination of teens like Williams.[60]

Restless of body and spirit, Claude left home in 1910 to explore the tumultuous world beyond his parents' homestead. Like most teenagers, he craved adventure and asked curious questions his family could not answer. Perplexed by Claude's queries, his parents and neighbors concluded that Claude must be destined to preach, the one rural avocation that allowed such heady pursuits. Williams had attended church with his parents since before he could recall. He was devout, he prayed, and he read the Bible. But he had never experienced what he imagined to be the full glory of God's blessing. His growing impatience led him to the road. What he really wanted was the satisfaction—not fully known by his parents—"of being his own master."[61]

As a first stop, Claude moved in with the Stover family, cousins who owned a farm near Martin. Also devout Cumberland Presbyterians, the Stovers provided Williams with moral guidance and plenty of work on their farm. Their earnest strivings impressed him deeply, but he sought to find his own way. With the Stover farm as a place of respite during the winter months, Williams worked variously as a railroad laborer, assistant carpenter, and painter, and as a coal-heaver on steamboats plying the Mississippi River. None of the jobs paid well and none seemed to offer any permanent satisfaction, but Williams enjoyed roaming because it allowed him to meet people. He often slept out of doors and dabbled in the delights of the tramp. Booze, cards, and women answered many of the questions he had about the contours of life off the farm. He learned "the taste and smell" of the world and liked it. Yet, at the same time, a sense that God had called him lingered in the back of his mind. When Williams stumbled on religious revivals, he would enter the tent and participate. But the ultimate moment of conversion remained elusive.[62]

Seeing opportunity for greater adventure, Williams enlisted in the U.S. Army in 1916. In training camps in Texas and Minnesota, he reveled in the camaraderie of the barracks with men who came from all parts of the country. Passing the time between training exercises over hands of blackjack and poker, Williams learned through frank conversation about the common aspirations and frustrations of other young men. He also admired and adhered to the discipline of the army and earned promotion to drill master. Further rewards followed, including entry into officer corps training that he hoped would take him to Europe to join in the Great War. The German Kaiser abdicated only days before Williams graduated as a lieutenant; he would not see combat. Nevertheless, Claude had grown in the army, becoming a leader and experiencing life far away from Tennessee. When his service ended in 1919, Williams reenlisted for two more years, which he spent at Fort Dix, New Jersey.[63]

Extensive demobilization measures introduced by Congress in 1921 threatened Williams's military career aspirations. Rather than fight for a rare officer's commission, Claude chose to reenter civilian life. His army career had gained him an offer of employment with a British fruit company in South America, likely one similar to the United Fruit Company, which controlled massive banana plantations, as well as domestic politics, in Guatemala and British Honduras. It was a booming business in the 1920s. Williams saw the job, a sinecure of U.S. imperialism, as a chance to enjoy the international adventure that he never got to experience in the military.[64]

On his way to New Orleans to embark for points south, Williams stopped in Weakley County to say farewell. His extended family congregated to congratulate him and remind him that their prayers always accompanied his travels. Williams had done more than could have been reasonably expected of a child from rural western Tennessee, especially one with a limited education. He had served with merit in the army; had risen into the ranks of officers; and now had promising work in a far-flung land. Despite these accomplishments, Williams was unsatisfied. He would later call the period from 1914 to 1921 his "lamentable years" of "emptiness and futility."[65] The question of his calling to preach loomed. Finally, Claude's uncle asked him directly: "When are you going to take up your work?" "What work?" he wondered. The reply struck every nerve in his body: "Preaching." Masking his insecurity with cockiness, Claude shot back: "Never!"⁶⁶

The farewell stop in Weakley stretched from days to weeks. Whether caused by his mother's fervent prayers, his uncle's challenge to take up the ministry, or the Stovers' example of simple devotion, Williams finally decided not take the job in South America. Instead, he put himself forward on September 27, 1921, as a candidate for the ministry. Soon thereafter Williams enrolled at a Cumberland Presbyterian school, Bethel College, in nearby McKenzie, Tennessee. Claude's transition to God's plan was not easy or clear-cut. He felt foolish at times for turning down a lucrative job, especially since he had had no specific revelation about his relationship to God.⁶⁷

Williams began studying at Bethel in January 1922. Founded in 1842 as a seminary to serve the Cumberland Presbyterian Church, Bethel College primarily trained young men for the ministry while also offering a general academic degree for those aiming to join the professions. It was not a large school. The lone building on campus could accommodate three hundred students, but enrollment rarely filled it to capacity. Although small in size, the college was important as the last independent Cumberland seminary. In 1906 a majority in the Cumberland Presbyterian Church voted to rejoin the Presbyterian Church (USA), the so-called "northern" branch of the denomination, after the main body had sufficiently amended the Confession of Faith to abandon strict predestination. About one-third of Cumberland churches, most of them rural, chose to remain independent; these included the congregations attended by the Williamses and Stovers. As a result of the union, all ten of the Cumberland seminaries closed. Bethel, however, reopened as the sole bastion of Cumberland theological training.⁶⁸

Relegated to a backwater of American Protestantism, Bethel's students took pride in their school's stubborn independence. Solitude had strange effects. On the one hand, the Cumberland faithful adhered to a strict code of conduct that forbade alcohol, smoking, gambling, or dancing. These prohibitions, along with a fervent belief in the literal truth of the Bible as God's word, placed Cumberlanders in agreement with the then inchoate but growing set of evangelical believers who described themselves as fundamentalists. On the other hand, the Cumberlanders embraced controversial theological ideas. By 1920 Bethel admitted female students, some of whom went on to preach in the church, which was a radical departure from most southern denominations, while others entered the missionary field or became teachers. The instruction Williams received at Bethel, at once strict and liberating, drew on the strong convictions of a self-perceived righteous minority. In classes dealing with topics from the Bible to Greek to American history, Williams's teachers railed against the influence of wealth in society, and in the Presbyterian Church (USA) in particular. Bethel's theologians claimed that mainstream Presbyterians worried more about the grandeur of church buildings than they did about eternal salvation, more about their place in the local Chamber of Commerce than in the battle against Satan. At Bethel, Williams came to understand himself as part of a new generation of Cumberland leaders, who as a righteous remnant had the potential to speak God's truth to a wayward, self-obsessed world.[69]

No class or book, however, influenced Williams as much as did one of his fellow students, Joyce King. Born in the Ozark Hills of southern Missouri in 1897, Joyce had grown up in a Cumberland Presbyterian family that traced its roots to the denomination's founders. Small, quiet, yet confident and intelligent, she entered Bethel to become a missionary. Williams, by comparison, was tall, talkative, and prone to exuberant argument. They became inseparable. Their match, they soon came to believe, portended more than mere chance; faith had melded them together. Although they had known one another for only a few months, Claude and Joyce sealed the union in marriage on May 16, 1922.[70]

To the college elders, the couple's quick courtship and marriage seemed less to do with faith than a preoccupation with the cravings of the flesh. Bethel's elders feared that sex among some students, even in marriage, would distract others. They questioned Williams about his personal life, but levied no punishment. Still, the nosiness of old men angered him. Should not a man who was twenty-seven years old be able to make his own decision about marriage? Williams's grades certainly suffered after his marriage; his middling record of Bs and Cs (with As in ethics and algebra) suggested a desire to move on to less academic endeavors.[71]

As a trainee, licentiate preacher at Bethel, Williams was assigned to serve at Pilgrim's Rest Cumberland Presbyterian in rural Carroll County, not far from where he grew up. In October 1922 he began preaching there weekly because the church had no permanent pastor. The elders and congregation liked him so much that they asked the presbytery to grant his full ordination in March 1923. If the presbytery agreed, Williams would have had open to him a lifetime of service among the people he had grown up with, no doubt including many of his kinfolks. It would have been a proud achievement, but the Committee on Literature and Theology thought otherwise. The committee was "of the opinion it is not best and just to Brother Williams, and that the request be not granted." They saw a young, undoubtedly gifted preacher who did not seem ready to shoulder the burdens of full-time ministry. The decision forced Williams to continue his education.[72]

The experience awoke a prophetic voice within Williams. In the grand scheme of Presbyterianism, Bethel was tiny and unnoticed, a forgotten relic of the nineteenth century. Williams had given up a potential army commission and a good-paying job to attend a school located on the fringe of the fringe. Cumberland Presbyterianism, like the families who made up its congregations, remained poor and marginal compared to modern American life in the 1920s. After the run-in with Bethel's elders and his rejection by the presbytery, Williams realized that his role as a preacher lay not in the narrow space of Cumberland Presbyterianism but in assailing the false optimism of American society. He decided to adhere to the Cumberlanders' original charter, "to preach the redemption of men's souls from hell to heaven," which meant that Williams would have to escape the strictures of the church in order to speak the truth of the Cumberland faith in the face of mainstream Christianity.[73] Thus, in 1923 the Williamses left Bethel. Claude and Joyce resolved that the best they could do as Cumberlanders would be to take the church's beliefs as missionaries into unfriendly lands. In October 1923 Williams requested and received letters of "dismission and recommendation" from the local presbytery.[74]

Wasting no time, Claude Williams applied to the Presbyterian Church (USA) for a preaching assignment the next year. The denomination gladly accepted the young couple and assigned Claude as a licentiate preacher to a series of rural churches in the Nashville hinterland. By 1926 Williams had been welcomed as pastor of three rural churches outside the towns of Lebanon, Auburntown, and Lascassas, Tennessee. Working from a "deep, personal religious conviction" to proclaim "the horrors of hell and the hope of heaven," Claude preached "till they could feel the flames lapping around their legs." Joyce, meanwhile, conducted her ministry in the homes of member families. Together, the Williamses brought members back into the churches, which delighted the local elders, because members meant financial stability.[75]

In preaching solely of "repentance and salvation by faith in Jesus Christ," the Williamses consciously challenged the logic of ecclesiastical divisions between Presbyterians. The lesson of Bethel had been to escape the narrowness of denominations. The Williamses now counseled tolerance among all Christians. "If a man says, We and only we are right, he is following Churchanity and not Christianity," Claude preached. Such theological hair-splitting wasted time that should be spent making religion relevant to ordinary people. "We spew and spit, quarrel and cuss and damn about theological propositions which are not clearly set forth," he preached, "and absolutely ignore the plain teaching of God's word." That word was as simple as "he that believeth Jesus is the Christ is born of God."[76]

Williams's quest for universal Christian truths attracted him to the burgeoning fundamentalist movement. During the 1920s, fundamentalists emphasized the interdenominational "fundamentals" of Christian belief over false, worldly divisions imposed by denominational bodies, which led to liberal, errant theology. A turning point came in 1927, when Claude and Joyce heard Billy Sunday. America's most sensational evangelist, Sunday delivered a sermon in Nashville on the basics of Christ's salvation and the alternative, eternal hellfire. In the overflowing audience, Claude and Joyce felt "set on fire." They returned to their churches determined to preach the "roots" of the Christian faith. They were successful; by late 1927 the Williamses served five rural churches.[77]

In this "fire" the Williamses saw a flame of Christian universalism that would burn away artificial social boundaries. Most controversially, the Williamses offered fellowship to African Americans, who made up roughly 25 percent of the population in Rutherford and Wilson counties where they preached. Invited personally by Claude and Joyce, a few African Americans attended the regular service. After one such Sunday sermon, Williams shook the hand of a black man in front of his white congregation. The act of politeness, he later recalled, confronted his childhood fear of touching people with brown skin and seemed to open new truths about Christian fellowship. Soon thereafter, Williams gave a sermon at a small church in a nearby black community. The religious devotion of the people there impressed Williams, though he did not feel comfortable among them.[78]

The implication of Williams's message about the openness of salvation to all who repented and accepted Christ discomfited many and aroused suspicion among his regular congregants. Although inculcated with white supremacist belief from an early age, Williams now began to question segregation in religious services. Was this practice not just one more social affectation that repudiated God's teaching? The church elders balked at raising such a question but could do little to dissuade Claude's strategy of broad outreach since it filled the pews and the offering plates.[79]

Following his inspiration by Billy Sunday, Claude enrolled in two correspondence courses on evangelism and "Practical Christian Work" that were offered by the Moody Bible Institute in Chicago. Founded by Dwight L. Moody, the most famous evangelist of the late nineteenth century, the institute provided interdenominational training for aspiring evangelists. Although its teaching broadly supported the antiliberal, antimodern fundamentalist consensus, the institute's correspondence school, founded in 1901, attracted a variety of preachers who expressed interest in universal Christian convictions and Moody's main goal of the "evangelization of the World."[80]

Williams thereafter also educated himself by reading theology, philosophy, and history texts. With polymath sensibilities, he joined the Religious Book Club, a series that published scholarly works that were not overly academic. Club choices introduced Williams to new studies in liberal theology that ran counter to Moody's fundamentalism. The first book he received was *The Modern Use of the Bible* by Harry Emerson Fosdick, a professor of practical theology at Union Theological Seminary in New York, who reached a national audience through his weekly radio sermons on biblical liberalism.[81]

In *The Modern Use of the Bible*, Fosdick provided a framework for ministers like Williams who wanted to make the holy inspiration of the Bible more relevant in contemporary society. As the record of Christian ideals and development, Fosdick contended, the Bible offered a practical guide to modern moral behavior and action. Fosdick's teaching was based on a belief that God did not want men to preserve outmoded traditional views. He urged ministers "to handle the Bible with new zest, freedom, honesty, and power" and transform themselves to be "of such a spirit that God can work his victory in and through us . . . to strive for the better organization of society that the divine purpose may be furthered, not hindered, by our economic and political life." Moreover, Fosdick instructed, preachers might follow Christ's example by shaking off "the formalities of popular religion" in order to "bring men into more abundant life." Such a task was neither easy nor comfortable. In fact it was a "revolutionary business" since it would alter the church, society, and the economic system. But these preachers would have considerable, even divine, support. "God is a living God, not far off, but here," Fosdick reassured readers.[82]

The book was a revelation to Claude and Joyce, who stayed up all night together reading it. They immediately understood what Fosdick meant when he called his vision a "revolutionary business." Fosdick's call to lead believers toward a more "abundant life" confirmed their own desire to make Christian belief more relevant. In the mission work that the Williamses sought to carry out, it was not enough to preach a generic heaven and hell; one had to show how Christ could work in and through people's actual lives. They aimed to offer faith as Fosdick did—as a "spiritual adventure into the release and use of divine power in our own day."[83]

The Williamses also sought a wider circle of religious scholars to discuss theology, and Claude received such an opportunity when Vanderbilt University in Nashville hired Professor Alva W. Taylor. A minister in the Disciples of Christ, Taylor preached a version of the Social Gospel, an early-twentieth-century urban development in American Protestantism that looked to social democratic thought as a way to reorient Christian belief. "When science gives the technique and the Church gives the social passion," Taylor wrote in 1931, "we will possess power to make the world over into the kingdom of God." He shook the intellectual world at Vanderbilt, which was, like most other southern universities at the time, bound by a "rigid orthodoxy of thought and opinion" that meant "academic freedom was perpetually endangered." An Iowan by birth, Taylor wanted his Vanderbilt course to broaden the minds of his southern students, particularly rural preachers from the surrounding area for whom he ran special summer sessions on the Social Gospel. He aimed to bring Christ's teaching to life by making it applicable to the problems of the day. "Making the community Christian is not only to practise the gospel of preventive morality," Taylor instructed, "but it is to build up the Kingdom of God."[84]

Claude enrolled in Taylor's first summer session and was not disappointed. Taylor, Williams recalled, "had a way of removing the theological debris from the Son of Man under which he's been buried for all these centuries and making him appear human." Christ had engaged people where they were, with their troubles and joys. Moreover, he had taught the "basis for a programme of action," for the improvement of this world. This kind of "social evangelism" brought people closer to God by bringing God closer to them.[85]

Joyce, now the mother of two daughters under the age of five, Constance and Cornelia, kept up with her husband's training. Although she was as talented and committed as Claude, Joyce was expected as a woman to devote her main energies to caring for her family and running the household while he preached and studied. Neither she nor Claude disputed these gender roles. Nevertheless, she read the same things he did, debated them with him, and came to many of the same conclusions.[86]

At Vanderbilt, Williams discovered that he was not alone in his hunger for a more relevant Christian ministry. In the summer of 1929, two other white southern preachers—Don West and Howard Kester—joined Taylor's seminar. These preachers formed a fast friendship that liberated Williams from the sense that he and Joyce were alone in their beliefs. West, born in northern Georgia in 1906, would go on to a lifelong career as a labor organizer, preacher, poet, and champion of Appalachian culture. Kester, born in 1904 in the Virginia hills, also dedicated his life to fighting racism. Intellectual and social support emboldened Taylor's students. Not only did this school of thought obliterate denominational boundaries, but the religious conversations Williams enjoyed with his classmates extended to questions about the very structure of southern society—its politics, its economics, and its ideas about race. These debates among Taylor's pupils made an odd contrast to the ideas generated by the Nashville Agrarians, then the intellectual doyens at Vanderbilt. While Williams, West, and Kester may have shared the Agrarians' concern about the acceleration of industrialism at the expense of southern farmers, they differed in the remedies they prescribed. The Agrarians pined for the preservation of traditional white southern culture, even if it had perpetuated slavery and a master class of planters. The "South itself has wavered a little" from its desire "to live its own kind of life," the Agrarians stated in their 1930 manifesto. "The younger Southerners," they argued, "who are being converted frequently to the industrial gospel, must come back to the support of the Southern tradition." The budding radicals in Taylor's seminars, however, eschewed southern traditions that prevented the making of "a Divine republic."[87]

The fellowship Williams experienced at Vanderbilt led him to finally reject white supremacist ideas. In the summer of 1929 Kester encouraged him to attend a conference for racial reconciliation organized by the Young Men's Christian Association (YMCA) and the Fellowship of Reconciliation in Waveland, Mississippi. In the late 1920s southern college students looking for an alternative to white supremacy were attracted to both groups, and the YMCA was particularly popular among students like Kester, who got involved at his college in Virginia in 1922, and Myles Horton, who was an active member at Cumberland University in Lebanon, Tennessee.[88] The first night at the conference, Williams's roommate arrived late, and seeing that Williams was asleep, slipped quietly into their shared bed without waking him. The conference, which featured an integrated group of pacifists, had been a challenge for Williams, whose upbringing proved resilient. When Williams awoke the following morning, however, he saw that he had slept all night in the same bed with a black man. "It was a brand new experience for Claude," Kester remarked, "but he made it through all right." Williams had been gradually moving toward a liberal view of race, but the surprise and embarrassment of this event, coupled with the good-humored support of his friends, convinced him of the ridiculousness of his racial fears.[89]

But this intellectual trajectory made Williams's pastoral assignment around Nashville increasingly untenable. When Claude confided to Joyce that he no longer knew how to preach to his congregants with a clear conscience and that he was considering enrolling in nearby Cumberland University to study the law "because I can be a lawyer without being a hypocrite," she encouraged him to "preach what you believe" and "whatever happens we will share it." At a revival in Auburntown in late 1929, Claude preached a single sentence that summed up his new faith and stunned the congregation. The Bible "is not given to us to tell us how God made the earth," he said, "but to tell us how the Kingdom of God can be brought to the earth."[90]

During the winter of 1929, as the Great Depression cast a dark shadow over the nation, the Williamses decided it was time to move their ministry. Claude's preaching had strained their relations with church elders. But more importantly, they believed that their calling required them to take their religious convictions to the frontlines of southern deprivation. God seemed to open a door that autumn when the Presbyterian Church (USA) adopted a new mission to carry Christ into "the field of social and economic relationships." Through the denomination's Board of Missions, the Williamses learned of a church in the mining town of Paris, Arkansas, in need of a permanent minister. The parish was in disarray: the church's roof had begun to fall down and few people attended anymore. Bolstered by the recommendation of M. L. Gillespie, the head of the Arkansas Presbyterian Board of Missions, Claude took the job. Headstrong and filled with missionary zeal, the Williamses headed to the Ozarks.[91]

III

The Whitfields, meanwhile, left Arkansas in favor of a new land that they hoped would yield some milk and honey. Along with thousands of other black farmers, they moved upriver in late 1922 to the new cotton frontier in southeast Missouri. Covered by swamps and old-growth forests, the lands of the Bootheel—like the alluvial lowlands of Arkansas and Mississippi—caught the eye of investors who financed the transformation of the swamped woods into rich farmland. The crash in commodity prices following World War I forced the owners of these farms to switch from wheat and corn to cotton production. In 1923 landowners doubled cotton acreages and looked to "import a large number of experienced cotton growers" to ensure profitability. They expected that these migrants would be "mostly colored families."[92]

Over the next three years, more than 15,000 enterprising African American farmers moved to the Bootheel.[93] The Whitfields took a sharecropping arrangement near Charleston in Mississippi County. The newcomers were "well dressed and every one of them self-sustaining and with bank accounts," one local newspaper reported. They came from the lowlands of Arkansas, Louisiana, Mississippi, and Tennessee, regions where the shrinking availability of land, continuing problems with the boll weevil, and increasing white racial violence had undermined their economic and political autonomy. One newcomer reported leaving Arkansas because "conditions were so he could not make a living there." Good farming, however, meant more than profitable crops. He was glad to be in the Bootheel, the man said, because here he could prove "that he was a good farmer and a good citizen." There were no Jim Crow disenfranchising laws in Missouri, so most migrants had the right to vote for the first time. Moreover, the migrants had the goodwill of local landowners and investors, who needed their labor. In the words of one local editor, the settlers were the "saviors of agriculture in this section."[94]

The agrarian ambition that attracted black farmers like Owen and Zella Whitfield to Missouri's cotton fields also pulled them toward the nationalist ideology of Marcus Garvey's Universal Negro Improvement Association (UNIA). Founded in Jamaica in 1914, Garvey's organization attracted the attention of black Americans after he arrived in Harlem in 1916. From there he transformed the UNIA into a worldwide movement to build "a strong and powerful Negro nation."[95] Garvey argued that economic strength was the best way for black people to realize "a country of their own where they should be given the fullest opportunity to develop politically, socially and industrially." This message captured a sense of urgency among black farmers like the Whitfields in the years after World War I, especially those who suffered violence, debt, and privation in the South. "If at any time in the history of the Negro race men were needed for service," Garvey argued, "that time is 'Now.'" "Whatsoever my future is to be is my own creation," he concluded, and "as of the individual so of the race."[96]

Often seen as an urban phenomenon, the UNIA movement that the Whitfields witnessed showed the vitality of Garvey's ideas in the rural South. African Americans in the Bootheel established 15 divisions of the UNIA in the 1920s; altogether, southern farmers formed 354 divisions from Virginia to Oklahoma, which made up half of all divisions in the United States.[97] While most of these divisions were small—anywhere from seven to fifty members each—those who joined had immense influence in their communities. Rural Garveyites were mainly prosperous men along with a few women: they were small landowners, successful renters, teachers, and preachers, usually over thirty-five years old who claimed personal property. Their property provided them with important protection from white interference, insulation from expensive credit and crop liens, and a sense of family and community autonomy. Although they shared these aspirations, Owen and Zella Whitfield had not yet attained them. They never became official members of the UNIA—perhaps because they could not afford to pay the monthly dues of 60 cents—but Owen and Zella discussed Garvey and his program and frequently went to UNIA Saymos Division 706 meetings. Like hundreds of other young families, the Whitfields sought to emulate and learn from the UNIA, even if they did not have the means to join.[98]

Garvey's emphasis on self-defense as a pillar of autonomy and manhood resonated with farmers like the Whitfields, particularly following the Elaine Massacre. "If some unfriendly acquaintance of yours threatens to burn down your house," Garvey advised readers of the *Negro World*, the UNIA's newspaper, the sensible man "will surround himself and his home with sufficient protection as to make it impossible."[99] Nearly all southern blacks would surely have agreed with Garvey's message about self-defense, since each person knew well about white acts of terror.

More than a decade after his high school graduation, Owen Whitfield finally found in Garveyism a suitable vehicle for fulfilling his Okolona charge that God helped "them who help themselves."[100] Unwittingly, the Whitfields had come to interpret this adage over the intervening years in the same unsuccessful way as Owen's parents. Like them, Owen and Zella had believed that their individual family effort would be enough to acquire land and achieve independence. By 1920, however, repeated setbacks pushed them closer to a collective solution. Where the Whitfields as a family had failed, the race could succeed if it had proper leadership. Farming for a black landlord in Arkansas made this kind of race-based solution clearer in their minds. Garvey's program of racial solidarity and self-determination also furthered Wallace Battle's admonition in terms of one's duty to the race as a whole. "If you do not exercise your own will," Garvey cautioned his followers, "you will be lost."[101]

Local preachers echoed Garvey's message by absorbing and refashioning it for black farmers in the South. Speaking to a UNIA meeting in Mississippi County, Rev. L. W. Johnson preached "in strong terms" against "the Negro depending upon God to do for them that which they themselves can do." He challenged the assembled Garveyites "to do greater work."[102] Owen Whitfield found the Garveyite call for race leaders to undertake that "greater work" to be a revelation of God's purpose for himself. A common search for land and opportunity had made Bootheelers neighbors, but these settlers knew little of one another at first. When not laboring on their crops, African American migrants built churches where the UNIA had beckoned people in common cause.[103] What solidified black nationalist politics among rural farmers in the Bootheel was the UNIA's ecumenical religiosity. Division meetings were usually held on Sundays, often in churches; each division had a chaplain; and Garveyites sang hymns, heard sermons, and said prayers.[104]

To do his part in bringing these people together, Whitfield began preaching among his fellow farmers in Mississippi County sometime in 1924. With

Garveyite ideas and Battle's "spirit of service" in mind, Whitfield accepted his duty to serve his new neighbors as a preacher. He found people hungry for religious fellowship, and he preached to ad hoc gatherings. With no formal theological training and no denominational affiliation, he had nevertheless imbibed much about righteousness from his mother. At Okolona, moreover, he had learned that in order to make good the privileges of his education, he needed to serve some greater purpose. Whitfield began to consider himself as marked for leadership, by his own conscience as much as the appraisal of others. When he spoke, people listened; when he preached, people believed.[105]

Whitfield's early sermons dwelt, as Zella later recalled, on the necessity of people doing things to help themselves, and on God's insistence that works must validate faith. In denominational terms, Whitfield identified himself alternately as a Missionary or Primitive Baptist. This identification aligned him with the black Baptist majority but did so while claiming a tradition fiercely insistent on congregational autonomy. Missionary Baptists resisted all efforts from larger denominational bodies to regulate their worship, which they believed should be emotional, auditory, and focused on simple, direct communion with God. These demands for independent, free spaces, as well as for an authentic voice, mirrored the bedrock belief among Garveyites and educators like Wallace Battle in the power of individual responsibility in service to racial destiny. In this view, no one, not even God, would save African Americans if they did not help themselves.[106]

The Whitfields' first few years of diligent work in the Bootheel brought reward. They cleared over $900 on their first crop in 1923, when cotton sold at 32 cents per lint pound. Although with lower prices the family only broke even the following year, Owen's preaching brought in additional money from the offering plate. He extended his ministry to more church groups, and parishioners responded by supporting his ministry with what little cash they could spare as well as food and clothing. Whitfield tapped into shared black nationalist aspirations, which led to the flourishing of both his congregations and the Garvey movement in Missouri. As J. L. Simmons, a UNIA leader in Mississippi County, informed the UNIA national convention in Harlem in the summer of 1924, the organization in the Bootheel "was getting along nicely and becoming a power in the community."[107]

Owen was a rising leader in that community, but preaching at several churches made it difficult to devote his full energies to sharecropping. Zella, meanwhile, had seven children under the age of ten to care for by 1925. Although they could have used extra money, Zella and Owen rejected the possibility that she might work for wages in the casual wage market. Garveyite thinking reinforced the traditional view since the Civil War that freedom meant black women should work only for the family and not under the control of white men, and it reinforced the couple's resolve following their ordeal with Dr. Hardin. To allow her husband to pursue his career, Zella tended their small patch of cotton on the riverside and cared for their large family. To help make ends meet, Owen took a job working on the Missouri Pacific Railroad lines that ran out of Cairo, Illinois, and Charleston, Missouri.[108]

The vision of collective prosperity that Missouri Garveyites shared soon faded. A collapse in cotton prices in late 1925 made the Whitfields' delicate balancing act much more difficult to sustain. Usually when cotton prices fell, a sharecropping family could earn extra money by sending children to work in the peak labor seasons. But the Whitfields' children were young, and Owen and Zella hated the idea of sending them to work for others. Still, the kids had to be fed. "Had a great big family that couldn't do nothing but slaughter me at the table," Owen later quipped. In early 1926 the teetering family economy suffered its first major hardship when Zella, heavily pregnant, tripped and fell as she was cutting dried cotton stalks in the fields. She dusted herself off and continued to wield her hoe until she felt contractions. Later that day, the Whitfields' eighth child, Ruth, was stillborn. The loss cast a pall over the family. Owen kept preaching, but alongside this test of personal faith, economic prospects darkened. The price of cotton fell to 10 cents per pound that autumn, the lowest the Whitfields had seen in their adult lives.[109]

The spring of 1927 brought new catastrophes. Following heavy rains across the Midwest, the swollen Mississippi River ripped a gaping hole in the levee protecting Mississippi County. Onrushing waters displaced over 31,000 people in the Bootheel, including the Whitfields, who fled to Cache, Illinois. Most of these were tenant farmers who lost what little they owned to the flood. "Though they did not suffer a great loss," one local writer noted, "it was to them a painful situation because it . . . hurt them as much as it would hurt a man who owned $10,000 worth of property and lost that."[110] But unlike many African Americans further south, those displaced in southeast Missouri chose self-help over paternalistic relief. In Arkansas and Mississippi local landlords used provisions from the Red Cross as a means to gain more control over black workers. In the Bootheel, by contrast, many African Americans organized community relief through local UNIA groups. The strain of this effort and the slow recovery of the local economy, however, dealt successive, withering blows to black farming families. Six of the fifteen UNIA divisions in the Bootheel survived the flood, but the movement suffered irreparable damage as economic disaster and Garvey's deportation from the United States in the autumn of 1927 sapped its lifeblood. Even the divisions that remained went into terminal decline. Unable to find an adequate sharecropping arrangement in 1927, the Whitfields remained in Cache, where Owen worked on a steam shovel crew through 1928.[111] The economic crisis forced him to flee at his congregants' hour of greatest need. Still steadfast in his dedication to serve, Whitfield became a minister without a ministry.[112]

In 1929 Owen and Zella Whitfield finally returned to the Bootheel, but their timing was inauspicious. The collapse of the abstract and distant New York stock market that autumn ignited the very real economic kindling that had been piling up in the rural South since 1926. The Whitfields watched as the nation's financial crisis devastated planters throughout the region: banks closed, credit disappeared, and cotton prices plummeted further. Owen managed to return to preaching, but 1929 was a year of sustained hardship. Not long after moving back, the Whitfields' youngest child, one-year-old John Marshall, died of pneumonia.[113]

As the couple struggled to cope with the loss of yet another child, climatic disaster heaped misery upon misery. The summer of 1930 brought the worst drought on record. The Bootheel's crops dried up as high temperatures baked the region's soil to a crust. Like thousands of others, the Whitfields could not afford to buy cornmeal, the main staple in rural diets, as prices on foodstuffs rose due to shortages in supply. The physical and mental anguish took a toll on their marriage.[114]

Throughout these crises, Whitfield continued to preach, but family survival now mattered more than being a community leader. In contrast to other rural black preachers, Whitfield made no effort to support either of the two political groups that had replaced the UNIA in Mississippi County: the National Association for the Advancement of Colored People (NAACP) and the National Federation of Colored Farmers. Worse still, his congregations dwindled as black believers rejected mainstream denominations like the Baptists that they perceived to have failed to address the Depression. "The 'old line churches' are evidently not meeting the needs of a certain class of people," noted a team of sociologists working in the Bootheel at the time.[115] Disaffected Christians looked instead to new revivalist groups, especially Pentecostal-Holiness congregations. These "new-sect" churches emphasized the process of sanctification, which, according to one historian, stressed the experience of "the Holy Spirit descending upon them, purifying them of sin, blessing them with supernatural powers, and assuring them of eternal reward."[116] The most prominent of these churches in the Bootheel were the Church of the Living God, the first black holiness group, and the Church of God in Christ, a holiness church that would become the largest black Pentecostal denomination in the United States.[117] These "new-sect" congregations in the Bootheel were, by 1935, "made up chiefly of share croppers, tenants, or farm laborers."[118]

In the early 1930s, with cotton prices at a record low, the family managed to make money some years, while breaking even or losing money in others. Crucially, the Whitfields now had five teenaged children able to work in the cotton-chopping and -picking seasons.[119] And by 1933 the Whitfields had saved enough cash to make theirs a "two-mule farm."[120] With these mules (the favorite called Beck) and a large family workforce, Owen and Zella gained status with white managers on local plantations. The Depression had forced many Bootheel landowners to default on their mortgages. The banks and insurance companies that took control of their farms wanted skilled tenants like the Whitfields who would pay rent and require little supervision. Successfully renting 120 acres near Henson, the Whitfields earned little more than they had as sharecroppers, but they found a rare measure of independence. The following year, they even employed two sharecropping families, one of them their daughter Cora and her new husband. Ironically, the greatest economic crisis of their lifetimes had enabled the Whitfields to become semi-autonomous black landlords.[121]

The election of Franklin D. Roosevelt in 1932 did not bring much change. The main agricultural program of the early New Deal, the Agricultural Adjustment Act (AAA), boosted cotton prices in 1933 by reducing the acreages planted. The Whitfields, keen to rely on themselves and steer clear of government schemes, did not participate in the voluntary program and profited. But government policy the following year left them no choice. The 1934 iteration of the AAA, the Bankhead Cotton Control Act, made acreage reductions of 40 percent mandatory for all growers. This required cut handicapped the Whitfields. The government money meant to compensate for their lost income got hung up in the hands of the landowner, as money often did. They felt cheated and, once again, the family suffered a tragic personal blow that autumn when their eleven-year-old son, Excel, contracted malaria and died.[122]

The Whitfields' brief independence had been illusory. Owen now realized that however hard he and Zella worked, white people profited far more than they ever would. Their joy or sorrow depended on the whims of white landowners. "You're the best damn nigger I've got," the landowner at Henson had told Owen, "now I want you to set the pace." And, despite all that he had learned from his parents, from his uncle Chuck, from his teachers at Okolona, and from fellow Garveyites, Owen Whitfield did as he was told. A white man dictated the pace of his work, and the pace at which Owen required his sharecroppers to work, including his own daughter and son-in-law. "Now I was out there with old Beck when the sun would come up," he explained, "and I come to realize that I was just what he said I was, I was the best damn nigger he had."[123] His three buried children belied his feeling of independence; he reckoned that to be the "best damn nigger" on a cotton farm was not to be very much at all.

These insufferable injustices pushed Owen Whitfield back toward political activism. When in March 1934 a stranger named Ashima Takis began speaking to crowds of former Garveyites in Mississippi County, Whitfield took pause and listened. Takis urged sympathetic black nationalists to join his organization, the Original Independent Benevolent Afro-Pacific Movement of the World (OIBAPMW). This group, Takis said, was meant to support Japan, which was the "champion of the colored races," and intended to crush imperialist white supremacy. "You are the most oppressed people on Earth," Takis informed crowds, but "if you will join the Japanese and other colored races you will be in command of the whites."[124] By July he had organized OIBAPMW lodges throughout the Bootheel. This was not a small group—the lodge at Charleston boasted over six hundred members, including Owen Whitfield. Takis's magnetism derived in part from his ability to evoke Garveyism: solidarity and self-determination among people of color.[125]

New members pledged to "protect and preserve the legitimate rights of their race." Owen Whitfield later recalled that "this jap specialized in pointing out to Negroes the unfairness and brutality heaped upon us by the American white man." People responded with "great bursts of applause," he said, when Takis "pointed out the great things that awaited us when Japan would come to America to free its black brother from modern slavery." In the midst of the worst year to date in the Great Depression, such talk of an imagined community of international racial solidarity had broad appeal among black farmers. Even relatively well-off tenant farmers like Whitfield believed for a time that revolution, spurred by far-off allies, was the only way to bring change to the Jim Crow South.[126]

Takis's rebellion died quickly. By the autumn local police had broken up the OIBAPMW. Some organizers went to jail, and followers across the Bootheel recanted their membership. Whitfield explained later—after the Japanese attack on Pearl Harbor in 1941—that the only reason he had joined was to make sure that people did not lose their dues money. More truthful, perhaps, was his admission that his churches would have been completely empty had he not taken part. Takis in many ways modeled himself as a revival evangelist, and his popularity no doubt made clear to Whitfield how marginal his own ministry had become. Whatever his subsequent explanation, Whitfield could not deny the sense of frustration he felt during this period. He had lost children, his dreams, and his youth. Later, the OIBAPMW came to represent an outlandish and embarrassing episode, but the desperation and anger that drove him there was real.[127]

Although he continued to preach, Whitfield recoiled again from civic life following the OIBAPMW debacle. In 1935 he and Zella left the farm at Henson to rent land east of Pinhook, in the southern part of Mississippi County. Whether they moved because of Owen's support of Takis—which would have certainly raised white doubts about him—is unclear. The twin tolls of economic crisis and the exacerbating Bankhead Act could equally have encouraged them. Whatever the case, Owen again took the pulpit in scattered Baptist churches in the area.[128] But Pinhook was different. In the countryside the Whitfields encountered an unfamiliar rural world where white share-croppers predominated. They had always lived in plantation districts where African Americans made up the majority of the population; whites, in their experience, owned farms or lived in town. But here only one-third of tenants were black. Although the Whitfields had always known poor whites, they saw there for the first time the depth of rural white poverty.[129]

Yet, the new racial context of Pinhook did not immediately soften Owen's distrust of whites, which explained his skepticism when some of his white and African American neighbors joined the Southern Tenant Farmers' Union (STFU) in 1936. Founded by a small group of white and black sharecroppers in northeastern Arkansas in the summer of 1934, the STFU aimed to secure economic and social justice for landless farmers. In the short term, the union pushed for the reform of New Deal agricultural policies, beginning with the AAA; in the long term, it looked to establish full democracy for the mass of southern people.[130] Approaching the agricultural crisis in the South as a class rather than a race problem, the union's socialist leaders allowed local groups to organize along racial lines, or integrate, as they saw fit. Many whites and blacks segregated themselves; others, however, formed mixed locals. Black tenants near Charleston formed the first STFU locals in the Bootheel in the summer of 1936, having learned of the union through word of mouth. Hundreds more farmers, mostly black and a few white, soon joined after the union sent John Handcox, a black Arkansan, to organize in the area. While most of this activity took place in the northern part of the county, two locals, East Prairie and Crosno, formed in the vicinity of the Whitfields' farm.[131]

Owen and Zella stood apart from the growing union movement that entire summer. But as the STFU gained support among their neighbors, and among Owen's parishioners, pressure built on the couple to attend a meeting. Late in October a member of Whitfield's congregation requested permission to host a union meeting in the church. It was to be a special affair, the man said. Among those scheduled to speak were E. B. McKinney, a black Baptist preacher, former Garveyite, and STFU organizer from Arkansas, and Claude Williams, a popular preacher, regional union organizer, and, to Whitfield's chagrin, a white man. Whitfield consented to the meeting and even agreed to attend. He had much in common with McKinney and was interested to hear him speak. As for Williams, Whitfield asked, "What can that white pecker wood say to me?"[132]

2. Seeking the Kingdom of God

In June 1930 Claude and Joyce Williams and their two daughters moved to Paris, Arkansas. The family drove west from Nashville across the Arkansas–Tennessee border and the plantation lowlands bordering the Mississippi River, through Little Rock, and then up into the Ozark hills to their new mountain home. Founded in the 1870s as the seat of Logan County and originally a cotton market town, Paris became the mining capital of Arkansas in the 1920s. By the time the Williamses arrived, a dozen mines produced 400,000 tons (6,500 train-car loads) of coal annually. Of its 3,500 people, a third worked in the mines, with many more dependent upon the wages of miners for survival. Paris had no library, no city park, and no place for family recreation. The Presbyterian Church (USA) of Paris was without a pastor and had only a handful of active members. L. E. Blakemore, a Presbyterian minister, had described the people of Paris as being "lost in a fog." "They need leadership," he told Williams.[1] Claude and Joyce wanted a challenge for their ministry; they found it in the depressed mining country of western Arkansas.

I

To interest people in the church, Williams decided to concentrate on recreation instead of wrath. After working long shifts underground, male workers congregated at a pool hall that was operated by a local bootlegger. The town's clergy hoped their new colleague would support their ongoing campaign to close it. Rather than join the chorus of condemnation, though, Williams decided to bring recreation into the purview of the church. He appropriated leftover money from the church's building fund and bought a pool table as

well as decks of cards, chess and checkers sets, and an assortment of maga-
zines and books. "Play," Williams told those who entered his recreation room,
"is divine instinct, found in birds, babies, and lower animals, and is not immoral." It worked. More and more people, especially young people, entered
the church. They played games, borrowed books, and engaged in casual
conversation, and they generally took a liking to Claude, who increasingly
became known simply as "preacher."[2]

The popularity of Williams's recreational program also brought on criticism.
It was bad enough, the leaders of the rival Baptist and Methodist churches
thought, for this outsider to offer sinful games. But when these games led to
organized girls and boys clubs and defections of their own members, Claude's
peers vowed to stop the "preacher." During the winter of 1931–32, Williams
proposed a weekly charity event of Sunday afternoon movies to the Kiwanis
Club, a local fraternal organization, and the Parent-Teacher Association. The
proceeds, Williams explained, would provide clothing and shoes for children
in need. His fellow religious leaders opposed the proposal because it represented a direct challenge to the dominant "blue laws" that restricted activities
on the Sabbath. A Baptist minister circulated a petition that called Sunday
pictures antireligious and convinced 1,300 people from Paris to sign it. Yet,
after Williams wrote an article in the *Paris Express* to explain the idea and its
charitable intent, the townspeople changed their minds, and the conservative
American Legion even agreed to sponsor it. Not to be defeated, the Baptist
Church flexed its civic muscle; on the first two Sundays the electricity mys-
teriously stopped working right before the movie began.[3]

Unbowed, Williams redoubled his efforts by organizing a weekly Sunday
charity baseball game. Sunday baseball was progressive; northern states had
legalized it in the 1910s, so long as it did not occur too close to a church.[4]
Williams's now familiar opponents led a delegation to the district attorney's
office to demand the arrest of anyone who tried to play baseball on the Lord's
Day. When the attorney came to warn him, Williams was defiant: "do your
duty," but "I'll be on the field Sunday with the boys." Seven hundred miners
assembled to play; half ringed around the baseball field and the other half
assembled in front of the Paris jail. Although activities like a Sunday picture
show and baseball game seemed innocent, the leaders of Paris rightly interpreted them as a challenge to their authority. What made Claude's outreach
so appealing, and thus so suspect in the eyes of older preachers, was that he
willfully blurred the boundaries that divided the secular from the sacred.[5]

In the months that followed, Williams elaborated on the teachings of Jesus
in relation to the everyday lives of the people of Paris. He set up a proper
library in the church—open to anyone—that included all sorts of books

and literature, from Harry Fosdick's works to pamphlets on disarmament to literature published by the Socialist Party.[6] In Sunday school classes for teenagers, Claude and Joyce introduced the idea of equality between the sexes and championed the new 1920s idea of "companionate marriage," a view that marriage should be based on democratic family organization and emphasize the emotional and sexual needs of both husband and wife. "A good marriage is simply a good union," the Williamses taught.[7]

The couple became so popular that their students asked them in the summer of 1932 to chaperone a public dance. The Williamses agreed. A week later, the now predictable backlash struck when a minister condemned the dance in the local paper as a "hell hole." Not to be outdone, Williams used the article for discussion among his youth and philosophy clubs at the church; they decided that Claude should preach the following Sunday on the topic "OUR DANCE AT THE HELL-HOLE." The provocative title resulted in an overflowing audience, and Williams used the opportunity to discuss social interaction. People, he said, should not deny the existence of sex, because shame led to unwed mothers and disowned sons and daughters. Williams's argument and the enthusiasm of the local youths won support for chaperoned dances thereafter, but it also further infuriated the opposition. A church elder sent one of the fliers that advertised the dance "AT THE HELL-HOLE" to the Presbytery of Arkansas as proof of Williams's strange ideas. M. L. Gillespie, a leader of the Arkansas Presbytery who had helped recruit Williams to Paris, reassured Claude of the "sympathetic interest" of church leaders but advised him not "to stoop to the plane of your critics at the expense of the dignity of the church."[8]

Williams remained uncompromising because he believed that his ministry was working. "I stood outside [Williams's service]," one miner explained, curious but too skeptical to go in. By the end of Claude's sermon, however, he became "so interested that I got closer." What impressed this miner and others was Claude's ability to discuss the religion of Jesus rather than the religion about Jesus. The message was of a practical faith that had relevance for working people. "After a sermon on Sunday," this worker recalled, "we talked about it all week in the mine." As a result, "miners go to hear Williams preach," another one said. "He compares the problems of labor with the teachings of Jesus."[9] Williams's Presbyterian allies lauded this success. Warren Wilson, secretary of the Presbyterian Church (USA) national Board of Missions, wrote to M. L. Gillespie in late 1932 in support of "a daring and radical thing" Williams was doing. Gillespie relayed Wilson's sentiments in order to reassure Williams of the church's support: "He has some of that breath-taking courage that the greatest Christians have had," Wilson wrote.[10]

Williams displayed that courage by reaching out to African American cotton farmers who labored in the nearby "bottoms" along the Arkansas River. Williams preached against racism, both to his regular white Paris congregation and during his sermons in rural villages like Roseville, Driggs, and Scranton. With Joyce he also went into the plantation district to hear sharecroppers speak about their plight. One black woman from "the bottom" recalled that after Claude and Joyce visited her, they in turn invited her family for dinner. When the family arrived in Paris, Williams led them through the front door and opened the blinds as they dined. The racial logic of Jim Crow, Claude had concluded, stemmed from skewed religious understandings. His critics argued that Williams needed to preach about Jesus as crucified, and not worry about current conditions because the separation of the races and social classes was part of God's plan.[11] As one historian concluded about many ministers in this period, "Church leaders gladly cast the authority of religion into the support of these upper-class dictums, preaching as essential the virtues of a society strictly articulated by class and race."[12] Williams fumed at this interpretation of Christianity and told his parishioners to ignore the popular view and instead listen to the teachings of Jesus. "May we not dare to hope there are revolutionary fires already kindled . . . which are destined to bring a new renaissance, a new reformation, yea a new penticost which will equip us for our age?" he asked his mentor Alva Taylor.[13]

What followed for Williams was a growing conviction that the gospel of Christ should overturn southern orthodoxies of gender, race, and class. He believed that the people themselves held the power to break away from old injustices and sensed a latent rebelliousness in western Arkansas. Williams surveyed the plight of area miners during the worst year of the Great Depression. In 1932 mine operators closed the mines for months at a time because of low prices, which left workers and their families in poverty. Struggling fathers and husbands sought Claude out as a friendly confidant, someone to whom they could reveal their stories without shame. In these sessions, older people recalled when the miners of western Arkansas had confronted injustices. In the 1910s they had embraced the Socialist Party of Eugene V. Debs and, through militant action in the United Mine Workers (UMW), had won better wages. The miners had made their stoutest defense in a 1914 strike at the Mammouth Vein in adjacent Sebastian County, when miners, socialists, and tenant farmers had banded together to declare western Arkansas "Union Man's Country." By World War I their struggle and the wartime need for coal earned the miners record wages of $7.50 a day. When operators tried to push wage scales back to prewar levels, the miners went out on strike again and won. Yet, in 1925 the Southwestern Coal Operators used declining economic conditions, the weakening of the UMW, and the withering of the Socialist Party to withdraw from union agreements. By 1927 they had crushed the UMW locals and established an open shop across the Ozarks.[14]

This hidden history captivated Williams, who was looking for a way to broaden his ministry. He envied his friends Howard Kester and Don West, who were in the thick of activist work elsewhere. "I believe that you have a big contribution to make," Kester wrote, "and I feel that you should begin to contact such groups as we have"—referring to the Socialist Party and the Fellowship of Reconciliation, interracial groups promoting progressive causes. "We need your brains and brawn in a radical movement now." Meanwhile, West was creating an educational institute with Myles Horton, another Cumberland Presbyterian from west Tennessee who had turned radical. Their Highlander Folk School admitted students in late 1932.[15]

Spurred by his Vanderbilt cohort, Williams invited labor organizers and UMW district leader David Fowler to use his church in their effort to reorganize the UMW locals. Area miners agreed with Fowler's proposal to form provisional UMW District 21, which encompassed the coalfields of western Arkansas and eastern Oklahoma, and strike until the mine operators recognized it as their bargaining agent. The strike call went out in May 1932. Williams joined the miners, accepting their invitations to speak in Russellville, Clarksville, Midland, Jenny Lind, and points west in Oklahoma. He talked to the miners about God in relation to the union. The preacher showed how verses in the sixth chapter of the Gospel of Luke explained that workers should live by the words and deeds of Jesus despite the enviable position of those who prospered as sinners. "Blessed be ye poor: for yours is the kingdom of God," Jesus had said to his followers. "Blessed are ye, when men shall hate you, and when they shall separate you from their company, and shall reproach you, and cast out your name as evil, for the Son of man's sake. . . . But woe unto you that are rich! . . . Woe unto you that are full! for ye shall hunger" (Luke 6:20–26). Poverty, Williams preached, was a sign of righteousness. It was up to the poor, though, as Christ had said, to lead men and women forward to make the Kingdom of God on earth. Williams had found his audience, even if sometimes he preached under cover of darkness so that miners could attend without fear of company spies reporting them to the bosses, or marking them for physical retribution. The miners, in turn, deemed him an honorary member of their newly revived union.[16]

The strike also brought Williams into contact with another small group of kindred souls. During his travels among the miners, Claude met Lucien Koch and others from Commonwealth College, a small socialist school in Mena, Arkansas, about eighty miles south of Paris. In late 1924, students and teachers had hacked the Commonwealth campus out of the wilderness after it relocated from Louisiana. Now situated in a valley at the foot of Rich Mountain near the Oklahoma border, Commonwealth prospered under the inspired leadership of Koch; his brother Raymond Koch; the college's executive secretary, Charlotte Moskowitz; and Clay Fulks, an Arkansas socialist who stood as the party's candidate for governor in 1928 and 1932. By the early 1930s they had recruited nearly fifty students—many of them Jewish and from northern cities—into the college's labor activist program. When Williams met the Commonwealth contingent in the spring of 1932, they were on their way to support striking miners in Harlan County, Kentucky, then the site of a brutal war between unions and company-backed militias. Next to these hardcore activists, Williams felt conservative. Williams asked them where they got their courage, thinking them to be excellent Christians. The Commoners—as those who lived at the college called themselves—replied that they believed in Marxism, not Jesus. They explained that they were communists and socialists who believed that poverty, hardship, and violent struggle resulted from the despotic ownership class under capitalism. While there were not many communists in Arkansas at the time, it was not illegal to be one. The Communist Party (CP) ticket received only 175 votes in the state during the presidential election of 1932. That the CP even made it on the ballot was remarkable, considering that the party's vice-presidential candidate was James Ford, a black man. Williams listened intently to what the Commoners said. Faithless or not, Marxist or not, he hoped that in the future he could work alongside these brave young people.[17]

Curious about the Commoners' ideological motivations, Williams began studying Marxist thought. He steeped himself in the writings of Bolshevik leader V. I. Lenin, who interpreted Marx and Frederick Engels through the lens of imperialism. Williams was learning a new language; a new framework with which to think about current problems. Alva Taylor supported Williams's nascent commitment to the working-class movement, but warned Claude that his frequent use of the "red rag" word "proletarian" in his letters "gets you misunderstood by a lot of good folk" and "renders you liable to attack by the wolves who yelp bolshevik at everything in sight and thus poison minds unaware." Williams had already faced the wolves in Paris, however, and while he did not ascribe to Marxism as a sectarian philosophy that explained all of human nature, he began to see its value as an ideology that challenged and sharpened his own spiritual faith. That intellectual step drew him increasingly into alliances with socialists and communists alike.[18]

Williams and his union colleagues wanted to enshrine the new relationship between local labor and the church with a new building that they dubbed the Proletarian Labor Church and Temple. During the summer of 1932, the workers pressed for immediate implementation, since they could use the space for meetings of their UMW Local 1116, whose 1,200 members suffered gatherings in a cramped forty-by-sixty-foot room. A local architect lent his expertise to draw the plans for the building, and Williams cashed in life insurance policies to buy cement for the foundation. His willingness to liquidate assets designed to protect his family in case of his untimely death testified to his commitment to the union movement. The miners backed him up when eleven locals in District 21 agreed to pay one dollar per member from their union dues and volunteered their labor. The people who came to Paris to work on the Labor Temple were black and white, miners and farmers, who had traveled as far as forty miles to help. The new church was to be more than a simple structure. Williams intended the Labor Temple to be a refuge, worship house, and school for workers, modeled in part on Commonwealth College.[19] Williams also aimed to begin a labor newspaper, "the South-West Proletarian" and asked Alva Taylor and Howard Kester to edit it.[20] He hoped that the Labor Temple would "at once occupy the minds of the strikers, produce something worth while, and dispel the popular fallacy that striking workers are destructive."[21]

With construction underway that August, Williams and several of the workers penned the charter for this new church. The Labor Temple would "proclaim the Kingdom of God: that in a system founded, in fact and practices, upon the principles of righteousness, equality and brotherhood there should be no hunger, cold nor nakedness." This meant honoring the dignity of labor by treating all workers, men and women, as equals. By "seeking the Kingdom of God," the charter stated, "we are to seek to change the conditions which give rise to want, suffering, insecurity and crime."[22] Williams's overall goal for the Labor Temple, written on a sign at the building site, was "That They Might Have Life, and Have It More Abundantly," as Jesus had said (John 10:10).[23] This scriptural inspiration flowed directly from his reading of Harry Fosdick's *The Modern Use of the Bible*, which had challenged preachers to seek to "bring men into more abundant life," even if it meant following Christ's example by throwing off "the formalities of popular religion."[24]

Williams sought to expand the denominational church because "if the Church is to be the CHRISTian Church it must lead the way." He did not want to break from the denomination. This strategy stemmed from something Alva Taylor had taught Williams at Vanderbilt: "one can accomplish more fighting within than without. The very opposition one may incur will be educational to the group while if one is independent very few are concerned about what he does or believes." An "extra-denominational movement," Williams told

Taylor, would be "futile," so instead, Claude appealed for the support of church allies.[25] "You need have no worry about the support of the Board," wrote M. L. Gillespie of the Arkansas Presbyterian Synod, because it would back his "sane, aggressive application of the Gospel to social conditions."[26]

The Labor Temple, however, had barely risen from its foundations before progress stopped. David Fowler, the District 21 boss, had ruled that using the UMW dues check-off for contributions to the Labor Temple building fund violated the UMW International Constitution, which did not allow "donations to be made for other than legitimate purposes." Fowler was also wary of Williams, who, he pointed out, was not actually a member of the UMW, or a miner. Fowler was an experienced union leader and politician. A native of the Rhondda Valley in Wales, the site of decades of bitter union struggles, Fowler had defended the interests of miners for eight years in the Pennsylvania state legislature before moving to Oklahoma. He knew that union organization in the coalfields was usually a protracted battle that required pragmatic leadership. One year earlier, UMW efforts to secure a union contract in Harlan County, Kentucky, although ultimately successful, had been jeopardized by communist activists working independently among the miners. Fowler thus rejected the possibility of using the union to aid the preacher's projects. "We appreciate your efforts in behalf of the workers in the past," he wrote, and "I have no objections to any individuals in our organization who may choose to assist you." But Fowler's main point was clear: "I trust that you will discontinue your activities along this line for the best interests of the United Mine Workers."[27]

Writing to the leaders of District 21 locals, Fowler made his irritation more obvious. In a letter to R. F. White of the Jenny Lind local, Fowler dismissed questions about the Labor Temple, demanding from White "more cooperation in carrying out the policies of the United Mine Workers, and less attention paid to those who have fanatic ideas and less to some of the students who are parading this district from the Commonwealth College." The "fantastic ideas" of Williams and the Commoners, Fowler told his boss, John L. Lewis, are "great ideas but they do not realize the cost of putting [them] into effect."[28] The resounding victory of Franklin D. Roosevelt in the November 1932 election had raised the political stakes for the UMW. With a Democrat in the White House, union leaders rightly saw a perfect opportunity to push for protective legislation for organized labor. The UMW would need to appear like a responsible voice for working people for that lobbying campaign to work. In the view of union leaders like Fowler, union approval of, let alone direct support for, mercurial figures like Williams would not help.

As Fowler impeded Williams's work with District 21, the preacher noticed in May 1933 that the half of his salary that came from the local Paris church elders vanished from his paycheck. He made an inquiry and was told it would arrive "soon," but "soon" eventually became "later," and he realized that all of this likely meant "never." Williams assumed that his support for the strike and his plans for the Labor Temple must have resulted in the pay cut.[29]

Despite these troubles, the UMW national office sent word in October 1933 that the coal operators had recognized District 21 and that the strike had been settled. The contract stipulated a wage scale of $4 a day. After the initial elation wore off, Williams and others did the math: $4 a day meant that a family could not earn more than $300 a year on the current mining schedule, which was still limited due to the reluctance of operators to open the shafts. The new scale did not seem to put miners, who needed around $340 a year for basic survival, in a better position to stave off hunger. To make matters worse, three mine companies had not settled with the UMW, and the workers in their pits remained outside the union body.[30] On a speaking engagement in Hackett, Arkansas, soon after the strike ended, Williams was approached by three workers from Hartshorne, Oklahoma. They said they represented the relief committee there, and since the strike had not been settled in their coalfield, the people had become desperate. After hearing their stories, Williams canceled everything and rode back with them to eastern Oklahoma.[31]

Williams had seen hunger in his life, but never anything as dire as in Hartshorne. Replacement workers from other towns worked in the mine next to armed guards with machine guns. People looked hollow-faced, had barely enough clothing to cover their bodies, and felt abandoned by their union. The miners trusted Williams and invited him to a secret meeting. He attended and learned they intended to make bombs out of kerosene, phosphorus, and "high life." These bombs, the men explained, could be planted to explode hours later. They planned to put them in the mine as well as the homes of the mine managers. Up to that point, Williams had been a pacifist. In discussions with his Vanderbilt cohort, he had always agreed that "individual violence and terror defeats the end of the worker."[32] But events in Hartshorne made Williams so angry that he now reconsidered the morality of political violence. "I was desperate," he recorded in his diary. After deep deliberation, however, he preached against the bomb plot.[33]

Williams and the miners eventually reached the conclusion that they needed to transform their union to change their deplorable conditions. When negotiating the recent union contract, the national UMW leadership did not consult the rank and file, and many miners thereafter criticized the union for its lack of internal democracy. At Williams's urging, the miners of District 21 appealed to Fowler for a greater say, including official UMW recognition of the Labor Temple.[34]

Williams's efforts to encourage an autonomy movement in District 21 angered Fowler. Bad blood had been brewing between them since their clash over the Labor Temple. Williams represented a dangerous distraction from the difficult work of organizing a miner's union, and the UMW was fortunate to secure "an organizing contract" that Fowler considered the "best contract that we could [reach] under the present conditions" even if it left out some miners. Local mine operators had destroyed the previous union in the area a decade earlier and would not hesitate to use violence to fight unionization. Moreover, the Arkansas and Oklahoma state governments were more than willing to use their legal power to help the mine operators keep the fields unorganized. Employer recognition, a union contract, and a union wage scale were notable gains in this context. Recognition bound the miners of District 21 into the national body of the UMW, whose leaders carried significant political weight in the Democratic Party. Moreover, President Roosevelt had strong support throughout Arkansas, which he had taken with 86 percent of the vote.[35] Although the initial contract was not ideal, Arkansas miners could reasonably expect a stronger contract in the near future. Fowler did not want to do anything that jeopardized the bread and butter of the union: wage gains, union recognition, and union dues check-offs by companies to sustain the UMW's coffers.

It is little wonder that Fowler moved swiftly to neutralize Williams, but the UMW leader misjudged the extent to which Williams had helped build District 21, as well as his influence among the miners who started the autonomy movement. Twenty-four locals endorsed autonomy by 1934. These workers wanted better health conditions, union democracy, and the Labor Temple as a base for their struggles because the meaning of the union encompassed their whole lives—not just the time they spent in the pits. That more holistic understanding of the connections between work, faith, family life, recreation, and citizenship stemmed directly from Williams's ministry and contained an emotional appeal and vision that Fowler's pragmatic agenda lacked.[36]

Aspects of President Roosevelt's New Deal widened the rift. Under the auspices of the National Industrial Recovery Act (NRA) that Roosevelt had signed into law in June 1933, the miners in District 21 took advantage of their new collective bargaining rights, provided in section 7(a) of the NRA, to hold an election of their own in early 1934 on the issue of union representation. Of approximately 7,000 votes cast in the district, 5,254 miners voted for the right to elect their own leaders. Much to the chagrin of those who rejoiced in this expression of democratic unionism, NRA officials rejected their claim for new leadership on the curious grounds that such a decision was an "internal matter" not relevant to the NRA.[37] The miners of District 21 realized that NRA officials were loyal to the national UMW leadership, because John L. Lewis and his deputies had lobbied and shepherded the bill through the Congress during President Roosevelt's first hundred days.[38] Such was the political power of the UMW in the New Deal. Whatever the miners of District 21 had expected from the close relationship between organized labor and the new president, this was not it.

The Ozarks rank and file revolted. According to the miners of the autonomy movement, the UMW, the capitalists, and the government seemed to have agreed upon a "marriage" without including the workers, or indeed, even inviting them to the ceremony. Determined to stop such attacks, Fowler wrote a letter to District 21 members that accused these "unproved, untried" men of "slandering its officers" to "Russianize all on board" the "good Ship Unionism." These men, he railed, wanted "to be an oak without commencing to be an acorn," which "can have only one end—DESTRUCTION." More direct, Fowler phoned Williams to warn him to "keep his head out of labor" or he would suffer the same fate as local activist Jeff Thornton, who had been recently beaten by a group of thugs. The union boss also stated that the NRA board would decertify all of the UMW's union local contracts if the rebellion succeeded. Did Williams want to continue with his antics and risk the collapse of District 21?[39]

Fowler was keen to establish his authority whether it meant coercing local members or not. In February 1934 Williams convened an autonomy convention in Fort Smith. Fowler countered by orchestrating a government trial of the autonomy leaders on the charge of operating a "dual union." In front of NRA Board Number Four, authorized by the Code of Fair Competition of the Bituminous Coal Industry, Fred Howell, Harrison Tuggle, and Bert Loudermilk stood accused of being elected as rebel leaders of a shadow District 21 who sought only to line their own pockets from salaried offices based on the Fort Smith convention. The board sustained the charges, expelled all three men, and declared the autonomy convention illegal. To the miners of the autonomy movement, the verdict confirmed Fowler's dictatorial powers. Fred Howell responded with an open letter that argued that like the American founders, the miners of the district deserved consensual representation. Dues-payment, Howell and others reasoned, led to a simple "right to elect officers of our choice." The miners did not want "dualism," they explained, but only a modicum of control over their own destiny within the UMW.[40]

With half of his salary withheld by the church and Fowler bearing down,

Williams considered leaving Paris. For the second time in his life, he wondered whether or not he could better follow his calling and support his family outside of the denominational church. Williams applied for work with the Arkansas arm of the Federal Emergency Relief Administration (FERA), a New Deal creation that aimed to help the unemployed. He believed himself to be well qualified considering his work "since 1927 has been with the indigent, the workers and the under-privileged." M. L. Gillespie urged him to take the job. "If ever a man fought for his ideals and sacrificed everything for them anywhere you have done it at Paris," he wrote, but the endeavor was not worth continuing without church support. As Williams pondered leaving, he balanced "the things sane people usually consider on one side": a good salary, family security, and his physical health. On the other side he contemplated "the things fools, fanatics and failures usually consider," like pursuing an ideal vision of the world despite the consequences.[41]

During this period of doubt, Williams received a boost with the arrival of Ward Rodgers, a young Methodist preacher from Combes, Texas, who had studied with Alva Taylor at Vanderbilt in the early 1930s. Rodgers had taken up a preaching position near Paris in late 1933 and was immediately drawn to Williams. An active member of the Socialist Party, Rodgers was also well connected to leading theologians like Reinhold Niebuhr, a Social Gospel intellectual at Union Theological Seminary in New York. Rodgers encouraged Williams to parry the opposition from within the denomination. In the end, Williams decided not to take the government job. "I resolved with myself and before God," he declared in the end, "to go all the way." "We are no different than others if we accept the easy, the certain, and the secure," Williams concluded. "Christians daringly gamble with ultimates, flout the secure and live dangerously for the uncertain."[42] With a fresh wind at his back, Williams restarted efforts to build the Labor Temple.[43]

Despite his involvement with the union autonomy movement, with the Labor Temple, and with the Commoners, Williams still considered the Presbyterian Church his base. Much to the chagrin of the Paris church elders, Williams opened a membership drive in early 1934 that brought in new congregants by the score, many of them miners. Their enthusiasm heartened the preacher, as did the support of Rodgers, who had quit his pastorate and now lived with the Williamses. Additionally, the opposition of hidebound local elites confirmed to Williams that his preaching was true to the Gospel of Christ. What Paris needed, what the Presbyterian Church needed, Williams concluded, were "good healthy radicals who 'could take it on the chin.'"[44]

Williams believed that his national Presbyterian allies supported him. Warren Wilson admitted that Williams had the "gospel spirit in him" and

reassured him that "the people of Paris need you." "I praise you for your loyalty to the working people and I hope it will have success," he wrote. Williams
noted that the national body seemed to be moving in his direction. At the
General Assembly of the Presbyterian Church (USA) in Denver in May 1932,
it had adopted a set of sixteen ideals that included calls for the "subordination
of profit to the creative and co-operative spirit" and "the right of employees
and employers alike to organize for collective bargaining and social action."[45]

Consistent with this mission, Williams called a meeting in April 1934 in
which his newly enlarged congregation demanded a greater voice in the direction of the church—a strategy that bore close resemblance to the autonomy
movement in District 21. "The proletarians believe this is their opportunity
to take over the program," he informed Roy Burt, a socialist leader from
Chicago. The board of elders offered them four new deacon positions. Once
the congregants learned that the deacons held no real power, they voted for
an expansion of the board. With great hesitation but without recourse to deny
the democratic vote, the elders agreed to expand the board by seven members. The congregation, many of whom had joined from the Labor Temple
project, proceeded to elect two students, one woman, one businessman, and
three miners.[46]

Eager to build on this momentum, Williams conceived of a big meeting
of labor and religious activists that summer to bring Christ's Gospel into the
hostile terrain of the Ozark coalfields. He called it the New Era Forum and
invited speakers to join local activists and workers in dialogue. These national
speakers included religious activists such as Willard Uphaus of the National
Religion and Labor Foundation (NRLF) in Connecticut, theologian Reinhold
Niebuhr, and representatives from the Federal Council of the Churches of
Christ and Union Theological Seminary. For his part, Ward Rodgers founded
a Socialist Party local (which Williams joined) and planned to start an Ozark
folk school along the lines of Commonwealth and Highlander to work with
the growing socialist movement in Arkansas. "I am here for a show-down,"
Williams declared, and "if the religion of the Nazarene cannot be expressed
through, or championed by the church, then I am through with the church
and institutional Christianity."[47]

The showdown came days later. Fourteen members of Williams's church
(out of 112 total tithed members) signed a petition in May 1934 that called
upon the presbytery in Fort Smith to end Williams's pastorate. They charged
their preacher with dereliction of duties to the church, with the espousal of
communism, and with the preaching of heretical doctrines. At the hearing in
Fort Smith, the Presbyterian judges hardly discussed the charges and barred
sympathetic congregation members from testifying. The presbytery avoided

controversy by declaring the pulpit vacant on the argument that Williams had left his contracted duties in Paris to work for the UMW and organize the Labor Temple. Feeling vindicated, the petitioners, who owed their preacher hundreds of dollars in withheld salary, presented the Williams family with an eviction notice. The blow was stunning. "I am out," Williams informed Sherwood Gates of the NRLF: "down for the count."[48]

II

Williams dropped his plans for the New Era Forum to rally support for an appeal to the highest church body. The Socialist Party of Arkansas, in response to requests for help from Rodgers, warned the state's Presbyterians that it would "publicize and take an aggressive stand on this matter" if his appeal failed.[49] Letters of support poured in from Howard Kester, Willard Uphaus, and other prominent allies, including a fiery note from Highlander's Myles Horton, a Presbyterian himself. Writing to Warren Wilson, the usually calm Horton fumed that "if Williams' type are not encouraged to stay in the Church, there will be no argument against the charge that the Church is a tool of the owning class." "This is a case," he warned, "where neutrality is impossible." According to Horton, the only crime that Williams had committed was to dare "to draw into his church miners and tenant-farmers. Because of this the 'Pharisees' have thrown him out." Gospel preachers across the South were "waiting to see with which class the Church will side in Paris Arkansas," he concluded.[50]

The appeal failed nevertheless. Sherwood Gates immediately promised to use the NRLF to "make an appeal to our constituency through the bulletin, and to certain Eastern leaders . . . for financial support of your endeavors."[51] At the urging of Lucien Koch, the International Labor Defense (ILD), a communist-led legal advocacy group, planned "a nationwide campaign" on behalf of Williams and sent two organizers, Bob Reed and Horace Bryan, to confer with him on local action.[52] Meanwhile, Uphaus went to Paris to investigate, and arrived to find an unbowed Williams still preaching to hundreds of people in the local movie theater, which they now dubbed the "Labor Auditorium."[53] In what would become a theme of his career, Williams was gaining national fame in his hour of defeat. Reinhold Niebuhr, for example, wrote an article in defense of Williams in *Christian Century*, the nation's leading ecumenical journal.[54]

The most important new relationship Williams established during his ordeal was with the Socialist Party. Socialism had virtually died out in Arkansas in the late 1920s; having attracted over eight thousand votes in the state in the presidential election of 1912, the party netted fewer than five hundred in 1928.[55] But the Depression caused people to consider socialism again. Party locals sprang back to life around the state in the early 1930s, including one in Paris led by Ward Rodgers. Socialist contacts had put Williams in touch with Highlander's Myles Horton, who had studied with Abram Nightingale, Williams's old friend from Vanderbilt. These radical circles were tight-knit. Williams attended a worker's education conference at Highlander in Monteagle, Tennessee, in July 1934, where he conferred with Horton about possible collaboration.[56] Williams's new socialist connections also went right to the top of the party. Norman Thomas, the socialist presidential candidate in 1928 and 1932, wrote to him expressing sympathy and support.[57] But most important in convincing Claude that the socialists were on the right track was their role in founding the STFU in eastern Arkansas. Earlier that summer, four white Socialists, H. L. Mitchell, Clay East, J. R. Butler, and Ward Rodgers, wrote the union constitution. Mitchell had since convinced Williams's old friend Howard Kester, whom Mitchell had met at a socialist event in New York, to pay a visit to the Arkansas lowlands to "see what Ward Butler and I have got started." Even Lucien Koch, the communist from Commonwealth, "attended one of our meetings and remarked that the Revolution started in Arkansas," Mitchell boasted.[58]

STFU leaders wanted Williams to get back into the fight. Mitchell and Rodgers wrote to him asking for information about his future plans now that he was out of work. Williams replied that his "life is in the radical movement" and noted "with savage delight . . . the constructive hell [the STFU] are raising in Eastern Arkansas." Williams suggested several avenues of cooperation with the Arkansas socialists and the STFU, including running for the governorship on the Socialist Party ticket and hosting a big workers' conference along the lines of his postponed New Era Forum. He had ambitious plans, but his health waned. Williams had suffered a bout of tuberculosis in the late 1920s, and now his troubles had caused further deterioration in his lungs. "My physician has frankly told me that I was going at too fast a pace," he informed Mitchell and Rodgers, "and that I must stop now or be undone later." Although he wanted to run for office, Williams admitted that he might not have the energy. He decided to run anyway, but got knocked off the ballot because of a lack of a poll tax receipt.[59] Mitchell rallied to his side in these difficult months. He spent several days with the Williamses in Paris, when "we talked damn near all night." Claude and H. L. struck an immediate bond, particularly because they were both sons of west Tennessee sharecroppers. Mitchell, who had grown up in Obion County not far from where Claude's father was raised, looked up to Williams, who was ten years his senior. After his all-night talking session with Williams, Mitchell urged Kester to help to provide Claude "some sort of support so as to continue his work" and wrote to Norman Thomas to inform him that Williams, "a natural leader of men," was "with out means of living and will soon be forced out unless some sort of support can be secured." He asked Thomas to canvass his liberal and radical friends to provide "a few hundred per year" to keep Williams going.[60] Without the help of sympathetic socialists, Claude's career might have ended in premature retirement in the last months of 1934.[61]

Bolstered by his friends and followers, Williams turned his attention to organizing a "Conference on Economic Justice" in Paris that November. In consultation with Myles Horton, he had decided that the conference should focus on how to make "the revolutionary program of Jesus become effective in the life of the world," whether in existing churches or in "independent labor churches."[62] He now believed more in the independent variety. Williams thanked Horton for the "FELLOWSHIP IN REVOLUTION" they had shared at Highlander that summer, which helped "to drive me forward with curve to left sharpening."[63]

Williams was also becoming a lightning rod for southern youth who were moving left too. Zilphia Mae Johnson, the daughter of a Paris mine owner who gravitated to Williams's preaching and led the youth group at his church, moved to Highlander at Claude's urging because her parents had disowned her for her activism. She went on to a celebrated career as an educator, musician, and civil rights activist, and married Horton in 1935.[64] Lee Hays, who had no living family when he enrolled at the nearby College of the Ozarks in Clarksville, Arkansas, became a devout follower of Claude in the summer of 1934. The Williamses virtually adopted him when he moved in with them to learn how to organize. Hays later achieved fame as a folk singer with the Almanac Singers and the Weavers and considered the preacher his "surrogate father."[65]

The loyalty of young people like Hays and Johnson encouraged Williams to follow the leftward curve with local miners. Williams traveled throughout District 21 during October, meeting miners to discuss union developments, the availability of work, the standard of government relief, and the "the underground movement for autonomy." Williams also spent a lot of time with the Commoners, particularly Horace Bryan and Bob Reed, both of whom had come to support him on behalf of ILD in the summer. Together they discussed the autonomy movement and plans for the upcoming conference. The Commoners helped Williams attain new credentials, by making him the president of their local of the American Federation of Teachers and by arranging for him a commission to organize on behalf of the Workingmen's

Union of the World, a new organization of relief workers and unemployed people. With Williams's prodding, all of these groups focused their immediate attention on the Paris conference.[66]

On November 9, 1934, over three hundred delegates met in the Paris grade school auditorium to "face together the problem of creating a just society." The conference featured an array of speakers, including Uphaus; Sherwood Gates; Arkansas Democrat and New Deal administrator Brooks Hays; and James Workman, a Methodist preacher from nearby Conway, Arkansas; as well as local African American and white tenant farmers. The second day of the conference featured field trips to "study and investigate the actual conditions of the state," including the Eureka mine and a local cotton plantation. Williams kept a low profile during the conference, only speaking when he led a discussion on resolutions. Those resolutions included calls for an "old age pension, workingmen's compensation and general social insurance"—the same causes the miners of District 21 had been calling for over the previous three years. Williams counted the conference a success. For one, it had actually gone ahead, when most of his other plans had not. Second, "Negroes and whites participated on same program," he recorded in his diary, "sat and mingled together in audience" and even ate at the same table. Williams seemed unhappy with the tenor of the discussion, however. The final resolutions were timid compared to "the revolutionary program" Williams had discussed with a group of students from Commonwealth on the eve of the meeting. His biggest worry was Uphaus, who he thought "split the middle" and was "compromising." He privately "determined not to go further with [the] Religion and Labor Foundation under Uphaus' leadership."[67]

In the weeks following the conference, Williams increasingly had "revolution" on his mind. His diary entries for this period include almost daily references to conversations he had about communism, socialism, and dialectical materialism, the theoretical basis of Marxism. Not only was he reading Lenin's *State and Revolution*, but he also had frequent meetings with Horace Bryan, a communist well-versed in Marxist theory. His growing advocacy of revolutionary action mirrored his family's increasingly dire financial position. Williams had no work and obtained what little money he could from the support of sympathetic patrons and by selling seals for a tuberculosis charity. "I am too 'radical' for anything with remuneration," he joked. Had economic conditions been better, Joyce might have taken a job, but she did not. With no shortage of free time, Williams packed in entire days of discussion, debate, and reading. On November 29, for example, he talked "revolutionary socialism" with a student from 8:30 P.M. until 11:00 P.M. "We are almost persuaded,"

Williams noted, "as is Rodgers, that it is the most consistent and most hopeful position and program." The ideal form of political organization, he recorded elsewhere, was "anarchy."[68]

In late 1934 Williams began a peripatetic scramble to continue his preaching career. Despite medical warnings to take it easy, Williams attended the Conference of Younger Churchmen in Tennessee. The conference in early December brought together an interracial, interdenominational group of Christian social activists, reuniting Claude with his mentor Alva Taylor and his friend Howard Kester, with whom he "talked of future program" into the early hours of the morning. At the conference he heard several African American speakers, including Dr. Fortner from Fisk University on "What it Means to Be A Negro in America," as well as the black socialist intellectual George Streator, who discussed the "Causes of the Crisis." Williams spoke "on Class Struggle in Specific Phases," reflecting his recent study of Marxist thought. All of the presentations apparently had a distinct radical edge. Nat Ross, a white district organizer for the Communist Party in Alabama, quipped "that he felt like a conservative in such a crowd," most of whom were southern preachers like Williams and Kester.[69] Williams then hitchhiked to Fort Smith three days before Christmas for a labor conference, where he wrote several resolutions. One of these demanded that the federal government take over relief in the state of Arkansas, or else his new union, the Workingmen's Union of the World, would mobilize to protest their lack of wages and poor conditions. "Resolutions revolutionary; Speeches revolutionary," he noted with satisfaction.[70]

Williams masked whatever worries had afflicted him since his ouster by the Presbyterian Church with constant work that gave the outward appearance of empowerment. His diary entries, however, reveal a state of manic desperation. Williams could claim some contribution to an emergent movement of southern radicals, but he also had to admit anguish over where his family would live and how they would eat. Joyce was not well physically. "It is a revelation," Uphaus wrote, "to some [of my Yale divinity students] that a wife could stand so much for the sake of a cause."[71] But her illness did not stop Williams from furious travel that winter. His ideals often clashed with quotidian reality, particularly in regard to Uphaus. In his diary, Williams wrote several times about how he wanted to reply to Uphaus, not to thank him, but to part ways. Williams could not stomach the liberal pat on the back, the go-it-slow approach that he believed Uphaus represented, but did not know how to express this frustration to someone who had stood by him financially and emotionally. When Uphaus telegrammed Williams to ask about rumors that he "had repudiated Foundation's leadership," Williams could only reply that he had "serious reservations."[72]

Williams found his family suffering from cold, hunger, and sickness when he returned from the Fort Smith convention. As Claude and Joyce awaited the final appeal of their eviction from the Paris pastoral manse, local supporters—people who had very little themselves—brought them food and money. On Christmas day, Montgomery Bird, a seventy-three-year-old African American, brought them a sack of turnips and dried peas. "I didn't have anything to bring but sentiment and I'd thought I'd just bring it along in a sack," he explained. A young miner left them 15 cents because he "just want to give it." The man told Claude that he had been "waiting all his life to hear the things [Williams had] been saying." The spirit of fellowship that underpinned the generosity of these poor people gave the Williamses hope, and they continued to serve their followers up until the last. One day Claude married a young couple, and on another he performed the funeral of a ten-month-old child. The latter he said was "not the will of God . . . but an outright case of murder by our economic system, as eight million other undernourished babies were being murdered." These represented the final acts he would perform in Paris.[73]

On January 8, 1935, the hearing convened to decide the dispute over the manse. The lawyer for the local church set out to discredit Claude by asking questions about his beliefs on religion, monogamy, and race. Williams answered truthfully. As expected, the ruling that came down cast the Williamses out and required them to pay back rent, plus interest. As Claude prepared to appeal, the NRLF thought it "unwise." Uphaus nevertheless offered to help them move into a new home and to send money. Whether or not Uphaus was too liberal, Williams had to rely on his generosity.[74] Joyce, who, in the face of poverty and eviction, had looked after the children while Claude traipsed across the South, believed it was a blessing. In all of these struggles she never wavered from their conviction that "a good marriage is simply a good union."[75] Although she remained behind the scenes caring for the couple's children, Joyce was as committed a religious activist as Claude; her private work enabled his public campaigns. "We are free," she told Claude after the eviction. "Free of institutions. Now you can really work."[76]

Amid the rubble of the Paris ministry, Claude and Joyce conceived of a new mission. They now believed that only revolutionary struggle could bring the nation's poor into the "abundant life" of Christ's intention. One could not champion justice and advocate the slow reform of the oppressive Jim Crow system. Bitter fighting with the religious elders of Paris and the Presbyterian

Church board had strengthened the Williamses' core religious convictions. Confident now that denominations restrained true Christian action, they vowed to work among the poor, the hungry, the marginal. After all, it was ordinary people and not institutions, they believed, who would be the ones to "create the new society."[77]

III

In early 1935 James Dombrowski, a Methodist preacher and Highlander's manager, invited Williams to a conference "against the rise of Fascism and terror in the South" to be held in New York.[78] Williams went, despite his family's trouble in Arkansas. On his first morning in the city, Williams attended services at Harry Fosdick's immaculate Riverside Church. Located in Morningside Heights, Manhattan, Riverside was one of the richest churches in the nation. Claude was dumbfounded by the "million-dollar" building that towered over West 121st Street. Although he had traversed a great distance in his thinking since first reading Fosdick's *The Modern Use of the Bible*, he still expected much from the man who had been so influential in his life. But Fosdick's sermon, "Can We Be Christians in Our Society?" seemed to Claude like nothing but a "good opiate." In essence, Williams summarized, Fosdick argued that the poor should be content because it was they, not the rich, who "have the promise of the kingdom of God." By submitting to God even a "southern tenant farmer girl in Arkansas may have spiritual victory," Fosdick preached, because "it is easier for a camel to go through the eye of a needle than for a rich man to enter the kingdom of God." The massive building, the finely dressed parishioners, the timid sermon all underlined for Williams the inability of well-meaning liberals to understand, let alone change, conditions in Arkansas. Fosdick's point of view contrasted sharply to Williams's recent struggles, and Claude left the church "desperate."[79]

While conference attendees discussed fascism in tranquil New York, violent conflict erupted in Arkansas. Williams received word that his close friend Ward Rodgers had been arrested following a speech in Marked Tree, a cotton town in the Arkansas Delta. The local police charged Rodgers with barratry, which in Arkansas meant conspiring to disturb the peace, and the promotion of anarchy. Authorities also raided the STFU's office in Tyronza. When Lucien Koch, Bob Reed, and Atley Delaney from Commonwealth College rushed to Marked Tree to help Rodgers, thugs abducted and pistol-whipped them. "They slugged us around pretty bad," Reed reported, "with threats of killing us." Reporters from Memphis picked up the story, and within days it was national news: "Minister Accused of Anarchy in Arkansas."[80] Sharecroppers, like the miners of District 21 before them, had disturbed the status quo, and the violent reaction had been swift. For Williams, these events signaled a new phase in the battle against Jim Crow and class tyranny in the South.

Stuck in New York, Williams searched for allies to boost his ministry. He met an array of activists at the conference, including Roger Baldwin, the head of the American Civil Liberties Union (ACLU); Ben Davis, the African American lawyer, communist, and editor of the *Negro Liberator*; Harry F. Ward, the influential professor of social ethics at Union Theological Seminary; Winifred Chappell, a female Methodist deacon and activist in Ward's Methodist Federation for Social Service; Norman Thomas, the Socialist Party leader; and Earl Browder, secretary of the CP, who talked about "Socialists coming [into] the party." These leaders impressed Williams, who had begun to judge people not by their affiliations but by their commitment to action; he was ready to collaborate with Democrats, socialists, and communists alike if they were bold. Claude also met Warren Wilson, his erstwhile supporter on the church's national Board of Missions, but concluded that he was "liberal—no good." Before leaving, Williams met again with Thomas, who approved Williams's work with District 21 and the Arkansas Socialist Party.[81]

On the return trip, Williams and Uphaus stopped in Washington, where they presented petitions on behalf of the miners to officials in the NRA and the FERA. Although sympathetic, the policy makers they spoke to complained of an inability to do much to help people at the local level. The southern authorities who controlled the agencies under their jurisdiction made it impossible to do anything. Richard Brown of the NRA urged them to "force the issue."[82] Williams thought that this last piece of advice had the ring of gospel in it—it was what Christ would have done.

Williams returned to Paris at the end of January 1935 to relocate his family to a new home. With borrowed money and a borrowed car, the Williamses moved to a building in Fort Smith that was big enough "for both residence and classes."[83] Claude, Joyce, and Lee Hays, who had dropped out of college to help them, decided the building would house a new project, the New Era School of Prophetic Religion, a school that would offer "classes in trade union history, organization and tactics, in the Christianity of Christ, and in political and economic subjects." Although Williams still thought he should "force the issue" to provoke federal authorities, he decided to proceed quietly for a time to give the new school a chance to succeed.[84]

Despite the uncertainty of his own affairs, Williams savored the new connections he had made in New York. Eager to establish ties with both socialists and communists, Williams wrote similar follow-up letters to Norman Thomas and Earl Browder. Profuse in his flattery, Williams thanked Thomas for giving him a signed copy of his recent book, *Human Exploitation in the United States*. Although Claude had actually lost the book on a bus in Washington, he promised Thomas that he would long "treasure it"—a white lie designed to help his New Era plan. To Browder, Williams bolstered his communist credentials. He had been ostracized by government officials in Arkansas, Williams claimed, for being "a RED—A Communist." He hoped that both leaders would look favorably on the draft curriculum for New Era that he had enclosed, and told each what he thought they wanted to hear. To the socialist leader, Williams explained that the weekday classes would promote "timely issues and movements through teacher's unions, student groups, labor meetings, civic clubs, church circles; efforts in behalf of American Civil Liberties Union, Socialist locals, etc." Saturday events, he informed Thomas, would be "open for work with the under-privileged and Sunday for message of a distinctly religious tenor." To the American communist leader, Williams explained that the weekday classes would promote "the issues in Teacher's Unions, student groups, labor meetings, and . . . civic clubs, luncheons, church circles" with teaching "developed from the Communist view point." Saturdays, he informed Browder, would be "open to work with the Unemployed League and Sunday morning a message with a semi-religious tenor." Sundays would be "a front," he added, hoping to obviate Browder's concern over funding religious activities that he assumed all communists disdained. Williams concluded both letters by stating his main purpose: he needed their financial support for supplies, equipment, and "a minimum family budget."[85]

Fort Smith provided no respite for the Williamses, who arrived in the middle of a strike by unemployed workers over government relief. The state authorities who administered FERA funds kept relief wages meager because, they argued, southern workers did not need as much as northern workers. Too much charity, local officials contended, would make them lazy, and so the unemployed had to be paid just enough to survive. Relief workers could endure this rationale no more when state authorities cut their wages from 30 to 20 cents per hour. "This wage rate is totally insufficient," the strikers declared, "to maintain a decent standard of living for our families." The militancy of the relief workers was rooted in the past efforts of the Workingmen's Union of the World and the recent "revolutionary" Fort Smith conference where Williams had sponsored demands for FERA to improve conditions. By February, under the leadership of Horace Bryan, over 4,000 people from throughout Sebastian County had joined the protest. Given Williams's earlier support, the strikers appealed to him for advice. Claude spoke out in support of the strike, but having just arrived in Fort Smith the previous week, averred against further involvement so as "not to isolate myself from [the] community before New Era Program [is] established."[86]

The police forced matters. After the arrest of Horace Bryan and then Ray Koch, Lucien's brother and Bryan's replacement as strike leader, Claude felt he had no alternative but to assume the leadership of the strike. The news of the arrests, coming so soon after the attacks on the STFU in eastern Arkansas, brought reinforcements from Commonwealth College and the College of the Ozarks.[87] Over the course of the next week, Williams led the strikers on a series of daily "hunger marches" through the streets of Fort Smith. Such tactics, albeit peaceful, provoked the mayor to warn Williams of further arrests. Williams told him to "do your duty, and I'll do mine." He was clearly worried about violent repression, however, and sent notice of the strike action to John Gans, a National Labor Relations Board official he had met in Washington, "as precaution." With Williams in the lead, strikers carried banners, sang hymns, and displayed excellent discipline. He ordered everyone to obey Exodus 14:14, "The Lord shall fight for you, and ye shall hold your peace." It was not easy. The police and local thugs threatened the marchers with bodily harm, but the strikers, whom the state deemed both unruly and lazy, remained disciplined.[88]

The police attacked anyway on February 18, when the strikers assembled for a rally. George Edwards, a Texas-born activist for the socialist-led League for Industrial Democracy (LID), gave a fiery speech in which he told the strikers that the state of Arkansas spent more money to feed the mules on its county farms—$9 a month—than its relief workers. Before the crowd assembled to march again, they sang the national anthem and then kneeled to pray. As they bowed their heads, the police arrested Williams, Edwards, and a handful of others. As the police hauled the men away, Joyce rushed forward shouting, "You've got to take me if you take him." She shared his activism and now wanted to share his suffering. The police saw only a hysterical wife not an activist, however, and shoved her back. In desperation, Joyce sent an emergency telegram to George Edwards's father, a prominent attorney for the ACLU in Texas, that read: "PEACEFUL MEETING GEORGE EDWARDS CLAUDE FRAMED IMPRISONED NONE TO PROTEST." On the way to the jail, one officer told Williams that he ought to be lynched for using Christianity to incite a riot. The next day the defendants were charged with the same offense that jailed Ward Rodgers and Horace Bryan: barratry. With Claude in jail, the police raided the Williamses' home and took all the literature they could find, as well as his Socialist Party membership card. Officers also menaced Joyce. "You won't live in this house long," they told her. "When you see him again it won't be in this town."[89]

Given the unwanted national attention that included the elder Edwards's arrival as counsel, Arkansas officials now had to crush the uprising legally. Their charge of barratry, which was typically defined as an offense by lawyers who filed frivolous lawsuits, served a much broader function in Arkansas because it included any act by a "disturber of the peace who spreads false rumors" to create "discord and disquiet."[90] The trial was a sham, Edwards Sr. noted, with a "poorly tried case" by the prosecution and the "mood hysterical" in the Fort Smith courtroom. It shocked even Samuel Teitelbaum, the Austrian-born and Harvard-educated rabbi of Fort Smith, who had seen plenty of abuse, much of it personal, since he moved to the South in 1927. Like Williams, he refused to call a black man "boy" and invited African Americans to services and dinner. As a result, he had received threats on his life and complaints from other religious leaders as well as from his own congregants. Teitelbaum knew southern injustice, but the frivolous charge of barratry, the judge's decision to bar any witnesses for the defense, and the fact that no other clergy supported the defendants, left the rabbi in anguish. He had "never witnessed anything as unfair and as unjust in a court of law."[91]

Williams and the others were convicted and sentenced to ninety days in jail and a $100 fine. In a cell with a nonflushable commode, dirty blankets, and cellmates afflicted with untreated venereal disease, Williams's faith in humanity was severely tested. Day after day he heard the limp arguments of Salvation Army preachers, and night after night the screams of deranged inmates. "I am in the fight," he reminded himself, "not for romance, but because of conviction." But the experience wore him down.[92] Williams feared for his life, since imprisonment rarely stopped lynch mobs from seizing their victims. He went so far as to write to Kester to make sure that someone would "care for my 'little girlies' (god how I love them) and not let them suffer" if he "should '86' [die] and it is likely I know—Sentiment is high."[93] H. L. Mitchell worried about his friend. "Williams isn't in the best of health or spirits," he informed Thomas, "and if left in jail will be a wreck."[94] Claude later described the ordeal as a "post-graduate course in the pain of the despised and rejected."[95]

Edwards secured Williams's early release on bond in March. The STFU, the Socialist Party's Emergency Committee for Strikers' Relief (which Norman Thomas chaired), and the NRLF all contributed to his bail bond. Upon release, Williams relocated his family again, this time to Little Rock, where he met extensively with his socialist allies Kester and Mitchell. Williams owed them for their personal support but also wanted to attract their help for the New Era project, which he now planned to restart in the state capital. His connections with Uphaus, whom Williams now managed to pull leftward, also proved valuable. Uphaus later recalled that "Claude rubbed my nice Yale nose into the dirt until it hurt," after which he helped create the National Committee for the Support of the Reverend Claude C. Williams and sought funds for Williams with an appeal for "the support of friends across the nation who believe in putting religion into social action." The committee, which included Niebuhr, Winifred Chappell, and Kester, raised $160 over the summer to supplement the monthly disability pension of $50 that the Presbyterian Church finally awarded Claude.[96]

With this modest amount of funding, Williams inaugurated the New Era School of Social Action and Prophetic Religion in Little Rock in the summer of 1935. The school accepted African American and white students, male and female. New Era paid no salaries and charged no tuition fees. The first class consisted of ten blacks and nine whites. "Our job is not to teach abstractions," Claude explained. "We must grasp the total problem of fighting oppression in the South. Here are young workers, born of squalor and reared in hunger. . . . We have to show them why they . . . must work together for their God-given right to freedom and equality."[97]

The curriculum aimed to "train prospective leaders in social and economic thought and action." The weeklong courses covered international relations; the "human relations" of race, class, sex, and self-determination; political science; labor history and dramatics; Saturday outreach among the poor; and Sunday worship services. In addition to these regular meetings, Arkansas-based activists offered an array of special lectures: Rodgers gave a talk called "Tenantry and Share-Cropping in the South"; Lee Hays gave a lecture about "Labor Dramatics and Creative Writing"; Mitchell delivered a lesson entitled "Socialism in the South"; Kester gave a lecture called "Race Problems"; and Joyce Williams directed lessons that explored approaches to adult education. Claude Williams, for his part, offered talks called "Political Science and Mass Action" and "Prophetic Religion." He also promised students visits from national activists like Uphaus, Thomas, Chappell, Myles Horton, and Powers Hapgood, a leading socialist and trade unionist.[98]

The New Era School embodied what became known as the Popular Front: a coalition of communist, socialist, liberal, and progressive activists that coalesced in late 1935 to resist the rise of fascism in all forms. While most Popular Front activists focused on European fascism, Williams and his colleagues aimed to stop fascism in the South. At the center of this network in Arkansas, Williams went to New York again in the autumn of 1935 and the spring of 1936 to build on his alliances. To Williams the Popular Front was not just a slogan or a temporary tactic but a worldview that put sectarianism aside for the sake of unified action. "Claude is having a wonderful trip," reported Lee Hays, who served as Williams's traveling secretary. "He is growing in stature as a public speaker and everyone is showing him great sympathy, as well as giving him some cash." The ACLU, the Methodist Federation for Social Service, and the LID all contributed money and publicity.[99]

Williams used these Popular Front networks to introduce his revolutionary version of the Christian gospel to a wider audience of activists. With the help of Horace Bryan and Bob Reed, two veterans of the fight in western Arkansas, Williams also organized "joint classes" that connected New Era teaching to the local meetings of the Unemployed Council, a communist-led group, and the Workers' Alliance, a socialist-led group. Williams espoused his gospel to every organization that would listen. The influence of his ministry, cultivated at the New Era School, could be seen in the Workers' Alliance, for which he served as an Arkansas representative; in the American Federation of Teachers, in which Mitchell had helped get him elected national vice-president; and in the Socialist Party, on whose ticket he planned to run for state office in November.[100]

Williams worked most intensively, however, with the STFU. The violent backlash against the union that began with Rodgers's arrest in early 1935 had propelled it into national prominence. The union's actions, which included a victorious cotton-pickers' strike in eastern Arkansas, raised union membership to several thousand by early 1936 and gained the attention of New Deal officials in Washington. Not only was the STFU the most robust working-class organization in Arkansas, but several of Claude's close friends had put their lives on the line to support it. Rodgers, Koch, Reed, and Thomas all had suffered attacks at the hands of mobs while organizing in the Arkansas lowlands; other organizers and supporters lived under constant threat of death. Williams's attachment was thus highly personal, and he felt honored when the STFU commissioned him as an organizer. He did most of his work from New Era but made several speaking tours on behalf of local organizing drives. Williams did "a very effective job of it," Mitchell reported.[101]

The STFU provided a vehicle for Williams's ministry because it privileged the role of Christianity as an organizational tool. Although an atheist himself, Mitchell recognized the importance of religion to the lives of rural people. As a strategic measure to gain congregational support, he instructed all organizers to bring preachers into the union first. The approach worked, with local black ministers such as E. B. McKinney and A. B. Brookins emerging as powerful union leaders. Where Mitchell's atheism caused him to balk personally, STFU leaders such as Rodgers and Kester embedded evangelical Christianity in the ritual and structure of the union. Kester's "Ceremony of the Land," for example, combined Christian imagery and rhetoric to cast the union struggle as a godly one of black and white believers against the forces of tyranny in the cotton South. "Speed now the day," those reciting the ceremony concluded, "when the plains and the hills and the wealth thereof shall be the people's own and free men shall not live as tenants of men on the earth which thou hast given to all."[102]

As Williams's role in the STFU grew, his open alliances with communists concerned his socialist friends. While some socialists like Williams embraced Popular Front cooperation, others remained suspicious of communist intentions, since the CP had been generally hostile to the Socialist Party before 1935, and many socialists feared that communists would use cooperation as a means of subversion. Socialists in the STFU raised eyebrows when Donald Henderson, a CP official who had been involved in the creation of the Alabama Sharecroppers' Union, called for a reorganization of farmers' unions around the CP policy that owners, managers, and tenants should be in one union, while sharecroppers and wage workers should be in a different union. The STFU organized all classes of farm workers together and interpreted Henderson's proposal as "an effort to put the screws on the STFU." Suspicions were heightened further when Bob Reed requested permission to organize CP "cells" in STFU locals; Mitchell and Kester rejected the notion. They also suspected the political motivations of the Commoners, particularly Lucien Koch. Because Williams counted these activists as close friends and colleagues, his activities also began to receive ideological scrutiny. As the summer wore on, Kester grew increasingly critical of Williams's "positions and attitudes," particularly the way he pushed his agenda to the forefront of so many different groups. Although he did not say it, Kester seemed to fear that the New Era School was little more than a communist front and asked to no longer be associated with it. There was as yet no consensus within the union on such matters, however. Mitchell, for one, declared himself "willing to work with [communists] as long as they don't try to force their own policies on us." Rodgers, meanwhile, warned that it violated the STFU constitution to reject people on the basis of political persuasion.[103]

Williams soon gained a reputation among all parties as one of the best preachers of the union cause. Along with McKinney, he led worship at the STFU's second annual convention in Little Rock in January 1936. He became so popular among the rank and file that local organizers repeatedly asked for his presence on the trail. Williams was especially good at refuting the claims of "an international coloured fascism stimulated by Japanese agents"—the same OIBAPMW that had so intrigued Whitfield. Throughout the summer of 1936, for example, John Handcox practically begged Mitchell to dispatch Williams to southeast Missouri to extinguish the lingering appeal for blacks to join a worldwide anti-white alliance. Mitchell could not accommodate Handcox's request because he needed Williams for a more urgent matter. Frank Weems, a black union organizer in Crittenden County, Arkansas, had gone missing in June after being abducted by a vigilante mob. The presumed murder of a union organizer had become a national story, and the union aimed to make as much headway out of it as possible. Mitchell asked Williams, the union's most powerful orator, to preach the funeral sermon for the missing sharecropper.[104]

Making his way from Memphis to the funeral church near Earle, Arkansas, Williams entered into a trap. At the county line, vigilantes swarmed Williams's vehicle. They pulled him and his companion, Willie Sue Blagden, from the car to a nearby field where they whipped them with a leather strap made of mule belly. The mob put Blagden on a train back to Memphis and stuffed Williams in the back of their car, where they continued to pummel him. As he lay dazed in the back seat, they drove around discussing whether or not to kill him. They decided against it, releasing Williams with a warning to never come back to Crittenden County. He returned to Joyce bruised and shaken.[105]

There was nothing newsworthy in the beating of Williams, a known pot-stirrer, but the abuse of Blagden, a young white woman from a wealthy Memphis family, made national headlines. Photographs of her "plump thigh bearing a large black & blue mark," *Time* magazine reported, supplied salacious proof of the violent nature of the conflict in Arkansas. Local papers agreed with the national press, but interpreted the violence differently. "Outside agitators have felt the sting of the backhand where it would do most good," the *Earle Enterprise* boasted, and "where all other methods have failed."[106]

Williams used the incident to enhance the union cause, as well as his own celebrity. In early August 1936, the March of Time newsreel service reenacted the beating for an episode called "King Cotton's Slaves." Shown before feature films, newsreels detailed national and international events to packed theater crowds across the nation during the Depression. This episode focused on the problems of landless farmers in the South: their failure to receive the benefits promised to them by the New Deal and the "grumblings of revolt" witnessed in the ranks of the STFU. The film showed striking farmers marching and singing "We Shall Not Be Moved" as planters "close rank" "to teach 'em" obedience. Williams played himself in the film version, wherein the Earle beating took place off-camera. The film then cut to footage of J. M. Futrell, the governor of Arkansas, who called Williams and Blagden "outside agitators," just like the *Earle Enterprise* had done. The film ended with the muddied conclusion that "planter and sharecropper alike are the economic slaves of the Old South's one-crop system." This odd framing of the problem would foreshadow difficulties to come in regard to federal attention to rural poverty. For Williams, however, the film was an untrammeled success. When it debuted on movie screens around the nation and even overseas the following summer, he would become the recognized face of the STFU's southern struggle.[107]

Williams's beating bolstered STFU efforts to prevail upon President Roosevelt to intervene. Roosevelt had scheduled a campaign visit to the state in June—only weeks after Williams and Blagden had been thrashed—to support the candidacy of Senator Joseph T. Robinson. The president went ahead with the trip, during which he praised Arkansas and Robinson: "this is the first chance I have had to enjoy the generosity, the kindness and the courtesy of the true Arkansas hospitality," he said. In private, however, Roosevelt berated Governor Futrell for allowing "two citizens on an apparently peaceful mission" to be "subjected to cruel and inhuman treatment." Futrell obeyed the order to stop the violence and set up a commission to study the farm tenancy problem in the state. Furthermore, Senator Robinson—known above all else for his political loyalty to Roosevelt—adopted a friendlier attitude toward the STFU. That summer he met with Mitchell and Gardner Jackson at the Democratic National Convention in Philadelphia, where he agreed, surprisingly, to support legislation to give rural workers greater rights. Given that Senator Robinson was probably the most powerful Democrat after Roosevelt, his willingness to listen to the STFU reflected the political power the new union had accrued. In order to maintain pressure, however, the union's leaders now more than ever sought to distance the union from political controversies, particularly any relations with the CP.[108]

After several weeks of recuperation, Williams got back to preaching on the STFU circuit and put his hat in the political ring as well. In July he participated in a "traveling seminar" conducted by the NRLF in Little Rock that included the Arkansas Federation of Labor, the Bureau of Labor and Statistics, the Workers' Alliance, and the STFU. In the weeks that followed, Claude filmed the March of Time newsreel and lobbied unsuccessfully to be included in Governor Futrell's commission to investigate the tenancy problem. That autumn he put his newfound notoriety to use as the dark horse Socialist Party challenger for Joseph Robinson's senate seat. Although the STFU leadership was now negotiating with Robinson, they wanted to keep the pressure on him via Williams, whose beating had helped bring Robinson to the bargaining table in the first place. Williams lost badly, garnering only 1,587 votes to Robinson's 154,866 and the Republican candidate's 27,746. He ran well ahead of the Socialist ticket, though; Norman Thomas attracted only 446 Arkansas votes in his presidential bid. In fact, Williams received—on the basis of name recognition alone, since he did very little campaigning—more votes in Arkansas than any socialist since Eugene V. Debs's run for the presidency in 1920.[109]

In September, Mitchell finally acceded to John Handcox's requests to send Claude to Missouri. Williams gave a successful speech in Charleston; he knew the area well because his brother Daniel Williams lived in nearby East Prairie. "I think his speeches meant much to us," Handcox reported, in terms of an "increase in members and more interest in the old members." He proved so popular that local organizers wanted more. Two months later, Williams and E. B. McKinney, the union's vice-president, returned for a series of events at "the most strategic communities." On Thursday, the fifth of November, the fourth night of the tour, Williams and McKinney took the pulpit at Owen Whitfield's Baptist church, with word of Williams's quixotic challenge of Senator Robinson two days before no doubt at the forefront of discussions. Before them sat a packed house that included Whitfield.[110]

NOVEMBER 5, 1936

Claude Williams Preaches at
Owen Whitfield's Church, Crosno, Missouri

"Arrested by the tension" of speaking from Whitfield's pulpit, Claude Williams delivered his "message using the Bible with both barrels."[1] That message was now, more than ever before, a revolutionary gospel that challenged ordinary people to attack southern injustice in all forms. Williams's gospel was honed through years of study and struggle. Rejection, imprisonment, and physical pain had marked it with an authenticity that the faithful instantly recognized.

"We have to build the Kingdom of God on earth," Williams began. "The Kingdom is not of this world, but it is in this world. What Jesus meant by 'world' was the social order. 'Seek ye an order founded upon my principles'—an order of justice and brotherhood for everybody. There is an abundance for all if we seek this order.

"We pray to our heavenly Father—not the white man's father . . . not the black man's father—but our Father. We ask, Thy will be done on earth as it is in heaven. Thy will be done in the union.

"That's what trade unionism is—the most Christian thing in the world. My lying geography told me there were five races of people in the world. But I turned to the Bible and found there is no race, creed, or color in Jesus' religion. There is only one race—the human race.

"'Thy will be done,' we say. It is not God's will that men and women and children should toil in the fields from sunup to sundown to grow cotton, and go naked. It is the will of the planter, but it is not God's will."

The congregation warmed—while Whitfield looked on—as Williams reached an evangelical cadence: "Oh no! That's right!" they responded.

"It isn't the will of God that five million children should starve," Williams intoned, "nor that women should marry for a meal-ticket.

"I'm telling you what God has told me to tell you. And I'm not asking any man's permission to say it. I was jailed in Fort Smith for saying it, beaten in Earle for saying it. I had a church, but when I began to preach the religion of Jesus I was fired."

"Fired!" Whitfield's congregation cried.

"Preachers have been trained to tell you the soul is the most important. If you starve to death, your soul will go flying to the pearly gates a hundred million light-years away. But Jesus didn't put it in that order. 'Give us this day our daily bread'—the body first. A body without a spirit is a corpse, and a spirit without a body is a spook, and I've no use for either of them."

"Amen, preacher! Go on, preacher! Hear him now!"

"Jesus said, 'Blessed are the poor'—why? Because they are the ones that need the Kingdom—they are the ones that will bring it, because they need it. I preach this way because it's the way I have to preach," Williams explained.

"Go ahead!"

"They call their sermons good news. This darned stuff they preach isn't good news for the poor. It isn't good news that a man must die before he can get to heaven."

"Sure isn't! Amen! No good news there!"

"This is red—as red as the blood of Jesus. And that's how red I preach. Now there is a new Pentecost" in the land and it's the union, Williams preached, drawing on the spiritual power of the Pentecostal new-sect revivals that swept the countryside in these years. After "Jesus was lynched," the disciples "were told to go to Jerusalem and wait until they got the power," he continued, quoting the Acts of the Apostles, the scriptural heart of Pentecostal belief. "How did they get it? When they became of 'one accord'—when they were organized. It was when they were all agreed together that there was power. So Pentecost is unity—a condition met."

"Unity! Amen! Yea, Man!"

"We are getting this power—now what must we do with it?" Imagine, Williams preached, if the boss man wanted to get his cotton planted but all the black people were just sitting there, whistling, and all the white folks were just sitting there, whistling, and he couldn't do anything about it. "Cotton won't plant itself. Boss can't plant it. Cotton don't hoe itself. Boss can't hoe it. Cotton don't pick itself, and boss can't pick it."

"No, sir! Can't do it! Jest as helpless as a baby!"

"Well, we can do it!" Claude concluded. "But it's not going to be easy. Old boss don't care: he don't care if you starve. He's done it. Your babies have starved, and he starved them. His heart isn't going to melt, because he has a heart of stone. He don't care . . . unless we have unity. Unless we have the power. That's what we're going to do. It's time we got wise to this thing. Got to get converted."[2]

Williams's evocative southern rhythm, which inspired musician Lee Hays to dub him the "singing preacher," had drawn the black audience into a call-and-response usually reserved for one of their own preachers.[3] "Amen! I mean! Talk union! Preach union!" they shouted.[4] As Williams stepped down from the rostrum, stomps and cheers from the small band of believers shook the rafters of the little church.

Whitfield got hit by "both barrels." Claude's radical gospel convinced him, almost at a stroke, of the oppression that bedeviled him and his neighbors. There was more than race or tenancy to the troubles that stalked the Southland—the oppression that Whitfield lived was evil. And that a white man also knew this evil meant that the triumph of God's truth would require the faith of black and white alike. The old familiar expressions of that faith would not suffice. Williams's depiction of the working-class gospel as the "new Pentecost" confirmed what Whitfield already knew about the upheaval in his own churches. The popular demand for more responsive religion in the new-sect revivals had brought Williams into his church that very night as Whitfield's congregants appropriated the spiritual space for their own needs to hold a union meeting. People wanted a rebellious faith, and Williams gave it to them. What Claude Williams "the pecker wood" showed Whitfield the black nationalist was the revolutionary power of acting according to Christ's true gospel. At the end of the meeting, as congregants filed into the cool November night, Whitfield approached Williams. Fearing a clenched fist, Claude later recalled that "he took my hand and said, 'Man, I could hear you preach from here on out.'" Thereafter, Whitfield joined the STFU.[5]

3. Prophets in the Storm

In the weeks that followed his Missouri meeting with Williams, Whitfield worked as a part-time organizer alongside John Handcox, the STFU representative already in Mississippi County. Inspired by Williams, Whitfield brought the working-class gospel into his churches, where most people had heard of the STFU and some were already members. Whitfield's rapid conversion turned sporadic interest into communal support. Although his ministry had suffered in recent years, Whitfield was a well-respected leader in a mainstream denomination. His awakening to the union gospel, rooted in the potential of poor people to deliver themselves of oppression, renewed his confidence.

Just as Williams told audiences that he preached "red" because God demanded it, Whitfield expressed the urgency of the union by retelling his conversion as a moment of epiphany. In this allegorical rendition, Whitfield sat alone with his mule team on the turn row after a long day's work in the field. Suddenly the twilight quiet was interrupted by the cry of his daughter who ran from the house to tell him there was no food left for supper. Hungry, exhausted, and desperate, Whitfield fell to his knees and prayed to God for help. "You said the righteous and them that preached the Gospel would never go hungry," he complained. "But I done worked, behaved my self, kept Your precepts—and those that haven't is getting along much better."

At some point during his lamentation, an answer came to Whitfield from within, "like the common-sense part of me," as he described it. "But you ain't been preachin' the Gospel—just makin' a noise," the voice said. "I bless you with enough product to fill many barns. Somebody's gettin' it. If you ain't, that's your fault, not Mine."[1]

Whitfield told audiences that then and there he decided to stop "whoopin' and hollerin' at God" and start preaching the gospel of the STFU—economic and spiritual renewal through collective action. A preacher who will "tell you about Heaven and can't tell you how to get a loaf of bread here" was a "liar," Whitfield said. "A sermon," he declared, "sends you home happy. The Gospel sends you home mad."[2]

Whitfield's allegory was the work of a talented leader and thinker. His re-rendering of Williams's radical gospel consolidated the spiritual searching of his neighbors into his own narrative. Although highly personal, his story was one any cotton farmer in the 1930s could understand. Equally important, Whitfield omitted Claude Williams. He was, after all, organizing among African Americans who had given support to the UNIA and other adaptations of black nationalism whose adherents carried a distrust of white people. As a personal experience of God, however, Whitfield's moment of epiphany fused the teaching of Williams into a black theological tradition that enlisted union members as agents fulfilling God's will.[3]

I

Enthused by his tour of the Bootheel, Claude Williams returned to Little Rock to lead a New Era leadership training course for promising organizers. The union cause had been a central component of the New Era School since mid-1935, with Mitchell, Kester, and others providing frequent contributions to the curriculum. This session, the first dedicated to developing handpicked local leaders for the union, took the relationship a step further by making New Era an official educational extension of the STFU. "The purpose of this school," Williams informed one potential student, "is to offer intensive and practical training to an equal number of white and Negro members who wish to develop themselves for more effective field and administrative union work." The insistence on racial equality had been Williams's because he believed that the fight against racism was essential to the fight against economic exploitation, and the STFU's executive council agreed as long as it could choose those who would attend. Initially the union chose an all-white teaching staff, which included its president J. R. Butler, Mitchell, Myles Horton, Winifred Chappell, the secretary of the Arkansas Socialist Party Don Kobler, and Williams. Now far more progressive on racial matters than his white colleagues, Williams denounced the "conspicuous absence" of black teachers and appointed John Handcox, Whitfield's organizing partner in Missouri, as a staff member. Williams was forcing the white leadership of the STFU to publicly attack white racism, something they had hesitated to do for fear of antagonizing potential white members.[4]

The ten-day session commenced at the New Era School at 912 West 7th Street in Little Rock on December 13, 1936. Eighteen men and women—ten black, eight white—attended. "These people came eagerly from the cotton fields of eastern Arkansas and Missouri," reported Kobler, the New Era secretary, "hungry for knowledge as to how they might make their instrument of action, the Southern Tenant Farmers' Union, more effective." The students grasped with both hands the opportunity to do something that life in the rural South had generally denied them: get an education. They attended sessions led by a member of the teaching staff but also assisted in the running of the courses so that all "were partners in learning." Horton covered the "purpose and program" of the STFU. Williams "frankly discussed the friends and enemies" of the STFU and gave the students a sense of how their struggle attracted the support of national progressive groups. Butler and Kobler taught the nuts-and-bolts of union business, from writing minutes to negotiating tactics. For his part, Handcox taught music and familiarized the students with his original compositions, such as "Roll the Union On." After Chappell informed the group about "a concept of the broader struggle" and the union's place in that struggle, Mitchell closed with a lecture on the STFU, "today and tomorrow."[5]

The overriding educational message was the need for action. The enthusiasm of the students, Kobler wrote, was proof that "the South's final emancipation would never be signed in a state capitol, but was being born in just such groups as this and out of the bitter, blood-stained struggles of the oppressed." Meeting only blocks from the building where Arkansas's Jim Crow laws were made, and less than two miles from Central High School, a key site in the battle for desegregated schooling twenty years later, the New Era training course was integrated, largely because of pressure from Williams. "Tradition and law may have been flaunted," Kobler reported, "but a more fundamental law of brotherhood was respected in holding classes with Negro and white together." One black student said that the school's "sociality"—emphasizing the direct assault on the segregationist taboo of "social equality"—was "truly remarkable."[6]

Music was central to Williams's teaching methods. Lee Hays recalled that "all Claude's meetings were singing meetings." "He has dug up folk singers and songwriters [like Handcox] and set them to work fashioning songs for particular meetings or causes," he explained, usually out of the traditional music that people already knew. Williams, Hays, Handcox, and others created "zipper songs" by altering the verses of well-known tunes. This way, audiences knew the melodies but the lyrics became relevant to the current struggle. At the New Era session in 1936, Williams, Hays, and the students adapted the hymn "I Will Overcome," giving it a message about the saving power of the union. This song would go on to become the classic civil rights song "We Shall Overcome."[7]

Williams aimed to harness the natural talents of ordinary people to specific political causes. He collaborated closely with Handcox, whose discussions with Williams prompted new working-class cultural creations. Williams later recalled driving in a car with Handcox, who was singing the well-known hymn "O, Freedom" to himself, when it occurred to Williams to suggest a minor change to the lyrics so that the song implied earthly freedom as opposed to heavenly reward. "As we talked," Williams explained, "we decided that people who first had sung that song could not have really have lived unless they fought. So John wrote Freedom After While using 'fought and gone before' instead of 'died and gone before.'"[8] The new song, "No More Mourning," was Handcox's when he recorded it for Charles Seeger and the Library of Congress in 1937, but its message was also a product of Williams's work.

Williams believed that musical and educational collaboration enabled true religious fellowship. "For the first time in their lives," the New Era students had "the opportunity to worship the same God at the same time in the same place. Jim Crow was not present." The effect was powerful. "Never in history has we had the opportunity to meet in a cooperative school," Mary Jones, a New Era student, informed Williams upon her return home. "Organization is the only way," she explained, and "economic is the only problem we are going to have to bring a world on common plain." Classmate Clayton Donald concurred. "Though words fail me . . . it is my honest opinion there is none that equals our New Era Training School it success is yet unforeseen. Thank God for its leaders and its Christlike principles," he wrote.[9] The results were seen soon enough. New Era students Leon Turner, Nellie Bee Taylor, Bob Miller, J. F. Hynds, Henrietta McGhee, and W. L. Blackstone would all go on to play influential roles in the STFU.

Williams hoped that collaboration between New Era and the STFU would vault him into the vacant directorship of Commonwealth College, a position that he believed would provide his ministry with needed stability. But Commonwealth itself was under heavy strain due to sectarian disagreements among its supporters and from attacks by a hostile Arkansas state legislature. Aggressive tactics by Commoners over the preceding years had raised accusations from local people that the college was a haven for communists. The Commoners also antagonized the leaders of UMW District 21, who feared that Commonwealth would prove toxic for all labor groups in the state. The issue became an embarrassment for the STFU, which was also under fire from Arkansas authorities.[10]

The STFU needed the sympathy of the UMW because it was negotiating to join the Congress of Industrial Organizations (CIO), headed by John L. Lewis, the UMW boss. The CIO offered a powerful new vehicle for labor unions in different industries and regions to combine their forces in one organization for maximum political leverage. John Lewis had started the CIO in late 1935 after he became disillusioned with the policies of the American Federation of Labor (AFL). Lewis and others believed that all workers in each industry should be organized into one big union, rather than into separate unions based on their skill levels. As an autonomous body within the AFL by early 1937, the CIO offered an expansive idea of democratic empowerment that meshed well with the local struggle in the South to secure rights from the federal government. The CIO's stunning victories over General Motors and U.S. Steel in 1937 galvanized its members in the belief that their union possessed unprecedented power to reshape American democracy. "The C.I.O.," John Lewis declared, "has let loose great forces."[11] The STFU did not want to make any moves that jeopardized their chances of joining those forces.[12]

The caretakers of Commonwealth, Charlotte Moskowitz and Raymond Koch, sought to secure the college within this political matrix by reorganizing it under a new director in 1937. Based on his popularity in the STFU and prior area leadership, Williams seemed like an ideal fit, especially following the success of the recent New Era–STFU collaboration. Williams, meanwhile, hoped that the directorship of Commonwealth would secure his position on the union's national executive council.[13]

This complex plot came to a head when the STFU convened its third annual convention on January 14, 1937, in Muskogee, Oklahoma. Both Williams and Whitfield were among the delegates: Williams as a veteran organizer with ambitions to climb into the upper echelons of leadership; Whitfield as a fresh face looking to acquaint himself with the movement he had only recently joined. The meeting was sour from the start. On the first day, a student from Commonwealth gave a loopy interview to the hostile local press, which then ran a story about how the STFU was overrun by communists, atheists, and free-love advocates. The timing proved disastrous in light of the STFU's efforts to court the UMW and the Democratic Party. Only days earlier, S. Herman Horton, an Arkansas state representative, announced that he would submit a bill to outlaw any teaching that was communistic or otherwise immoral. He designed the bill, which was officially introduced on January 19, to eradicate Commonwealth and the STFU. To make a bad situation much worse, David

Figure 1. Claude Williams (center, looking at camera), at Commonwealth College
in Arkansas. The courageous activism of the students and staff at Commonwealth
inspired Williams in the early 1930s. Williams later served as the director
of Commonwealth College. Source: Negative #23, Photo #1, 1937–38, Folder
"Campus," Commonwealth College Photo Collection, Reuther Library, Wayne
State University.

Fowler, the leader of District 21, declared that in the wake of the press exposé
he would not deliver his keynote convention speech because he valued "God
and country" too much to cavort with such dangerous radicals.[14]

Angered by the antics of his old nemesis, Williams addressed the convention intending to refocus attention on the moral imperatives of the union. His
effort became highly personalized and defensive. "Mr. Chairman," he said, "I
have been called a preacher, a bolshevik, and an atheist," and "many people
are spreading rumors that we are against the church and they are using this
against us. This is not true." "We try to follow the teachings of Jesus," because
"you are the Kingdom of God [and] you are in need of it." Trying to make
this country a more just place did not make them traitors, Williams said, but
rather "co-workers with God."[15]

The following morning's proceedings showed the imprint of Williams's
ministry and the parallel course taken up by Whitfield. The New Era School
chorus first sang a selection of songs written by Handcox. Whitfield then led
the delegates in prayer: "Heavenly Father," he intoned, "we are calling upon
You because You are a Union God. . . . Oh Lord, we have been in the storm

so long until we made up our minds to come into this Union, and to seek an end to our many troubles," Whitfield prayed. "Almighty God, we are asking You to give us guidance," not "to come down here and to think for us" but to help us help ourselves. "We have knocked around. Our children have been crying for bread for a long time," he continued, in an echo of his conversion allegory. "We have cried for bread, and every time You stretch forth Your hand to help us," someone stole this food. Whitfield hoped, in conclusion, that "we might come together and have one strong band of Christians march down the road" to stop the theft.[16]

While the radical gospel inspired delegates on the convention floor, Mitchell and Jackson frantically tried to patch things up with Fowler. Both were eager to affiliate directly with the CIO, and fearful that an angry Fowler, a close associate of Lewis, could damage that prospect. After intense negotiations, Fowler, Mitchell, and Jackson released a statement admitting that the STFU had been "placed on the spot by people attending this convention"—the Commoners. Vowing to "divorce themselves from this element," the STFU leaders pledged cooperation with the UMW "and all other legitimate labor organizations in furthering a campaign to the best interests of workers." They then submitted and passed a resolution dissociating the STFU from all political parties and labor schools, naming Highlander and Commonwealth.[17] Mitchell and Jackson had chosen the road of political compromise.

Williams cried foul. He interpreted the measures as a personal attack and responded with fury. He "became a real problem" following the resolution, according to an even-handed report by Aron Levenstein, who described Fowler's politics as "the most vicious sort of red-baiting." Williams simply fell apart with rage. He accused Mitchell and Jackson of appeasing fascists when they "proffered support of racketeering, red-baiting and dictatorial Dave Fowler." On the convention floor, he claimed, too loudly and to too many delegates, that this deal "sold the union down the river." That Williams would use a reference to slavery in an interracial, southern setting in order to denounce the STFU's deal with Fowler was out of character. More reasonably, he predicted that the pact gave tacit support to S. Herman Horton's "red-rider" bill and would "hog-tie" the STFU.[18]

Williams began to suspect that the STFU leadership was trying to push him away at Fowler's behest. He responded by putting his name on the ballot for the executive council, thinking that a democratic vote would insulate him from attack. The move gained the vocal support of the Commoners on the convention floor, but the push failed. According to Levenstein, Williams left for an East Coast speaking trip "disgruntled and angry, with the feeling that he had been sacrificed to reaction." In a letter to Jackson the following week, Williams vowed to support a "broad campaign to defeat" the Musk-ogee deal. "In this fight there can be no 'middle of the road' policies," he declared, referring to the tendencies toward political and racial appeasement he now saw gripping the union's leadership. "Friends and foes must take definite sides." What should have been a week of pride had turned into one of division and despair.[19]

By contrast, Whitfield returned to Missouri from Muskogee with new en-thusiasm for the STFU. His fellow members had responded warmly to his prayer and his contributions from the floor. He got placed on the committee on government programs and told fellow committee members, "You all know the average livin' conditions of human beins' in these Southern states of ours. . . . Everything is taken care of but the worker. The dogs sleepin' where I ought to be sleepin' and I'm sleepin' where the dog ought to be sleepin'," he explained, deploying the homespun wit that made him such an effective speaker. "Maybe what we need is the Humane Society. We ought to get the government Health Service on our side" because "our houses leak on the outside and rain on the inside." Turning from humor to earnestness, Whitfield reassured his comrades that "this here isn't just rattle talk and we're goin' to Washington and ther'll be hell raised. We expect to put up the fight of our lives."[20]

That fight arrived sooner than Whitfield expected. Just days after he re-turned to the Bootheel, Whitfield learned that the U.S. Army Corps of En-gineers had dynamited the riverside levee guarding Mississippi County in order to reduce the threat of flood elsewhere. After the flood of 1927, the corps created a small number of "spillways," which could be inundated to reduce pressure on the levees and prevent another regional disaster. The first of these was the Bird's Point–New Madrid Spillway in southeast Missouri. The blast that winter morning sent a torrent of icy, muddy water over the homes and fields of several thousand black sharecroppers, including nearly all of the STFU's Missouri membership and the Whitfields. The corps had given them a few days notice to move. Owen and Zella, who was heavily pregnant with their thirteenth child, fled with the family into refugee camps alongside their ragged, cold neighbors.[21]

Their lives shattered by federal dynamite, the spillway refugees, guided by Whitfield and Handcox, decided to make their own New Deal for landless farmers. Just as Whitfield sharpened his sense of the culpability of the federal government in rural poverty through the STFU, another story emerged in the camps. There, the American National Red Cross fed, clothed, housed, and vaccinated the refugees in close coordination with the Resettlement Administration (RA), which issued loans for feed and seed. This massive relief effort revealed to the refugees for the first time the potential of federal power to positively intervene on the side of rural workers.[22]

Whitfield and Handcox formed a refugee council to issue union demands. "The U.S. Government," the council announced, "blast the levee releasing the Ohio flood water into the Spillway in which we lived swept away the cabin in which we lived taking our household good with them." In "the most disastrous flood in the history of our country," the government's action had "taken from us almost every thing we possessed." They considered this immoral.[23]

The council declared that the federal government was morally obliged to offer redress for the damage it caused. The refugees, backed by the STFU, vowed not to return to the spillway and raise a crop until certain conditions were met. They demanded to be allowed to own hogs, cows, and poultry for their own consumption and sale, as well as to maintain sufficient land for gardens, free of rent. Echoing Whitfield's call at Muskogee to "get the government health service on our side," they called for assurances of "sanitary houses an out houses with screen window and door to protect our health." In addition, "we as farm labors and citizens" had the right to modern school buildings for their children. Finally, the council insisted that the RA issue cash loans and grants to small landowners and landless farmers affected by the flood.[24] Union members distributed the declaration throughout the camps and to relief officials in Charleston. The STFU's newspaper, *Sharecropper's Voice*, featured it on the front page.[25]

The floodwaters receded and the government, forced out of its lethargy, began to act. The refugees went home for the spring planting, and to aid the transition, the Red Cross distributed garden seed packages and tents. Meanwhile, the RA extended loans to landowners for the reconstruction of farm buildings, including tenant houses, and issued monthly cash subsistence grants. The Public Health Service carried out home visits with those who had been in the camps to finish inoculations, check on ex-patients, and report on the well-being of the refugees. On the basis of these tangible results, Whitfield and Handcox gained new influence in the Bootheel.[26]

Landless farmers now clamored to join the STFU, no doubt impressed by the union's bold stance in the midst of the flood. When the union recalled Handcox from the area in April to save money, Whitfield became the STFU's top organizer in the state. Upset at being replaced, Handcox warned the national office that Whitfield would not have much time to devote to organizing, "for he's farming and pastoring 3 or 4 churches." Handcox was partly right. "Been so busy working in the fields all day and roaming around at night," Whitfield reported in June, "trying to get these locals to functioning again." From the excitement of the Muskogee convention, Whitfield now experienced the grueling day-to-day struggle of grassroots organizing.[27]

In the months after the disaster in Muskogee, Williams redoubled his efforts to become the director of Commonwealth College. By this point the college was nearly bankrupt, so with the help of Willard Uphaus and the NRLF, he made a fundraising tour through the Northeast. He spoke to labor leaders, religious groups, and even to high school students. Although Williams may have felt like lashing out at the STFU, he remained disciplined. Citing the courageous work of the STFU, he called for northern workers and progressives to help southern workers, "to protest the unbelievably wretched conditions which exist in" the South because "reactionary forces [are] concentrating their efforts in the South to enact repressive legislation as an entering wedge technique in the nation at large." Williams had Horton's "red-rider" bill, and perhaps Fowler, in mind.[28]

Williams based his proposed plan for the reorganization of Commonwealth around the idea that the Popular Front fight against fascism had to begin in the South. He believed that the college should take the lead in training the activists, particularly native southerners, and especially African Americans, who would wage this struggle. Williams still envisioned a close working relationship between the college and the STFU. But he also looked for other allies who could help. Williams established closer ties to the CP, which he respected for its courageous stand against racial inequality and guiding belief that empowered black workers were the key to defeating Jim Crow fascism. He had added CP membership to his range of affiliations sometime in late 1936, eager to maximize the reach of his preaching. Williams's dual membership as a socialist and communist irked many on both sides, however, so he dropped his CP membership in 1937 to await "the outcome of the STFU-SP hysteria" that followed the Muskogee meeting. "The dual connection is too severe on my ethics at this stage of the game," Williams wrote Walter Bergman, a Detroit communist and future Freedom Rider, in April, "not considering the additional dangers of embarrassing involvements."[29] Williams was willing to consider any "involvements" that would further his ministry.

As part of his strategy for Commonwealth, Williams worked behind the scenes to discredit those in the STFU who supported the Fowler measure. Williams wanted to shift the union to a more radical course, in both economic and racial terms. He found an ally in E. B. McKinney; both preachers agreed, in McKinney's words, that "things are geting very bad under the rule of the present dictator," H. L. Mitchell. Williams kept close to McKinney, who claimed the loyalty of thousands of black union members, because he was a leading Mitchell critic who demanded more black representation among the union's leaders. In addition, Kobler, a leading Arkansas socialist and close associate of Williams, convinced the state party leaders to censure Mitchell for appeasing "reactionary forces" in Muskogee. Williams's strategy to divide his "friends and foes" was a clever and cunning one: court the STFU's allies and backers around the country, while privately attacking the individual enemies that he believed hindered the union's work.[30]

These tactics certainly hardened his foes. Mitchell was outraged that the party would turn on him without giving him a chance to defend himself and vigorously protested to Norman Thomas and the Workers Defense League (WDL) about the censure. Mitchell was shocked by what his one-time friend Williams had done. He now concluded that the worries of Howard Kester, Gardner Jackson, and even Fowler were correct, and decided to try to cast Williams out of the STFU. Mitchell vowed to a WDL staffer that "as long as I have anything to do with the work of the STFU, Claude will not be used with my consent for anything." Kester agreed, at least partially, with Mitchell's sentiment. He admitted to Roger Baldwin of the ACLU that Williams was "a valuable man and we want to use him, but it occurs to us that we should be able to suggest how best he and others can serve." Although Kester did not share Mitchell's total antipathy, he was now reluctant for Williams to remain in the STFU without strict controls.[31]

Bridges were burned, but Williams's strategy succeeded. His popularity and notoriety both peaked in the summer of 1937, as he became known nationally when the March of Time newsreel reached audiences around the country. Coupled with his speaking tour and local success as an organizer, Williams had become a prominent face of the struggle against southern injustice. He did not waste the advantage. Williams requested that the executive council of the STFU approve his reorganization plan for Commonwealth, and thus his candidacy for director, at its June meeting. The timing was perfect, as Kester was absent and Mitchell was not serving on the council at the time. With his two biggest opponents sidelined, the STFU officially endorsed "the reorganization of Commonwealth College as outlined by Claude Williams." Kester arrived later that day to realize that Williams could not easily be stopped and decided to nominate him to the executive council as a peace offering. The motion carried that night. It was quite a comeback. In the six months since the debacle in Muskogee, Williams had achieved all of his goals: the reorganization of Commonwealth along the lines of his New Era School, STFU backing for his directorship, and a seat on the STFU's national executive council. In August, Commonwealth College made it official: Claude Williams would become its next director. He was now perfectly placed to play a part in the STFU's dramatic final bid to join the CIO.[32]

II

By the summer of 1937 the only option left for the STFU was to join the United Cannery, Agricultural, Packing, and Allied Workers of America (UCAPAWA), a new CIO-affiliated industrial union of agricultural and packing workers. Donald Henderson, a communist who had led the CIO's rural organizing efforts in 1935–36, and Harry Bridges, the militant longshoremen's union leader based in San Francisco, had convinced John Lewis that an umbrella union of workers who picked, processed, and shipped food on the West Coast would provide a significant source of income to the CIO. Lewis agreed with the strategy, because workers who labored year-round in canneries and other processing factories would form a nucleus around which seasonal agricultural workers could rally. Henderson planned to launch the UCAPAWA at a special convention in Denver in July. He invited delegations from other communist-led unions, including the Alabama Sharecroppers' Union and the Louisiana Farmers' Union, as well as the STFU. Shocked by the unannounced about-face from Lewis—he had appeared liberal, but now backed communists—the STFU leadership reluctantly sent a delegation to the UCAPAWA's founding convention.[33]

Among them was Owen Whitfield, whose organizing successes after the flood had catapulted him higher into union leadership. The STFU chose him as a delegate to Denver at its June council meeting, and at the UCAPAWA convention Whitfield immersed himself in the culture of the CIO and discussed the plight of rural workers with veteran organizers, including the union's highest leadership. The experience impressed upon him the potential organizing power now available to the STFU through this link to the CIO. The STFU delegation voted to join the UCAPAWA on the condition that it remain autonomous within the new alliance. Whitfield left the convention confident that the strength of the CIO was now his strength.[34]

Whitfield launched a furious organizing campaign once he returned to southeast Missouri. "Whitfield come here," local organizer W. M. Harvey reported, "and said in a speech . . . that his credentials come now from the agricultural cannery union which was united with the C.I.O." Shocked by Whitfield's new allegiance, Harvey wondered, "What has happen in the convention that Whitfield met in Colorado?" Before Denver, Whitfield had relied on his role as a local leader. Through the CIO, Whitfield now realized, these community-based groups could be linked to a much broader network of working-class activists, several million strong, united in their collective search for justice.[35]

The STFU held a special convention in Memphis in September 1937 to ratify entry into the new alliance. Claude Williams clinched the deal. Once opposed to affiliation with the CIO on the grounds that he despised Fowler and the political stance of John Lewis's UMW, Williams now relished the possibility of allying the STFU with the communist-led UCAPAWA forces and their more radical racial and economic ideas. In the run-up to the Memphis gathering, Williams held meetings with organizers throughout Arkansas and Missouri in which they discussed how integration into the UCAPAWA would work. At the September convention, Williams used a religious argument to persuade members to back the move. "The Lord spake unto the children of Moses: Go Forward: He that putteth his hands to the plow and looketh backward is not fit for the Kingdom of God. Go forward, FORWARD INTO THE CIO!" Delegates responded by rising from their seats with throaty cheers of assent.[36]

Whitfield embraced the CIO's "culture of unity" with similar zeal. CIO leaders sought to mobilize a diverse working-class movement to achieve political as well as economic goals. Racial animosity had to be overcome, especially in the South. The CIO promised white and black workers deployable power if they would view one another with solidarity when it came to common concerns. The leaders of the UCAPAWA took this view even further. Himself converted to the radical gospel by a white man, Whitfield started preaching racial cooperation. "What kind of doctrine is profitable in the Bible?" he asked audiences: "the doctrine of brotherhood." But white preachers and black preachers alike failed to preach it. "There's people in America that's glad to hear you say you hate the white folks," Whitfield preached to audiences of former Garveyites. The plain truth, however, was that "workers who are separated can't do nothin'." If people wanted change, then they needed to unite around their common economic concerns.[37]

Still, Whitfield never relinquished the goal of black independence and assumed that whites did not want to change social relations. For either group to survive, he reasoned, both would have to pool their collective resources. To illustrate the point further, Whitfield frequently carried a cartoon to union meetings with one frame showing two mules, one black and one white, pulling in opposite directions toward different piles of hay. In the second frame the two mules were hitched together pulling toward one pile, then the other. Despite working toward separate goals, he argued, neither blacks nor whites would accomplish anything unless they combined strength.[38]

As the work gained pace, Zella Whitfield began speaking to union gatherings alongside her husband. She aimed her appeal at rural women. "I am the mother of eleven children," Zella explained, "and during my 26 years of sharecropping and raising my family, I had many hardships." Like other farming women, she had worked all of her life, healthy or not, pregnant or not (Zella Whitfield was pregnant for about half of those twenty-six years).

She had nursed dying babies, watched as healthy children weakened, and had buried the dead. The union could help, but not if whites and blacks opposed one another. "Your children is going hungry and barefoot and not getting their selves education," she told white women, "just like ours." Zella admitted that she did not care if white people thought they were better than blacks; neither did she want any social equality. "But I do want my children to get an education—and you want the same for yours," she explained. "Just as long as we goes against one another, neither of us is going to get it." Women like Zella Whitfield were often at the forefront of STFU locals, sometimes in leadership positions. Their experiences as workers, wives, and mothers gave them powerful authority when addressing southern problems, and provided common ground for women of both races to cooperate.[39]

Claude Williams spent the autumn of 1937 in Arkansas rolling out his plan for Commonwealth. It would now be devoted to providing "basic instruction for labor union activity" in the South. In an attempt to get past damaging sectarianism, Williams announced that the college would also be "non-factional," meaning no political affiliations would be recognized on campus. "Commonwealth College can and must play an advanced role," he declared, "broadening and extending the traditions that have brought it to the forefront as a progressive factor in the life of the South." Williams hired two old friends to help the college accomplish this big task: Winifred Chappell as the faculty chair and Lee Hays as the instructor of drama and music. At Commonwealth, Hays honed the musical component of Williams's preaching, particularly a repertory of working-class tunes that he called "people's songs"—music full of "blood and thunder" that united "people in love and understanding."[40]

Winifred Chappell became a key leader at Commonwealth. Born in Iowa in 1879, her career as a religious activist exemplified the practice as well as the preaching of equality. A Methodist deaconess, religious educator, suffragist, and part-time journalist, Chappell worked as research secretary for the *Social Service Bulletin*, the newsletter of Harry Ward's Methodist Federation for Social Service. Her experience as a journalist writing about labor strife, first in the strike of women textile workers in Passaic, New Jersey, in 1926, and then in coal mining towns in West Virginia and Pennsylvania, radicalized Chappell. "One cannot pity these women," she wrote of the Passaic strikers, "one can only feel admiration for their undaunted spirits." As this statement suggests, Chappell came to reject Progressive-era feminists who sought protection for women as dependents; she instead urged the church to take aggressive action to empower workers rather than offer them paternal instructions. Her fiery opinions drew allies among socialists and communists, including the Kochs at Commonwealth College, where she taught for a month in the summer of 1934. When she met Williams in New York in early 1935, Chappell was under fire from conservative Methodists. Like Williams, she lost her job because of her politics; the *Social Service Bulletin* announced that Chappell had taken leave for a "much needed rest" in June 1936. Rather than rest, she headed back south to teach at the 1936 New Era School. Williams respected her intellectual dexterity and her formidable experience with working-class causes, which predated his own. Chappell in turn saw Williams as a kindred spirit and proudly accepted the faculty chair at Commonwealth in 1937, a role that allowed her to run the college during Williams's frequent absences on union business.[41]

Williams aimed to use his position at Commonwealth to ensure that the STFU took full advantage of its new affiliation with the UCAPAWA and the CIO. The Commonwealth catalogue for the 1937–38 academic year called the STFU a "movement of historical significance" but stated that "now the transition must be made from a movement to a labor union which can be

Figure 2. Winifred Chappell teaches a class in the Commonwealth College library. Chappell served as the college's faculty chair under Williams. Source: Photo of C. C. Classes ca. 1936–38, Folder "Classes," Box 1, Commonwealth College Photo Collection, Reuther Library, Wayne State University.

used as an instrument by its members to improve their miserable day-to-day conditions." In an effort to strengthen ties to the STFU, Williams appointed J. R. Butler, the union president, as a nonresident instructor. He also met several times with Mitchell that autumn to try to convince him of the positive aspects of the new alliance, but Mitchell only listened in a way that "let [Williams] think I agreed with every thing he said."[42]

By this point, however, Mitchell downright hated Williams. Mitchell believed that joining the UCAPAWA had been a severe mistake for the STFU. He resented taking direction from Henderson and worried about losing his control over the STFU to the UCAPAWA.[43] Certain that Williams was the key to a communist conspiracy to take over the STFU, Mitchell informed Kester that "unless there is something done we are going to have plenty of trouble on our hands." Mitchell suggested going straight to Earl Browder, the head of the CP, to request that Williams be reined in. Claude had himself admitted, Mitchell revealed, that Browder had given him $500 during his fundraising tour and that he was a CP member under the name "John Galey," which is plausible since Galey was his mother's maiden name. If an appeal to Browder did not work, Mitchell wildly threatened to "recite the history of Commonwealth for the benefit of the sensation loving American newspapers—and expose Claude for what he is, a dammed double crosser masquerading as a Socialist."[44]

For his part, Williams had tried to topple Mitchell at the convention in Memphis, where he sealed the STFU's entry into the UCAPAWA. He based his attack on Mitchell's stance on union racial policy. Always fearful of antagonizing whites and blacks, Mitchell had insisted that the STFU follow a flexible line on integration—locals could be mixed or not depending on their choice. This policy was in the main a pragmatic one, considering that many of the southern workers the union tried to organize came from white supremacist or black nationalist backgrounds.[45] Williams, however, announced that the STFU should follow the example of the UCAPAWA and denounce racial segregation. He argued that a union that had only one elected black leader (McKinney), but legions of black members (more than half) should not stand. Trying to rally African American members against Mitchell, Williams backed the candidacy of Leon Turner, a black graduate of the New Era School, in the election for executive secretary, the post held by Mitchell. Turner lost 83 votes to 32. Mitchell survived, but was livid. Not only did he ramp up his red-baiting of Williams, but he also issued ugly race-baiting accusations. Deploying racist stereotypes about the childlike nature of blacks, Mitchell said that Williams had appealed to the "race prejudices" of African Americans, who, "all very religious," "were swayed at will by Claude Williams." His "emotional speech" brought "them to frenzy," Mitchell claimed, both in support of Turner and the UCAPAWA alliance. He believed that Turner had been victimized because, although a good union member, he was "entirely undeveloped." Mitchell now demanded that Williams "be exposed and expelled from the Socialist Party and branded as Communist" to stop the flow of money to Commonwealth "until he is removed and the place cleaned up, completely." The blows landed. Even Norman Thomas agreed that the CP had "used Claud Williams as their tool." Crucially, Kester also now agreed that Williams "be expelled from the Socialist Party." Only three years earlier, these men had been the closest of friends and comrades; now, they were at war.[46]

That winter Williams looked to capitalize on his big victory in Memphis by aligning his efforts more closely with the CIO. In October he attended the National Negro Congress (NNC) in Philadelphia and received an important endorsement from this organization of black workers and activists led by A. Philip Randolph. Support from the nation's largest body of CIO-affiliated African American trade unionists emboldened Williams's efforts at Commonwealth. Restating the college's new plan in November, he declared that "the South is strategic" because the standards of workers there "were a menace to the labor union standards of all workers." It was time, he said, for southern workers to use the UCAPAWA to confront the menace. Commonwealth would begin by training local black and white leaders for union action through two institutes for "pastors, church workers and rural school teachers." Williams himself made a speaking tour of the STFU's locals in eastern Arkansas to build enthusiasm for "the new plans and duties of the organization" now that it was part of the UCAPAWA and the CIO. "I am a man of action," Williams informed the national executive council, which, with Mitchell and Kester once again absent, approved his educational program in early 1938.[47]

Whitfield, meanwhile, mobilized a campaign in defense of threatened farmers. With the help of the STFU, he traveled to Washington, D.C., in December 1937 to lobby the Roosevelt administration to prevent evictions of sharecroppers in the Bootheel due to take place in January 1938. The pending evictions, unprecedented in number, stemmed from the new programs put in place after the AAA was declared unconstitutional in 1936 and revised for 1938. Paradoxically, the new measures gave more rights to tenants than earlier contracts had allowed under the AAA, but, in doing so, the revised policy created further incentive for planters to reduce tenants to casual wage work. The conditions of Whitfield's neighbors seemed to worsen the more the government intervened. Whitfield "made it plain to the Administration," he informed a local newspaper, that he wanted "adequate relief measures for this mass of people, white and black." Whitfield now believed that in years past the rural poor had kept too quiet, so quiet "that many people at large who would help us knew nothing of our plight." As "a Gospel minister" he found it impossible "to preach a gospel of peace and good will to people facing eviction, and facing winter without food!" Instead, Whitfield concluded, "We are compelled to cry out."[48]

Whitfield used his trip to Washington to intensify pressure on local and state officials to stop the evictions. His letter to the local newspaper warned landlords and the government that unless they provided landless farmers the "lease on life as we once had," they would witness the spread of "radicalism, and communism and all other 'isms.'" Whitfield denounced extremism and cast himself as an important guard against any radical turn among his followers. "Give us the right to till the soil that we fought and shed blood for," Whitfield demanded, "and thereby keep the spirit of Democracy foremost in the minds of the workers." If not, he warned, they would give their votes to "men that will hand us a square deal in return."[49] Whitfield lodged a last-minute appeal with President Roosevelt, urging him "to do all that is in your power to get protection for us." No federal support materialized, however, and planters evicted several thousand people in January.[50]

Amid the evictions, Whitfield renewed the campaign to organize the soil toilers. He later recalled that it was in the first few weeks of 1938 that he really grasped how politics worked in the United States. Whitfield told audiences that the rural poor had to "organize for power" before they could do anything to change their pitiable plight. He explained to potential members that they could not just join a "Santa Claus" union for seventy-five cents and then get "land, mules, and hogs. We must organize for power before we can obtain these," he argued. Whitfield increasingly believed that union members had to exert their united force politically and claim "the balance of power."[51]

Whitfield's star was certainly rising in the STFU. At the union's fourth annual convention in February 1938 in Little Rock, he narrowly lost in the election for vice-president, the only office filled by an African American, to E. B. McKinney. The obvious popularity of both McKinney and Whitfield gave added weight to Williams's complaints about the paucity of black leadership in the union. The position of vice-president now looked like tokenism, since two powerful black leaders had to fight over it. Fearful of antagonizing African American members, the executive council created the post of second vice-president for Whitfield. Less than a year after joining the union, Whitfield was now one of its four most powerful officers.[52] His organizing success in the Bootheel, meanwhile, made him a regional political player.

By the spring of 1938 there were over 4,600 dues-paying members in at least twenty-nine Missouri locals, the third-largest state contingent in the union. This grassroots surge caught the attention of New Deal agencies. Representatives from the Farm Security Administration (FSA), the successor to the RA, called on Whitfield to get "the lowdown on the conditions of the homeless people in S.E. Mo." "I am going places and doing things where a negro has not been allowed," he boasted to Mitchell.[53]

Whitfield's political husbandry seemed to bear New Deal fruit in June 1938, when the FSA opened La Forge Homes, a cooperative farm in New Madrid County to house a hundred sharecropping families with the purpose of "rehabilitating" them as stable farmers. La Forge provided its sixty white and forty black clients (including the Whitfield family) access to land, decent housing, production loans, and training, as well as cooperative marketing associations and tools for community self-government.[54] Word had it that Thad Snow, a local planter friendly with Whitfield and the STFU, had secured the Whitfields a placement on the project. With the blessing of La Forge's director, Hans Baasch, Whitfield used the colony as an organizing base. He formed a Good Citizen's League to encourage his neighbors to vote, and was elected to the previously all-white advisory board but refused the post for fear of creating racial tension.[55]

La Forge made tangible Whitfield's solution to the plight of the rural poor. Providing secure land tenure, a home, a garden, access to education, and a rich community life, it supplied everything Whitfield and Handcox had demanded after the 1937 flood, all protected by the federal government. Moreover, it established these resources on a family basis, not a communal one, as advocated by other STFU leaders. This mattered to farmers like Whitfield, who never lost his attachment to individual ownership. In this way, La Forge recreated the ideal rural black world that migrants had sought in Mississippi County in the early 1920s—an image bound by stable rural communities and cooperative associations. But it was limited, as thousands of families, in contrast to the one hundred at La Forge, remained locked in poverty and faced more evictions in January 1939. While proud of their place on the project, the Whitfields could not be happy so long as others suffered. "If'n the Garden of Eden an I heard a lil baby cryin on the other side o that door," Owen later explained, "I couldn't be happy less'n I got that baby in too." The possibilities suggested by La Forge brought together his dreams as a farmer and his mission as a union leader, and transfixed him for the remainder of his career.[56]

Political disagreements within the STFU, however, threatened to upend the struggle against poverty and homelessness. Butler and Mitchell were looking for ways to pull the STFU out of the UCAPAWA. They had never approved of the alliance and now resented the CIO's strict policy on dues payment, which they felt was too onerous on farmers. They also still believed that Henderson aimed to take control of the STFU on behalf of communists. Henderson, on the other hand, considered the STFU leaders to be politically naïve, parochial, and ineffective. Throughout the spring of 1938, Henderson sought to impose CIO standards on the STFU, and Mitchell, Butler, and Kester threatened to secede. Williams and Whitfield were among the most vocal proponents of affiliation with the UCAPAWA. "It was unthinkable," Williams declared, "that the STFU should withdraw from the International."[57]

Whitfield sought desperately to reconcile the two camps at the Little Rock convention by arguing that the STFU needed the UCAPAWA for access to the CIO. "It gives [the STFU] more power," he told his colleagues, by giving "us recognition all over America" and, more importantly, "it gives us not 40,000 but 40,000,000 voting power." To illustrate his point and reiterate the religious roots of the movement, he gave the STFU convention a sermon. "Let me tell you the story of a ship in a storm," Whitfield preached. "The ship was wrecked and a man was swimming about tossed this way and that," grasping at bits of wood that sank until he "felt something solid and held onto it for it was a rock and he was saved. My brothers that story is just like our union," he concluded. "We have been tossed about by many storms and often our support has disappeared from us . . . but we reached out and found a rock to cling to and I say to you brothers . . . that rock is the CIO!"[58] At an executive council meeting in May, Whitfield explained that he was "done in Missouri if we are not connected with the C.I.O."[59] The STFU-UCAPAWA alliance survived, but barely.

With these distractions looming, both Whitfield and Williams tried to focus on action in the field. Throughout the first half of 1938, Williams ran a series of extension seminars among labor activists in Oklahoma, Arkansas, Texas, and Missouri, including another special session for STFU organizers. He also aimed to help Commonwealth's ailing coffers during a West Coast fundraising tour, where he met with religious activists, other UCAPAWA organizers, and CP members. "We ain't got no money and thar hain't no money in sight," he informed one prospective donor. While at a fundraiser in Los Angeles hosted by film director Frank Tuttle, and attended by the Marx Brothers, Williams met Cedric Belfrage, a British author. Belfrage was so fascinated by Williams's story that he decided to write a book about him. Back in Arkansas, Williams ran an integrated "cotton preachers' institute" in Little Rock, where the delegates discussed the role of religion in union organizing. For the rest of the summer, Williams taught at Commonwealth and occasionally spoke at local union meetings to discuss how STFU members could get the most out of CIO affiliation. Belfrage, true to his word, joined him on these trips as he wrote what would become his first biography of Williams, *Let My People Go*.[60]

During this period, Whitfield withdrew from the internecine union battle to fight the upcoming round of evictions. In July he began a "speaking and organizing campaign getting the people in readiness for a drive on the federal government" to force the "FSA to continue its homesteading projects." In August, after a conference with La Forge director Hans Baasch, Whitfield contacted John Clark, president of the Urban League of St. Louis, and proposed a series of speeches there and in other cities that would "put the plight of these homeless people before the nation." Now wary of political sectarianism, Whitfield professed to Clark that he had "no desire to go out as an official or organizer of any labor movement, but as the voice of a people that is homeless and is drifting from place to place." In the meantime, he continued to hold organizing rallies and tried to bring Williams to the Bootheel to speak. The first attempt failed because of a scheduling error. Whitfield rescheduled Williams to join him in late August. "Well, we are looking for you on Aug. 25 without fail," Owen wrote. "I shall certainly be there," Claude replied, "ready to open both barrels at any enemy you may designate." But he never made it.[61]

On his way to see Whitfield, Williams stopped to visit J. R. Butler. Comfortable in the home of his long-time friend and weary from the August heat, Claude took off his suit coat to enjoy a day of restful fellowship. When he left, however, Williams forgot the coat, which Butler's nephew decided to wear into town that night. Before doing so, he removed a sheaf of papers from the inside pocket and laid them on the mantle. Worrying he had mislaid union documents, Butler had a look. What he found shocked him beyond belief.[62]

In the pile was what appeared to be a proposal from Commonwealth College requesting money from the Communist Party to finance the takeover of the STFU. The curious document, marked-up like a rough draft, advised that Commonwealth under Williams's leadership "carried the need for a militantly progressive program" to the union membership, "the most important step to date in building the Democratic Front in Arkansas." Now a wonderful opportunity existed to complete that work: Mitchell, the greatest opponent of the UCAPAWA, "the Party, and to Commonwealth," was on a leave of absence. Williams, moreover, was about "to conduct an intensive program of mass meetings throughout Arkansas and Missouri, beginning August 21st," which included his trip to help Whitfield. The time, the proposal stated, was perfect "for establishing a real party base in the STFU" and to "capture the union for our line at the next convention." All they needed was $500 from the Communist Party to fund the project.[63]

Butler flew into a rage. Without consulting others, he released the document to the press along with a statement demanding that Williams be expelled from the executive council. In a maudlin letter to Claude, Butler charged him with violating "every principle of friendship and every principle of trade unionism." "It pains me deeply," he said, "to have to break the friendship that has existed between us for so many years," and signed it "your one time friend." Confirmed in their suspicions, the enemies of Williams piled on. Thomas, Kester, and Mitchell denounced him. Jay Lovestone, the leading American follower of Nikolai Bukharin and opponent of the CP, applauded their battle "against the machinations by the Stalinite puppets." In order to ensure Claude's expulsion, Butler announced a special session of the national executive council in September. Williams hoped for Whitfield's support and wrote him in advance of the meeting to reemphasize his dedication to the STFU. "As you are aware," he told Whitfield, "I have consistently fought for a trade union policy in the union."[64] Even in the 1970s Williams maintained that his goal that summer had been "to solidify the STFU into the CIO as a labor union of struggling sharecroppers and tenant farmers."[65]

After more than a year of STFU hysteria over communist infiltration, a majority of the council at the trial was already convinced that Williams was guilty before he opened his mouth in self-defense. After Butler and Kester angrily read the charges, Williams summoned some gallows humor by remarking that he was "glad this started off in a friendly way." He went on to explain that the document was nothing more than a rough draft of a funding proposal, produced as part of a student exercise to explore solutions to Commonwealth's chronic lack of money. He had been clawing tooth and nail to raise money for the college, and this was simply one among many requests that had been written, including several to national religious foundations. Williams denied writing it and went on to reaffirm the nonsectarian policy at Commonwealth. "This is an awful document," he explained, "and I hate that it is out." After further questioning, Williams admitted that he had received $500 from Earl Browder and that he had also once held CP membership, although he claimed to have relinquished it after becoming director of Commonwealth to preserve the institution's nonpartisan stance. Whitfield remained quiet throughout the hearing, except to encourage a frank response from Ralph Fields, the Commonwealth student who claimed to be the author of the proposal. "There are statements in that document which are very damaging to our organization," Whitfield explained. In the end, Williams took full responsibility. To blame someone else, he reasoned, would have legitimized red-baiting tactics and could lead him to implicate others for their political views. All of this doomed Claude's relationship with the STFU. Kester himself stated that "the more I listen to Claude Williams the more I become convinced of the genuineness of the document." The council voted unanimously to expel him.[66]

Williams returned to Commonwealth "grieving," but planned to arouse the rank and file in support of an appeal at the STFU's main convention in Cotton Plant, Arkansas, at the end of December. In the weeks that followed, Claude, along with McKinney, who was expelled for his outspokenness on race issues, and W. L. Blackstone, who was expelled for demanding the autonomy of STFU members in Arkansas, made a call to reorganize the STFU with greater internal democracy and against "all Negro Baiting, Red Baiting, Jew Baiting and all other methods used by the bosses and the friends of the bosses . . . to defeat democracy, progress and justice." Williams was certain that he had been targeted by Mitchell and Kester not because of the Commonwealth-CP letter, but because he was one of the strongest supporters of the STFU alliance with the UCAPAWA. The affair with the letter, he reasoned, was a mere pretext for expulsion. Despite Whitfield's vote to expel him, Williams hoped that his most promising ally would come to his aid at the Cotton Plant convention. This time, however, it was Whitfield who would not arrive. With few friends in support, Williams watched his ouster ratified by the delegates, 58–7. His career in the STFU was over.[67]

III

Whitfield returned to the Bootheel in September to refocus his energies on the fight against the next round of evictions that would hit on New Year's Day, 1939. Now convinced that only dramatic action would stave off disaster, Whitfield held meetings throughout October to discuss possible strategies. At one of these meetings, a farmer facing eviction suggested jokingly that since his family had nowhere else to go, they would have to camp out on the side of the road. Whitfield latched on to the idea. A roadside protest of homeless, destitute sharecropping families, he reasoned, would publicize their poverty and their struggle, forcing the federal government to intervene.[68]

Whitfield designed the demonstration to be a grassroots, independent action of local people. The plan was simple. Evicted families, mobilized and led by local union activists, would form roadside camps consisting of neighbors, kin, and friends all along U.S. Highways 60 and 61 in the Bootheel. Once on the roadsides, local leaders would run the protest while Whitfield called upon northern audiences and government officials for action. In advance Whitfield got assurances of support from the Urban League, the Industrial Union Council, and other civic organizations in St. Louis.[69]

Deeply wary of union infighting, Whitfield approached the STFU and the CIO much like he had the Urban League, as sources of political and material support rather than direct leadership. Having corresponded with the STFU national office only twice since the expulsion of Williams, Whitfield informed Mitchell in December 1938 that evicted families would "pile their household goods on sides of the highway" to protest upcoming evictions. He asked for STFU help once the demonstration happened. Meanwhile, Whitfield attended the UCAPAWA's convention in San Francisco as an STFU delegate, where he informed the CIO leadership about the planned demonstration. Before leaving he was elected a vice president of the UCAPAWA. In these efforts to secure support, Whitfield positioned himself to act as a conduit between the unions and the demonstration.[70]

Whitfield marshaled his forces for the demonstration but still worried about potential union interference. After his trip to San Francisco, he avoided any contact with either the STFU or the UCAPAWA. Claiming that he was too busy searching for some mules, Whitfield skipped the STFU convention in Cotton Plant while pledging his support for the union. His absence, he knew, sealed the fate of his friend Claude Williams, but the fight against eviction was more important—service trumped politics in his mind. With the demonstration a fortnight away, Whitfield and his top assistants finalized their plans in the Bootheel, far from the leaders of the STFU and the UCAPAWA.[71]

Planters welcomed several thousand sharecroppers into the New Year 1939 by issuing eviction notices. As planned, evicted farmers and union members began their move to the roadsides under cover of darkness on January 9, the last day of grace in most cropping arrangements. At dawn, their plight would be visible for the entire world to see. To ensure the widest exposure, Whitfield had arranged a final meeting of about 350 core activists in Sikeston on the night of January 7. He also invited Thad Snow and Sam Armstrong, a reporter for the *St. Louis Post-Dispatch*. With Armstrong in attendance, Whitfield knew he had one chance to reveal to the public the moral imperatives behind the protest before planters denounced it. He took the pulpit that night and spoke not just to the gathered crowd but also to the nation.[72]

Between resounding prayers and hymns, Whitfield compared the plight of the rural poor to that of Christ, saying, "The foxes have holes and the birds of heaven have nests; but the Son of Man hath not where to lay his head." His audience, both black and white, responded enthusiastically. "How many of you got a notice to move?" Whitfield asked. Hands shot up. "How many have got a place to go?" he countered, and the room went silent. "That's why we're here," Whitfield thundered, to "bear our burdens together. So, he asked, "Where we goin' to go?" The response shook the rafters. "Sixty-one highway!" they shouted. Whitfield encouraged them not to be afraid, for they had history on their side. Just as the Lord had freed Moses and the Israelites from Egyptian tyranny, so God, if they acted, would free them now. "We also must make an exodus," he exclaimed. "You've got no place to go," Whitfield concluded, "and the only thing left for us is to move quietly like good citizens to the highway." It was time to make people "see what we're up against."[73]

On the morning of January 10, 1939, more than 1,500 black and white landless farmers huddled in well-ordered roadside camps. Whitfield was not among them. He had already left for St. Louis, both to coordinate relief and to ensure his own physical safety. Once in St. Louis, Whitfield met with Urban League officials and oversaw the establishment of the Committee for

Figure 3. Owen Whitfield led the 1939 roadside demonstration in southeast Missouri. Source: Farm Security Administration—Office of War Information Photograph Collection, LC-USF33-002927-M1, Library of Congress. Photograph by Arthur Rothstein.

the Rehabilitation of the Sharecroppers (CRS), with the support of author Fannie Cook and local CIO officials, which secured clothing, surplus commodities, and tents for the demonstrators and organized fundraising events featuring Whitfield. In the following weeks, Whitfield appealed to crowds in St. Louis, Chicago, Boston, New York, and Washington for their assistance. "Our wish is to get back to the soil," Whitfield told his audiences. "We don't want anyone to give us anything, but we want some kind of help to put us back to the soil," he said, urging the FSA to expand its programs in the Bootheel. Whitfield's contacts with the CRS and the UCAPAWA enabled his speaking tour, but it was Mitchell and the STFU, although resentful of recent slights, that set up meetings for him with members of Congress, director of the FSA Will Alexander, and the president himself.[74]

In early February 1939, Whitfield sat down with President Roosevelt in the White House to discuss a New Deal for the rural poor. As a national labor representative and leader of the famous roadside demonstration, Whitfield had to be taken seriously, even by the president. In the ensuing conversation Roosevelt attempted to unveil the source of the power behind Whitfield's sudden prominence. Suspecting political subversion, Roosevelt asked Whitfield if he was a communist. Feigning ignorance, Whitfield said that he had "spent my life on a cotton patch" and did not know what the word meant. Could the president explain it? Roosevelt replied by saying that a communist was someone who thought they could take someone else's property for free. Based on this definition, Whitfield deemed whites to be the real communists, having stolen so much land from the Indians. Whitfield's response, which made Roosevelt laugh, evinced not only his independent radicalism but also an outspokenness that did not stop at the White House door. The preacher was successful. President Roosevelt instructed Secretary of Agriculture Henry Wallace in a private memorandum to "do everything within our power to assist the families of the sharecroppers, farm tenants and farm laborers in southern Missouri who 'went out on the road.'"[75]

As Whitfield pleaded to the nation on their behalf, the demonstrators on the roadside suffered. After attracting considerable media and government attention, the state health commissioner declared the roadside camps "a menace to public health" on January 13 and ordered them removed. The highway patrol broke up the camps, scattering the demonstrators across the Bootheel into isolated camps, saloons, and a swampy site in the spillway. When informed that the removal was based on health concerns, Whitfield asked if "they think those shacks my people have been living in are any healthier?" Having left the area, his only recourse was to intensify his pressure on politicians. The local press, however, accused him of "living on the fat of the land" while his followers floundered. The notion that he did not share their suffering cut him deep. "If I go back South I will be killed because I committed the crime of attempting to wake up the cotton slaves," he told people at the African Methodist Episcopal Zion Church in New York. "By do- ing this," Whitfield explained privately to Thurgood Marshall of the NAACP, "I have lost my home and is without a job." Worse still, he was away from Zella and the children, who had remained at La Forge, where they received threats from the police and local thugs. In February they finally joined him in St. Louis, but earning only $40 a month in wages from the STFU and the UCAPAWA, the Whitfields lived hand to mouth. "Things look a little dark for me just now," Whitfield informed Mitchell.[76]

Whitfield relied on his religious conviction to keep him on course. He was proud, he wrote, that he dared "to do what no Negro Preacher has ever dared to do, and that is to wake up the slaves." He had struck "at the roots of a system that held our people in slavery for over 50 years and has sent our mothers and fathers to a paupers grave without enjoying any of the fruits of their toil," as his own parents had suffered and died. This cause was "worth everything I gave up," he concluded, "to put an end to this darn system. I know that God is pleased, and I feel that the American people will not let me starve."[77]

Amid this turmoil, Whitfield lost vital connections with the demonstrators, whose own internal organization collapsed. With the Whitfields absent, the demonstrators pleaded for help from the STFU and the UCAPAWA. Police blockades and intimidation, however, complicated union efforts to supply aid. Working from Blytheville, Arkansas, the STFU's relief committee, led by Howard Kester, could only reach the southern Bootheel, while UCAPAWA aid from St. Louis was limited to the northern camps. To complicate matters, local landlords got their congressman to force the FSA to stop providing the emergency food grants it had started issuing to the protestors. As a result, the money and supplies Whitfield raised fed into a broken relief structure, serving only to fuel competition between the STFU and the UCAPAWA to sway the protestors to their side. As the demonstrators divided according to which union met their expectations, Whitfield struggled to remain indepen- dent as a paid employee of both the STFU and the UCAPAWA. He found it increasingly hard to prove that "our people will stick together if they have a leader that they can trust, a leader that won't sell them out."[78]

At the depth of the crisis in early February, Whitfield reestablished contact with the Bootheel locals in two letters that were by turns defiant and confused, and together revealed just how detached he had become. "You have fought the biggest fight you ever fought in your life," he exclaimed, "and you have won." Whitfield knew that the authorities had tried "TO STARVE YOU TO DEATH" by breaking up the camps. Moreover, he knew how the police had tried to "make you lose faith in me and the union." He reassured them that he had secured support for the STFU's effort "to get land and homes for all of the union people," and he advised them "to get busy and build our frontline trenches and continue our fight for freedom from wage slavery." Since the STFU was working to get the FSA grant checks reinstated, Whitfield now advised the protestors to stand with the STFU rather than the UCAPAWA, which people "don't like," he said, because of its communist ties. With resurgent loyalty, perhaps influenced by his conversation with President Roosevelt, Whitfield promised that neither he nor the STFU would fail them.[79]

But the STFU did fail, and so, it seemed, had Whitfield. The STFU could not get the FSA grants restarted, and on February 18 the union closed its relief center in Blytheville. At this critical hour, Donald Henderson launched measures to take control of the STFU membership by holding a referendum on the leadership of Mitchell, Butler, and the rest. To do so, he cited examples of its malfeasance in getting relief to the demonstrators. Henderson's tactics hit directly at Whitfield's credibility with his own people. Whitfield's followers now lashed out at him, telling him "to go to hell" after his broken promises about the STFU. Bombarded with criticism, much of it from his closest followers in Mississippi County, Whitfield twisted in the unkind wind. In a cynical about-face, he blamed the STFU for betraying him and the protestors. Whitfield called a state convention of all Missouri locals in March in St. Louis, where they would decide whether or not they wanted "to go on with the great labor movement in America" or stick with the STFU. The CIO offered immense power, he reminded them, but the schemers in the STFU were determined to obstruct its work in the Bootheel just as they had, he accused wildly, blocked CIO relief from reaching the roadsides. "Are you with me," he demanded to know, "or are you against me?"[80]

Twenty-one locals stood by Whitfield by voting to remain with the UCA-PAWA. The national political power of the CIO and the strong stance on racial equality by the UCAPAWA proved far more valuable to black tenant farmers than the STFU, which retained only five locals in the area. "All of our members wants to be thoroughly identified with the big democratic labor movement," explained one activist who sided with the UCAPAWA. After the vote, Whitfield reorganized them into the Missouri Agricultural Workers' Council (MAWC), affiliated with the UCAPAWA and under the elected leadership of William Fischer, a white sharecropper, as president and himself as secretary.[81] With surprising confidence given recent troubles, Whitfield promised those who joined the MAWC that he would "lead you on to the land where I started to lead you."[82]

Whitfield spent the summer of 1939 working to reconnect with his people and secure a lasting victory from the demonstration. First, under Whitfield's direction, the CRS purchased a ninety-four-acre tract of wooded hillside near Harviell in Butler County, Missouri. Eighty black and fifteen white families, among the last of the demonstrators without homes, moved that summer to what they called Cropperville, ending what for them had been a decade-long battle against landlessness and dependency. Ever loyal to Whitfield, the residents of Cropperville established a MAWC local that became the hub of UCAPAWA activity in the area.[83] The UCAPAWA was then in the process of restructuring in the wake of the split with the STFU. In October, Whitfield met with UCAPAWA leaders from other southern states in Memphis to plan their future work. This resulted in December in the creation of the Southern States Cotton Council (SSCC), an executive working group of regional leaders that included Whitfield, William Fischer, Leon Turner of Arkansas, Harry Koger of Texas, and Otis Nation of Oklahoma. The SSCC was meant to coordinate UCAPAWA efforts among workers in the cotton industry from the fields to the oil presses. For Whitfield, the most pressing issue was the fight against evictions in Missouri and elsewhere, more of which were planned for early 1940. This combined effort, in light of his notoriety after the demonstration, placed Whitfield in the national spotlight.[84]

In order to avoid a repeat of the previous protest, Missouri governor Lloyd Stark convened a conference in St. Louis in January 1940 consisting of Whitfield, two Bootheel planters, and state and federal officials. The conference hoped to finalize unprecedented FSA plans to settle displaced Bootheel families on unused lands.[85] Despite negotiations, conditions remained bleak. The people at Cropperville lacked food, money, or adequate shelter. Whitfield admitted that they could not go on much longer, let alone support the several thousand additional families about to be evicted. "I am asking the world," he confided to Eleanor Roosevelt, whose sympathy he had gained during the protest and his trip to the White House, "what shall we do? We can't stay where we are and we can't use the highway."[86]

At least not the way they had before. On the morning of January 7, 1940, the second day of the Stark conference, motorists driving along Highways 60 and 61 in the Bootheel encountered large clearly worded signs where, a year earlier, landless families had camped in protest of eviction. "Lest You Forget," the MAWC-authored signs read, "One Year Ago, sat on this roadside, 1,500 croppers shelterless for days in snow and freezing cold." Since then,

Figure 4. Owen Whitfield preaching at the Cropperville settlement in Missouri.
Source: Folder 8, Box 26, Belfrage Papers, Tamiment Library, New York University.

little had changed, except "the abuses remain and grow." Landless farmers
had gotten "a Raw Deal," the message stated, and "it makes us desperate."[87]
Press attention to the signs gave Whitfield new leverage at the conference. If
Governor Stark and others wanted to avoid another protest, Whitfield made
clear, they had to make concessions. Unless he came away with something
significant, Whitfield could not predict how his followers might behave. These
tactics worked. The next day, Stark, backed by all the delegates, called on all
landlords to postpone evictions until February and requested that the FSA
draft plans for an expansive program in the Bootheel. The group planned
to meet again in a month's time to formally announce what the FSA would
do. The maneuver stunned the local press. "The movements of the Negro
Whitfield will bear watching," one editor concluded.[88]

Whitfield's next move flabbergasted them. While attending the UCA-
PAWA's National Cotton Conference in the nation's capital in late January,
Whitfield and other SSCC leaders delivered a petition to the White House
signed by twenty thousand CIO-affiliated cotton workers protesting the im-
pending evictions across the South and demanding new federal programs
to aid landless farmers. Whitfield, along with Zella, presented the petition
personally to Eleanor Roosevelt. Zella Whitfield stole the show during this
trip to the White House. She felt at ease with the First Lady, who seemed
like an "ordinary person" with a "friendly disposition." Zella began the con-

versation by pointing out to Roosevelt that they were both wearing hats with peacock feathers.[89] Soon the two were talking about the terrible living conditions of those who had been evicted. Roosevelt expressed sympathy and promised "to do all in her power to call attention to the sorry plight of the sharecroppers through her column in the daily papers."[90] True to her word, the First Lady wrote in her "My Day" column on January 19, 1940, about "a visit from a group of representatives of the southern Missouri and Arkansas sharecroppers." They had "serious problems," she explained, but hoped that "some light is breaking" after hearing Whitfield tell about the negotiations between Bootheel planters and the FSA in Jefferson City.[91]

Before going back to Missouri for the second Stark Conference, Whitfield delivered the keynote address at the National Cotton Conference. "I used to be considered a good preacher some ten years ago, but I preached a different kind of gospel from the kind I now preach," he told the delegates. "I am preaching now about a present God in the hearts and minds of men—the brotherhood of man and I am seeking to build a heaven here on earth," Whitfield declared. This was what he hoped to do through the UCAPAWA. "There is no one here in Washington to represent us," Whitfield continued, "so we came here ourselves . . . to hang our troubles on the White House door."[92] "We found Mrs. Roosevelt very sympathetic," Whitfield informed a Bootheel newspaper. The paper's editor could only ask, "What's Whitfield Got?"[93]

Back home, Whitfield successfully negotiated a generous FSA program at the meeting in Jefferson City. In addition to an array of loans and grants, the agency announced plans to build eight rural public housing communities for displaced landless farmers. Known collectively as Delmo Security Homes—but as "Whitfield projects" to some—they housed more than six hundred families, both black and white on a segregated basis.[94] None of it would have happened without Whitfield's leadership, although he was more humble. "It wasn't me they feared," he later explained, "but the organization behind me."[95]

Whitfield was now feted nationally as a great African American leader. Since early 1939 he had spoken in front of numerous northern audiences—black and white—to convince them to aid the rural poor. These speaking engagements raised much-needed money for Missouri's sharecroppers and made Whitfield a celebrity among African Americans. Following Whitfield's performances in the Stark conferences, the Schomburg Library in Harlem and the Association for the Study of Negro Life and History named him one of ten award winners, alongside such distinguished recipients as boxer Joe Louis, singer Marian Anderson, historian Carter G. Woodson, NAACP leader Walter White, and author Richard Wright, for "distinguished achievement in improved race relations during 1939." The *Chicago Defender* celebrated Whitfield as "a new kind of preacher—one who dared to challenge a regime of peonage and terror." He garnered yet more headlines in April at the NNC meeting in Washington, where he delivered a well-received address. Invited as the guest of Mayor Fiorello La Guardia in New York and at the White House, he had entered chambers of power that few sharecroppers ever imagined. Much to the chagrin of white supremacists in his home state, these events "made [Whitfield] so stuck-up," according to the *Sikeston Standard*'s editor, "that nothing short of him being returned to [the] plantation where he formerly worked with the riding boss back of him with a black snake whip . . . would satisfy a great number of citizens."[96]

But Whitfield was still learning to balance his new role as a nationally recognized spokesperson with his concern for poor people in the Bootheel. The FSA program he had negotiated would only cover a fraction of those in need. Although he liked adulation, Whitfield also often thought that the banquets, the awards, and the florid praise were worthless, especially coming from rich white people. To court northern white liberals, he told one confidant, was to "make yourself a nice hell and jump in it." He was not comfortable, and his uneasiness ate away at his patience with those who had been on the roadsides. Whitfield thought that they complained too much to local government relief offices and chastised them for it. With heavy condescension, he asked if they knew that they had among government officials "built up the best reputation of any group in the United States?" "And did you know that you are now tearing down that reputation?" "Remember this!" Whitfield instructed—as if they did not already know—"what we get from the government in the way of help and homes depends on the way we conduct our selves." Leadership was all "muddy water," he complained.[97]

Whitfield's strategy of working simultaneously as a national and local organizer was initially successful, mainly because Zella assumed a larger role within the MAWC. Drawing on her experience in the STFU, she served as the leader of women's auxiliaries and cosigned MAWC press releases. More important, she took control of MAWC policy and strategy during Owen's absences. Zella's main task was to keep the leaders at Cropperville on the right path, which was difficult to do from St. Louis.[98]

Whitfield's national prominence also brought newfound political scrutiny. Texas congressman Martin Dies placed him on the "red list" that his committee circulated to alert local and state authorities to potential communists in their midst. But Whitfield remained allied to communists who offered practical support, unlike other black activists such as A. Philip Randolph, who cut ties with communists in the months after the August 1939 nonaggression pact between Hitler and Stalin, when the CP abruptly halted criticism of the Nazis and fascism in general. To explain his relationship with the CP, Whitfield recalled when a plainclothes officer attended a MAWC meeting to warn about communists. No one responded until a sharecropper called "Big Boy" said, "we don't know anything about the Russians and reds you are talking about, but we do know the southern whites." We have "learned to love the things you white folks hate." Whitfield believed that if communists helped win "our wage scale," croppers would have no problem associating with them.[99] He may well have had Claude Williams in mind.

Although he never admitted it, Williams was deeply wounded by his expulsion from the STFU in late 1938. Now approaching his forty-fourth birthday, he had been forced out of yet another organization that he had risked his life to build up. The wound cut him two ways. Claude believed deeply in the STFU and its potential strength. He continued to reiterate this fondness for the STFU some forty years later. "I believed in the union," he told Mitchell in 1976, "its people and its possibilities." Although he disagreed with Mitchell "about direction and emphasis," he "supported, without fail, the stated policies and program of the union." To compound matters, Williams's sense of betrayal was personal as well as political. He felt that his close friends had stabbed him in the back. What hurt most was that Kester, his spiritual kinsman, had joined the attack. After his failed appeal in Cotton Plant, Williams cut ties with his old friend. "Kester," he told him, "you are a goddamned snake that never rattles." Kester bit him again in December 1939, when he denied Claude's application to join the Fellowship of Southern Churchmen, the inheritor of Alva Taylor's Social Gospel legacy. The fellowship was "not convinced about your readiness to give your undivided loyalty to the cause of prophetic religion," Kester cruelly informed him.[100]

Despite the events of late 1938, Williams applauded Whitfield's leadership of the roadside demonstration and his decision to stick with the CIO. Williams kept publicly clear of the STFU-UCAPAWA dispute that followed, because his involvement would only ramp-up the red-baiting of Whitfield. Still, he voiced support in the Commonwealth College newspaper: the leaders of the STFU "should have learned by now," Williams wrote, "that the red-baiting does them no good."[101] Williams had great hope that the UCAPAWA would succeed where the STFU had failed. He drafted a plan for Henderson detailing how the UCAPAWA could absorb the remaining members of the STFU and the Socialist Party in Arkansas. He advised that if McKinney and Whitfield would make a joint appeal on behalf of the UCAPAWA, their combined influence would be unstoppable. Williams also hoped to get a job with the union himself. "I presume to mention (for what it is worth in light of other things)," he wrote to Henderson, "the importance of some one like myself who is a minister, who has worked with them in class and institutes and who can make a peculiar approach to them by speaking their language getting them together." "Henderson never replied to this or to anything else I sent him," Williams noted.[102]

Williams had little time to follow up, since the allegations made at his trial devastated Commonwealth. He spent the first half of 1939 trying to save the college, but it could not be done. His problems had stricken Commonwealth with a reputation for incompetence and instability. Williams recalled that Congressman Dies had "released in the national press a red-baiting blast of Commonwealth and myself." Financial backers fled, while hostile Arkansas state authorities looked to destroy it for good. Even the CP refused to donate money. "They said that Commonwealth was not a good school of its kind," one correspondent informed Williams.[103] Although Claude remained defiant, the year's fights had taken a terrible toll on his body. His lungs had been bad since the 1920s, but recent stresses had made this problem acute. Williams was also likely depressed as a result of constant fighting against friends and colleagues. He accepted his doctor's recommendation that he take a three-month break and resigned from the directorship of Commonwealth in August 1939. Health was only part of the reason. Williams also believed that his association with the college was now its main problem and thought if he stepped aside that it might recover. But Commonwealth College closed for good in the summer of 1940.[104]

Williams's fall from grace could not have been more spectacular. By the time Cedric Belfrage finished his biography of the preacher, no American publishers would touch it. Entitled *Let My People Go*, it appeared in London in 1940 as part of publisher Victor Gollancz's Left Book Club series. Although the series reached over sixty thousand British readers, it was not the audience Williams and Belfrage hoped for. "It was taken by many of the British reviewers," Belfrage later noted, "as a novel."[105] An American publisher agreed to release the book in 1941 as *South of God*, but it quickly went out of print. The books were virtually identical, and neither covered Williams's expulsion from the STFU or the collapse of Commonwealth College.

Williams thus began a period of contemplation—the first in a long time— that reminded him that amid the wreckage of notoriety, mistrust, and ruined friendships, he could still claim a resilient ministry that reached ordinary southerners. It was not an easy winter, as the family remained at Commonwealth not knowing where they would go. To make matters worse, Joyce Williams developed tuberculosis and was in and out of the Arkansas Tuberculosis Sanatorium in the winter of 1939–40.[106] In these trying conditions,

Claude began to formulate the next stage in his career. He wanted to get away from union disputes, from executive councils, from the grandees of the Left and get back to grassroots religion. Before his rest had even begun, Williams already spoke of a "contemplated return to work among my own people—the working people of the South."[107]

As soon as his health permitted, Williams reformulated his New Era educational program, calling his new independent project the "people's institute of applied religion." It had to be independent, he explained, because his reputation was so toxic that direct affiliation with him would harm any organization. Williams longed to get back "to work with the working preachers" of the South. Rather than organize from a single location, however, Claude now envisioned a mobile training course that he could take to flashpoints of union struggle, whether in rural areas or in cities. He also hoped to use visual educational materials to bring "prophetic religion" to people in new ways. Mobility, at the beginning of the largest internal migration in American history, was certainly the watchword in 1940. The war in Europe spurred a dramatic industrial expansion throughout the country, but particularly in southern cities like Memphis and Little Rock. Many migrants to the cities were former cotton farmers. Williams designed the people's institute to use the revolutionary aspects of Christianity to illuminate the practical struggles these workers faced. At a meeting of the NRLF in Chicago, Williams explained that "the greater number of untrained, laboring tent-preachers . . . may well be used as instruments of reaction" by right-wing activists and that his proposed work would "employ visual aid and capture the religious drive for labor organization and the correction of the many injustices that keep people in poverty and ignorance."[108]

Williams had been working on the idea, in consultation with Whitfield, since at least the first weeks of 1939. When a reporter had asked in the midst of the roadside demonstration about the topics of his sermons, Whitfield replied that he was "not preachin' 'bout heaven. No sir! I'm preachin' the brotherhood of man. I believes in the applied religion. Yes sir, I believes in the applied religion!" Whether the phrase was his or Williams's is unclear, but the two were united in their desire to take the radical gospel straight to the people. Whitfield could not commit much support to the project over the course of the year, consumed as he was with the aftermath of the demonstration. But the idea was never far from him.[109]

Williams was soon back to work. Using money donated by his old friends Willard Uphaus, Harry Ward, and Alva Taylor, Williams printed a series of five wall charts, drawn with the help of Commonwealth art student Dan Genin, to convey the radical gospel to illiterate and semiliterate audiences. These charts spelled out the biblical message and its relevance to current problems. With titles such as "Religion and the Common People," "King Cotton, His Lords and Slaves" and "Anti-Semitism, Racism and Democracy," the charts would become the key teaching tool for future institutes.[110] Williams held his first institutes in the homes of preacher friends in western Arkansas and eastern Oklahoma. After one such presentation at Samuel Teitelbaum's house in Fort Smith, the rabbi lauded Williams's program as "one of the few forces that is fighting racism and fascism and nazism of every variety in the South." Teitelbaum shared his "conviction that success in the struggle for freedom and democracy can be achieved only through an educational work among the masses."[111] Williams also welcomed long-time comrades as members of what by April 1940 was officially called the People's Institute of Applied Religion (PIAR). Lee Hays, Winifred Chappell, and Don West all signed a pledge to assist Williams "in formulating the plans and policies" of the PIAR "and to cooperate in its program."[112] Williams also sought outside support, despite his past problems working in other organizations. He informed A. Philip Randolph, the president of the NNC, about his new efforts to use "prophetic religion . . . for constructive social change" in the South, and offered his services for the upcoming NNC meeting in Washington, D.C., in April.[113]

On his way to the nation's capital, Williams attended the annual meeting of the Southern Conference for Human Welfare (SCHW) in Chattanooga, Tennessee, where the PIAR took on real life. Founded in 1938, the SCHW attracted business, labor, educational, and political leaders of both races from the across the South who were interested in improving conditions in the region. Chaired by University of North Carolina president Frank Porter Graham, the SCHW boasted a host of powerful supporters including Texas politician Maury Maverick, NNC leader John P. Davis, Howard University president Mordecai Johnson, and Eleanor Roosevelt, who delivered the keynote address in Chattanooga only a few weeks after meeting Owen and Zella Whitfield in the White House.[114] At the conference, Williams met and befriended Harry Koger, a UCAPAWA leader in Texas (where he worked with Horace Bryan, Williams's old friend). The plans for the PIAR interested Koger. Instead of joining Whitfield at the NNC in Washington, Williams accepted Koger's invitation to return with him to east Texas to put PIAR sessions into action. Koger also agreed to sign on as a sponsor of the new program.[115]

Williams excelled during this first real test of the PIAR. He held the institutes among African American preachers in and around Marshall, Texas. The sessions were a clear success. Vernon Olson, a UCAPAWA representative and recent graduate of Commonwealth College, followed Williams's tour and later thanked the preacher for his "positive approach, which emphasizes the

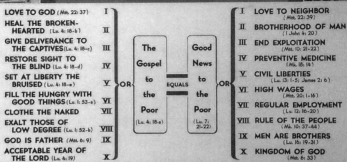

THE GOSPEL OF THE KINGDOM

SCRIPTURE: Luke 7: 19-30   TEXT: Mark 1: 14

LOVE TO GOD (Mtt. 22: 37)	I		I	LOVE TO NEIGHBOR (Mtt. 22: 39)
HEAL THE BROKEN-HEARTED (Lu. 4: 18-b)	II		II	BROTHERHOOD OF MAN (1 John 4: 20)
GIVE DELIVERANCE TO THE CAPTIVES (Lu. 4: 18-c)	III		III	END EXPLOITATION (Mtt. 10: 21-22)
RESTORE SIGHT TO THE BLIND (Lu. 4: 18-d)	IV		IV	PREVENTIVE MEDICINE (Mtt. 18: 14)
SET AT LIBERTY THE BRUISED (Lu. 4: 18-e)	V		V	CIVIL LIBERTIES (Lu. 13: 1-5; James 2: 6)
FILL THE HUNGRY WITH GOOD THINGS (Lu. 1: 53-a)	VI		VI	HIGH WAGES (Mtt. 20: 1-16)
CLOTHE THE NAKED	VII		VII	REGULAR EMPLOYMENT (Lu. 12: 16-20)
EXALT THOSE OF LOW DEGREE (Lu. 1: 52-b)	VIII		VIII	RULE OF THE PEOPLE (Mk. 10: 37-44)
GOD IS FATHER (Mtt. 6: 9)	IX		IX	MEN ARE BROTHERS (Lu. 16: 19-31)
ACCEPTABLE YEAR OF THE LORD (Lu. 4: 19)	X		X	KINGDOM OF GOD (Mtt. 6: 33)

The Gospel to the Poor (Lu. 4: 18-a) — OR — EQUALS — OR — Good News to the Poor (Lu. 7: 21-22)

PEOPLE'S INSTITUTE OF APPLIED RELIGION

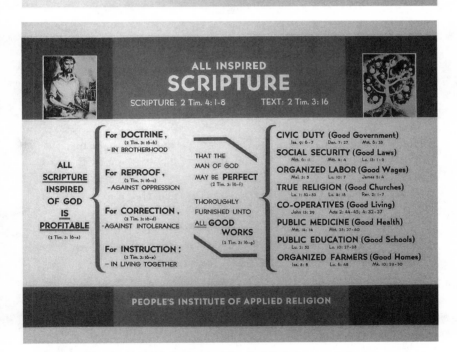

ALL INSPIRED SCRIPTURE

SCRIPTURE: 2 Tim. 4: 1-8   TEXT: 2 Tim. 3: 16

ALL SCRIPTURE INSPIRED OF GOD IS PROFITABLE (2 Tim. 3: 16-a)

For DOCTRINE, (2 Tim. 3: 16-b) – IN BROTHERHOOD

For REPROOF, (2 Tim. 3: 16-c) – AGAINST OPPRESSION

For CORRECTION, (2 Tim. 3: 16-d) – AGAINST INTOLERANCE

For INSTRUCTION: (2 Tim. 3: 16-e) – IN LIVING TOGETHER

THAT THE MAN OF GOD MAY BE PERFECT (2 Tim. 3: 16-f)

THOROUGHLY FURNISHED UNTO ALL GOOD WORKS (2 Tim. 3: 16-g)

CIVIC DUTY (Good Government)
Isa. 9: 6-7   Dan. 7: 27   Mtt. 6: 33

SOCIAL SECURITY (Good Laws)
Mtt. 6: 11   Mtt. 4: 4   Lu. 13: 1-9

ORGANIZED LABOR (Good Wages)
Mal. 3: 5   Lu. 10: 7   James 5: 4

TRUE RELIGION (Good Churches)
Lu. 1: 52-53   Lu. 4: 18   Rev. 2: 1-7

CO-OPERATIVES (Good Living)
John 13: 29   Acts 2: 44-45; 4: 32-37

PUBLIC MEDICINE (Good Health)
Mtt. 14: 14   Mtt. 25: 37-40

PUBLIC EDUCATION (Good Schools)
Lu. 2: 52   Lu. 10: 27-28

ORGANIZED FARMERS (Good Homes)
Isa. 5: 8   Lu. 6: 48   Mk. 10: 29-30

PEOPLE'S INSTITUTE OF APPLIED RELIGION

Figures 5 and 6. The People's Institute of Applied Religion used charts to communicate the working-class gospel. Source: Special Collections Library, University of Tennessee.

active philosophy of the Lord's Prayer 'let it be done on earth,' rather than
. . . waiting for a good life after death." "In your charts," Olson declared,
"you have armed the poor people of the South with a weapon of truth with
which to win a kingdom of brotherly love and freedom on earth where true
Christianity shall prevail."[116]

APRIL 27, 1940

Owen Whitfield Addresses the
Third National Negro Congress, Washington, D.C.

When Owen Whitfield took the floor at the third National Negro
Congress in the Labor Department's massive new auditorium at the
corner of 14th Street and Constitution Avenue in Washington, he
faced an audience as influential as any he had ever addressed. Friday,
the first day of the congress, featured a welcome by NNC president
A. Philip Randolph and a general session led by John L. Lewis, the
president of the CIO. The following morning, the congress's 1,285
delegates attended panels on the pressing issues of social security,
citizenship rights, economic security, and cultural freedom. Among
them were grassroots activists from across the nation as well as the
giants of civil rights organizing and trade unionism, including Randolph, Lewis, Philip Murray, chairman of the CIO's steelworker's
union, and NAACP legal architect Charles H. Houston. Whitfield
delivered the keynote address of the congress's second general session
that afternoon; his topic was "The Negro Farm Problem in America."
Claude Williams was not in the audience, having gone to Texas to
launch the PIAR instead. But Williams knew his friend would give
them "both barrels" in his speech to the boldest labor and civil rights
organization in America.[1]

Whitfield admitted to this august gathering that "after about 35
years of working in the cotton fields . . . today I feel as one who has
just waked up from a bad dream." With influence that his parents
could not have imagined, he thought not of successes, but of mistakes—"the many mistakes we [have] made in the past in all walks
of life." The biggest mistake was one of religion. Whitfield explained
that men of religion, including himself for most of his life, preached
"too much INSPIRATION and too little INFORMATION," which
led them to "preach Jesus Christ" but "refuse to accept the policies
of Christ." Whitfield claimed that most preachers had gone so far

astray from their mission that "if Jesus Christ would come to earth in 1940 . . . the church group would be the first to have him investigated by the Dies Committee." In such religious matters, Whitfield argued, African Americans had often only confused themselves. He lamented that "the Negro has been mislead by false leaders under the guise of champions of the race, but who, in reality, has only served as tools for the bosses." Questioning the path of black nationalism in the 1920s and early 1930s, Whitfield accused blacks of having "had more organizations than any other race on earth, but the bosses had no objections to these organizations, because of the fact that they consist only of Negro people." Now, he announced, interracial alliances and the "spirit of cooperation" were vital to cutting the "traditional rope called 'White Supremacy.'" Whitfield believed that in order to cut the rope, black people needed to get rid of "sky-pilot" preachers, "two-bit silver tongued schoolhouse political orators," and the folklore of "witchcraft and hoodooism" and demand leaders "who will not sell [a Negro] down the river."[2]

What African Americans really needed, Whitfield argued, were religious leaders who were not afraid to lead the way to "Brotherhood and concerted but peaceful actions for higher economics and a higher standard of living." Too often, he told the congress, educated blacks "high-hat or ignore the man who is not finished in learning." Too often, Whitfield continued, otherwise good leaders were scared to act for fear of losing their "status." "How can we win with status frights?" he asked. The answer, Whitfield explained, lay in the fact that "a man may be unlearned but there is a possibility of [him] getting up and doing unheard of things that may rock the nation." He offered himself as an example. "I think I proved this theory when I stepped out of my beautiful home, un-lettered, but with 45 years of practical experience, and led 1,700 white and black people to 60 and 61 highways" in an act of protest that "exposed the slave system and made it possible for the public to see with their natural eyes in one hour what it took them 50 years to read about." Intellectual and political leaders in groups like the NNC, he argued, had to join with ordinary activists to accomplish their goals. "With your learning and my experience," he promised, "we can end Jim Crowism." "With your learning and my experience we can tear down the whole slave system in the South and bring about to all civil rights" and "get back some of the good things that we worked, fought, bled and died for 74 years ago." Whitfield's efforts in 1940 were not just about poverty or racism but also about making right the broken promises of Reconstruction that had overshadowed the lives of his parents' generation.[3]

"The roadside demonstrations in Southeast Missouri proved many facts concerning the Negro," Whitfield concluded. It proved that African Americans were no longer afraid to "stand up and demand [their] rights" and would not "be misled again by a group of sky-pilots who can give only Inspiration." Most important, the protest had proved that black southerners would "not wait for bread to be shipped from Jerusalem by miracle from God, but will struggle to obtain some of the bread God has already provided for his people."[4]

The speech astounded the audience of prominent African Americans and labor activists. Reporting for *New Masses*, author Ralph Ellison deemed Whitfield the "hero of the convention." He explained: "[Whitfield] speaks with the skill of the Negro folkpreacher, in terms and images the people understand. The people from the farm country shout 'Amen!' and 'It's the truth!' Whitfield is of the earth and his speech is of the earth, and I said 'Amen!' with the farmers. . . . His is the pride of one who knows what it means to fight and win. He made the nation listen to the voices of his people." To the NNC audience, Whitfield personified the connection between militant rural sharecroppers and urban industrial unionists that CIO activists had been seeking since the mid-1930s.[5]

Whitfield returned to the Bootheel ready to drive the UCAPAWA forward. In June the MAWC hosted a mass meeting of 2,500 delegates at Cropperville, where he advocated for a resolution calling on the federal government to give more help to the rural poor. "In the past the government has done some good things for us," he said, "but now they seem to be shadow boxing and getting nowhere." It was time for serious action to address the "needless poverty and misery rampant among our people," Whitfield concluded. Following the rally, he attended a meeting of the Southern States Cotton Council at its new permanent headquarters in Memphis, Tennessee. Now chaired by Harry Koger, the SSCC had relocated to Memphis to initiate an organizing campaign among the thousands of rural migrants flooding into the city and its factories. The main component of that effort would be a new "workers training school" in the city, to convene in August. When it came time to appoint the person to direct the school and the SSCC's broader program in the cotton states, Whitfield and Koger had the perfect candidate in mind: Claude Williams.[6]

4. Religion Applied

Williams relished the chance to apply the ancient definition of religion, "to bind you to something," to Memphis workers. Through the revolutionary gospel, he hoped to stitch factory workers into CIO unions and achieve power through unity, the promise of Pentecost. Over the summer of 1940, Williams conferred with allies Harry Koger and Myles Horton about strategies for educating urban workers. In the final plan he sent to UCAPAWA head Donald Henderson, Williams recommended four staff members to run the sessions: Owen Whitfield, Zella Whitfield (to do important "womens work"), Harry Koger, and Winifred Chappell, the former faculty chair at Commonwealth College. On the banks of the Mississippi at the Inland Boatmen's Hall, these organizers planned a ten-day leadership training school to begin on August 5.[1]

I

The Memphis they entered in 1940 operated under the long shadow of two powerful white men: Nathan Bedford Forrest and Edward H. Crump. Forrest symbolized the Memphis of the past: a city built on unfree African American labor that became the largest market in the mid-South for slaves and cotton by 1850. He sought to protect its status. During the Civil War, Forrest infamously ordered his Confederate soldiers to massacre dozens of black federal troops who had surrendered as prisoners of war at Fort Pillow, Tennessee. After the military defeat of the Confederacy, Forrest helped launch the Ku Klux Klan to thwart interracial political alliances of workers, who during Reconstruction had managed to elect a reform mayor. Forrest's strategy succeeded, and he was rewarded with accolades. By 1905, when a statue was unveiled in a city park that depicted Forrest as a military hero on horseback, even the *New York Times* put aside its former nickname for him—"Fort Pillow Forrest"—to claim that he had "won quite as much appreciation in the North as in the South, though in the former, of course, the appreciation was a little slow in finding expression." National reconciliation around white supremacists like Forrest in the 1890s had allowed the construction of Jim Crow in Memphis alongside federal toleration for the violation of the Fourteenth and Fifteenth amendments to the U.S. Constitution.[2]

The imposition of Jim Crow allowed for the division of the workforce by race and gender, which set the stage for Crump. Born in Mississippi, Crump came of age in Memphis alongside Jim Crow. He first became mayor in 1909, and although he would step down from this position several times between 1909 and 1940 to pursue other political and business interests, nobody doubted who really ran the city. "Boss" Crump built a well-oiled Democratic Party political machine based on competing but loyal voting blocs. On the one hand, he catered to business leaders through the office of the County Trustee, which encouraged certain mortgage and insurance deals. On the other hand, Crump gave ordinary citizens concessions so long as they stayed in their economic and racial places. This meant reaching deals with the local AFL unions and with African American leaders in exchange for votes. Always willing to bend Jim Crow, Crump's machine often paid poll taxes so that African American allies could do their bit at the ballot box. In the 1927 mayoral election, for example, Memphis's black press hailed Crump's handpicked successor, Watkins Overton, because seven thousand black voters provided the margin of victory. In return, Crump opposed the city's hard-line white supremacists, denounced lynching as damaging to the city's economic fortunes, and brought thousands of jobs to Memphis by promising a plentiful labor supply to lumber and cotton processing firms, as well as to national corporations like the Firestone Tire and Rubber Company and Ford Motors. He consolidated his power during two terms as a congressman in the early Depression years when he fashioned a strong relationship with New Deal Democrats, including President Roosevelt. Crump supported the National Recovery Act so long as it did not raise minimum wages for black workers, and he backed the Works Progress Administration while requiring Memphis workers to make political donations in exchange for employment. To President Roosevelt, Crump delivered Tennessee votes for the Democratic Party, and that was what mattered.[3]

The city that deferred to Forrest and Crump seemed a poor beachhead for an interracial labor movement, but the same Mississippi River location that made Memphis a corporate hub also made it vital for CIO unions. In the late 1930s the CIO sent organizers from St. Louis. Early sacrifices by black organizers like Thomas Watkins produced gains for workers in the International Longshoremen's Association and the Inland Boatmen's Union. Watkins ultimately fled Memphis for his life, but his efforts gave the CIO a toehold in the city. When Harry Koger took up residence there, he did so about a block away from Watkins's former home in the working-class neighborhood of Fort Pickering. In August 1940 the only safe space for Williams to hold the forthcoming applied religion workshops would be down the street, in the Inland Boatmen's Hall.[4]

The five PIAR activists, as well as guest speakers Donald Henderson, Jack McMichael of the American Youth Congress, and Myles Horton, opened the institute by exploring the economic system of the South with their students, who were white and black, women and men. In the urban setting, their rural focus might have seemed odd to an outsider. Sessions called "King Cotton, His Lord and Slaves," "King Cotton, His Method: Divide and Rule," "The Plantation System, Its Victims," and "The South, Its People and Its Problems" made clear that there was no real dividing line between the injustices of the plantations and those in industrial plants.[5] Both were links in the great chain of commodity production that touched all southern workers through the cotton they picked in the fields or processed in the factories. In fact, most of the laborers in the factories of Memphis had only recently toiled on farms. "Many of these croppers are no longer on the plantations," Williams noted, but their movement had produced "fruitbearing branches" in cities.[6]

The second week of the institute asked the students to learn by doing. The PIAR instructors assigned the local preachers and workers in attendance to reflect on what they were learning in "house-to-house" discussions in the community. The point was to empower the students to empower others. Throughout the sessions, PIAR speakers interlaced passages from the Bible about brotherhood, unity, and earthly justice with discussions of labor history, union procedures, racism and anti-Semitism, and how to resist vigilantism.[7] Taken together, the lessons provided a spiritual and practical guide to the CIO's call for working-class unity. The PIAR approach, though avowedly nonsectarian, adopted the vocal, emphatic gospel-style of worship of the evangelical church that was familiar to many white and black Christians. This form evoked the same culture so recently emboldened in Pentecostal-Holiness revivals across the rural and urban South. Although similar in style to fundamentalist churches, the PIAR message differed. No longer would the poor gaze upward; instead, faith would lead them to seek liberation within earth's horizons.[8] This powerful merger of religion and

labor, previously dismissed by union leaders as an elite tool to make workers submissive, had immediate impact. In Memphis, the UCAPAWA won
recognition in three National Labor Relations Board (NLRB) elections in
the weeks that followed and soon had over a thousand members in sixteen
cotton-processing factories.[9]

Whitfield and Williams had worked out a model for tapping the religious
faith of workers so that the CIO was not just a vehicle for getting better wage
rates but also a moral cause that demanded the destruction of Jim Crow. In the
applied religion sessions, Williams later declared, "the people . . . experienced a
more profound unity or religious oneness than they had ever known before." In
their discussion of common problems, the students became "mutually aware of
a deep economic or class oneness . . . related to their mutual religious heritage
in words they had always heard but never before understood." Williams gave
the example of Mrs. Hattie Walls, a black sharecropper from Arkansas, who,
during a session where students were asked to identify the biblical passage
most relevant to contemporary problems, suddenly began singing the well-
known hymn "The Old Ship of Zion." Her rendition, which would become
the song "Union Train," evoked the hardship and hope of her life, which
Williams described as "an undefinable horizontal meaning" that echoed "the
tom-toms and the historic heart-beat of Africa." For Williams, spirituals and
hymns represented a grassroots language that "seemed to be saying something
about heaven and God" but "for those who 'had ears to hear'—were saying
something about earth and man."[10] The PIAR aimed to bring this indigenous
rural protest culture into urban, industrial environments.

The success of the Memphis institute gave the PIAR more secure official
footing. In the final months of 1940, the Williamses established a PIAR office in Little Rock and began producing literature about its "purpose and
program" to reach southern people "through their accepted leaders with
a positive religious message of active brotherhood, democracy and justice
before they are further deceived, victimized and utilized by pseudo-religious
and anti-democratic forces."[11] With the help of Winifred Chappell and Jack
McMichael, Williams gained the support of the Methodist Federation for
Social Service, a New York–based group led by Harry F. Ward, who called
the PIAR "the only way I can see to beat the fascists" in the South. Ward's
endorsement unlocked the financial and organizational resources of a range
of Christian activist groups, including the Presbyterian Fellowship of Social
Action, the Friends of Democracy, and the Home Missions Council of the
Federal Council of the Churches of Christ in America. Prominent activists,
many of them old friends, also rallied to the PIAR, including Willard Uphaus,
Alva Taylor, Max Yergan, James Dombrowski, and Liston Pope.[12]

Williams also made important new musical allies. During a late 1940 trip to speak at Yale Divinity School, Claude stopped in New York to visit Lee Hays, who had moved there after the collapse of Commonwealth. Hays introduced Williams to his new roommates, Millard Lampell and Pete Seeger, who were putting together a collection of labor songs (many of which Hays had worked on with Williams) and performing them in front of small gatherings of New York's nascent folk music community. Williams made an indelible mark on the group, particularly with his account of Hattie Walls's creation of "Union Train" from the traditional hymn "The Old Ship of Zion" at the recent PIAR institute in Memphis. "I pictured this scene the best I could to Pete, Lee Hays and Millard Lampell," he recalled later. Although he admitted that his "words and voice were a mere mockery," Williams communicated the song's power.[13] The Almanac Singers, the name the three young musicians chose for their group, included "Union Train" on their second album, *Talking Union*, released in July 1941. That recording session, and the group's late 1941 tour on behalf of the CIO, included a host of other songs handed down from the 1938 Commonwealth College songbook, including "Roll the Union On," "Join the Union," and "We Shall Not Be Moved." Through the Almanac Singers, Williams reached a ready group of activist artists, including Paul Robeson and Woody Guthrie. Guthrie, who later joined the Almanacs, wrote in 1941 that he wanted to use his music to give voice to the plight of ordinary people, like "Claud Williams and others have done."[14]

In early 1941 the PIAR planned an ambitious program of events to broaden its reach. In February Williams gave a speech in Detroit at the city's "Annual Civil Rights Institute," where he called for a "mass education" program for the "thousands of ex-southern people in Detroit 'served' by more than a thousand 'store-front' preachers." Unless progressive forces unified these people behind "their own leaders," Williams warned, others in the Motor City would goad them "to do a vicious job on a mass scale." The audience, mostly members of the Professional League for Civil Rights, a division of the Civil Rights Federation of Detroit that had supported strikes, academic freedom, and minority rights since 1935, responded enthusiastically. In February and March, Whitfield and Winifred Chappell joined Williams for two applied religion institutes in St. Louis. Among those at the St. Louis meeting was A. L. Campbell, a white preacher from Arkansas, who impressed Williams with his "great interest and ability." Williams supplied Campbell with a set of charts to take back to Arkansas. Williams also recognized five state directors whose jobs, although unpaid, would be to run institutes in their home states for "emphasizing . . . the teaching of the bible for this life" among the "untrained preachers." The first five state directors were Robert Shumpert, a black Arkansas Baptist; Don West, Williams's old friend from Vanderbilt who now preached in Georgia; Lawrence Lay, a white Oklahoma Baptist; Daniel Williams, Claude's brother who lived in Missouri; and W. L. Blackstone, a white preacher in Tennessee who had been a student at the New Era School in 1936 and a member of the STFU. As the new PIAR field representative, Chappell took charge of coordinating their far-flung efforts.[15]

That summer the PIAR activists looked to carry their work back south into the fields of Arkansas, Missouri, and Texas to reach rural workers before they moved into cities. In Longview, Texas, Harry Koger and a local African American preacher named Reverend Banks used a chart titled "Galilean and the Common People," which portrayed Jesus as the human leader of a poor people's movement against the divide-and-rule tactics of the Roman elite. In Hayti, Missouri, a Cumberland Presbyterian minister banned the PIAR from the church. Instead, Williams convinced a local merchant to open his picnic grounds. His message was "that the southland is afflicted with poverty, hunger, and crime . . . and that the oppressed people of the southland should organize and stand up for their rights as citizens, that it was not in accord with God's will and God's teaching that the workers should suffer such poverty while the landowners lived in luxury." "True religion," Williams concluded, "opposes slavery, yet slavery is still practically in effect in the south." Not far away, in East Prairie, Missouri—Whitfield's territory and home to Daniel Williams—local people worried so much about violence that they would only attend the PIAR meetings under cover of darkness. The next day, planters and a conservative local preacher confronted the PIAR staffers demanding to know if the "Nigger Whitfield" had anything to do with their program.[16]

Whitfield was fighting a bigger battle in his role as a UCAPAWA vice-president. In May he was in Louisiana to celebrate the anniversary of the Louisiana Farmers' Union, where he spoke alongside three dynamic young black leaders in the Southern Negro Youth Congress (SNYC), Edward Strong, Esther Cooper, and James Jackson.[17] Now with national visibility, Whitfield used what he learned in Memphis to transform the CIO's organizing approach in the South. In correspondence with the writer Harold Preece, Whitfield explained that CIO union members looked outward. "The people still outside the CIO are our brothers," he said, "we are going out to get them." Race, craft, and gender did not matter to him. "When men and women lay aside race hatred and organize and make up their minds 'we're going to do something,'" Whitfield declared, "then something is done." Religion provided the means for southerners to reach this stage, Whitfield confirmed. "It's time we opened our eyes and looked around—WATCH as well as pray." This faith is "the religion OF Jesus and it's what I'M preaching from now on out." In *The*

Crisis, Preece identified Whitfield and Williams as among those at the heart of the growing religious and working-class rebellion in the South, concluding that their work represented "the new covenant between white man and black man to free the South. And if the South is freed, what other part of America can remain in bondage?"[18]

The PIAR activists took their ministry back to Memphis in July 1941, defying a prior warning from a local official that the "streets of Memphis will run in blood" before the CIO could establish itself in the River City.[19] Harry Koger warned that the CIO's momentum made the city a "powder keg" where "we try not to go out alone, especially at night." But that tension proved that the union campaign was achieving success. In just under a year, the PIAR had gone from another seemingly wild dream in the head of Claude Williams to an effective vanguard in the CIO's drive to empower voters and workers to rebel against the Crump machine. The PIAR now wanted to take the campaign to a new level. On July 20 they held a session for hundreds of workers at an African American Holiness church and, in the days that followed, introduced the visual charts to smaller community groups. The PIAR attack now focused on civil inequalities. One chart in particular, "Anti-Semitism, Racism, and Democracy," dovetailed with the CIO's challenge to Mayor Crump, who played on ethnic and racial divisions to keep the city's workers quiet and pliant to the needs of the South's economic interests.[20]

Applied religion stuck like pine tar to southern workers. Williams had been struggling to find the right vehicle to deliver this radical gospel directly to the people since 1932, but his efforts—the Labor Temple, New Era Schools, and Commonwealth College—had all failed because his sense of mission had always clashed with other interests, whether the UMW, the Presbyterian Church, the STFU, or state and local authorities. Now with his independent PIAR ministry, Williams could finally preach as his conscience dictated. This point was reinforced by the theological temper of the congregations that hosted them—often Pentecostal and Holiness churches—whose members seemed most receptive to the PIAR message due to their fervent belief in the ability of individual believers to bypass denominational bodies and commune directly with God. The Pentecostal-Holiness revivals of the 1930s had roiled the old denominations by devolving intense spiritual power to the faithful like with the Apostles on the day of Pentecost, as described in the New Testament book of Acts. "The Bible is the heritage of the Southern masses," Williams concluded, and "we must speak to them in that language."[21]

The PIAR effort in Memphis proved longer lasting this time around. To facilitate common cause among urban workers and recent migrants from the countryside, the PIAR activists brought twenty rural church leaders into town to have sessions with urban preachers. These diverse meetings were popular; workers seemed to thrive in the PIAR's broad approach to southern problems. Harry Koger, now based full time in Memphis as an organizer for the CIO's International Woodworkers of America (IWA), held a picnic in August 1941 that over a thousand woodworkers and their families attended. Williams preached at the picnic alongside the black IWA organizer Ernest Fields. By the end of the summer, the IWA had won eight union contracts in the Memphis area.[22]

The PIAR momentum induced a counterattack by local authorities. The Memphis police detained Koger and Williams after the August picnic and held them without charge for two days of interrogation. The police had been informed by the FBI, who had originally been tipped by a still-vengeful H. L. Mitchell, that Williams was a communist troublemaker. Jail was not a foreign place to Williams, but he shocked the interrogators by engaging them in discussion and offering them his hand in brotherhood. The perplexed policemen eventually let both men out of jail on the recommendation of the FBI, whose agents would follow PIAR leaders, particularly Williams and Whitfield, for most of the next decade. Harassment from the police and vigilantes took a toll on the PIAR staff. Already in bad health, Joyce Williams suffered a relapse of her lung disease amid the anxiety and exhaustion of the campaign that summer. She decided to seek respite in the Sunset Sanitarium in Asheville, North Carolina, where she could rest her "tubercular" lungs. The Williamses sent their three daughters to study at the Bethany Home, an Episcopal boarding school outside of Cincinnati, Ohio, for their safety. While helping his daughters relocate, Williams met Joseph Moore, an Episcopal pastor from Evansville, Indiana, who told him his town needed the PIAR. Shaken by events in Memphis and the break-up of his family, Williams decided to relocate the PIAR's headquarters to Evansville. By the end of 1941, Joyce and the girls joined him. For the first time in years, the Williams family "settled down." The respite allowed Claude and Joyce the chance to build up the PIAR organization, send out new literature, and coordinate future activities. Most important, "the children were completely happy and adjusted there for the first time in their" teenage lives. The family would stay in Evansville for most of 1942.[23]

Whitfield, meanwhile, made a "dramatic plea" for the CIO to reinforce the PIAR work in the South at the union's annual convention in Detroit that November. In a speech to the five hundred delegates, he "declared that the CIO had done more to carry out the policies of Christ in the South than the church." But what the PIAR had accomplished was only the start of what would be needed to help the "five million workers . . . [and] the millions of hungry dispossessed farm laborers of the South who have no share in American democracy." Whitfield challenged those present to use the full power of the CIO "to smash the barriers of prejudice and poverty." The convention delegates agreed. President Philip Murray announced that "the organization of the white and Negro workers of the South is a big task for the CIO in the coming year." Even before the United States had entered World War II, the CIO, Murray pledged, would "defeat the little Hitlers throughout America."[24]

The success of the PIAR in Memphis encouraged the CIO to send more resources. Whitfield and Koger continued to hold applied religion institutes during the winter of 1941–42, and now had the help of emerging local leaders like William DeBerry, a black, Memphis-born activist. They were almost too popular for their own good. "People were joining up so fast," one organizer declared, "that the CIO had a hard time consolidating the gains they were making." As the war intensified abroad, demand for Memphis-made tires, steel, aircraft parts, cotton, and food products soared, triggering a greater migration of rural workers. Whitfield and Koger greeted these migrants with PIAR institutes and sign-up cards for the UCAPAWA, which by March 1942 boasted nearly eight thousand members in Memphis, the bulk of the city's CIO membership.[25] These gains meant that the PIAR was no longer the only union show in town; the PIAR crew now worked amid scores of other union activists and organizing campaigns, including educational seminars conducted by the Highlander Folk School. With more resources, the Highlander program tended to overshadow the PIAR, despite the former's struggles to attract workers with classes that focused on parliamentary and grievance procedures without a religious component. The PIAR lost its place at the forefront of the official union campaign, but it remained very popular at the grassroots.[26]

As Whitfield's speech to the CIO made clear, he viewed the struggle as a regional one of rural and urban workers. Still a leader of the Cotton Council and a paid UCAPAWA officer, Whitfield worked at a frantic pace that winter, shuttling up and down the Mississippi River between the Missouri Bootheel, Memphis, and his family's home in suburban St. Louis.[27] Surprisingly, the union's cotton farmers were pushing ahead faster than its city members. They won almost every demand in the autumn of 1941, as high cotton prices and a shortage of rural workers to bring in the crop (caused by migration to cities like Memphis) gave cotton pickers unprecedented leverage. "I am proud to report that bosses had to tuck in their tail to union forces," Whitfield announced in October. "Though suffering the pangs of hunger the people of our union stuck to their guns" and secured two dollars per hundred pounds of cotton picked, one of the highest rates in living memory. A reason for their success, one newspaper reported, "was the support of industrial workers, particularly in

Memphis, Tenn.," where "CIO members pledged to persuade all their friends and relatives to hold out for the union scale" in the cotton fields.[28]

The Japanese attack on the U.S. naval base at Pearl Harbor on December 7 shattered this run of good news and sharpened Whitfield's focus on the fight for democracy. His first thought as an organizer was not about Memphis but about the opportunity that the war created for rural workers to make new demands on the federal government. Writing to war preparedness officials in Washington just days after Pearl Harbor, Whitfield lambasted the Japanese as a way to demand that the U.S. government allow farmers to do their part for the war effort. Furious about "those ALMOND EYED MURDERERS" who "has leaped upon our people in our outlying islands and murdered them by the thousands," Whitfield nevertheless warned that rural blacks in the South might once again turn to subversive, pro-Japanese groups like OIBAPMW as they had in 1934. "These thousands of negroes," he wrote "are convinced that the JAP is the negro's best friend." On the other hand, if the government distributed needed supplies and aid, these farmers would become "an army behind the army."[29] He took this message personally to Secretary of Agriculture Claude Wickard in Washington before the end of the year. Whitfield pushed for new government programs for landless southern workers to help "us become food producers, instead of mere food consumers."[30]

Whitfield sensed that strong union pressure might bring quick gains. In February 1942 he bragged to Williams, "I stired up so much hell among the workers until they were going to shut down evry oil and compress in memphis friday night." According to Whitfield's account, representatives of the National War Labor Board (NWLB, the wartime successor to the NLRB) rushed to Memphis to begin negotiations after "the radio began broadcasting [news of the work stoppage] . . . and it stird up washington." "I had a hell of a time geting the men to wait," he reported, "but I suceeded in doing so negotiations is now going on for increase in wages better working conditions UNION SHOP ECT."[31] Although very much focused on union business, Whitfield understood these tactics in PIAR religious terms. At a UCAPAWA general meeting in Memphis in March, he praised the union for a policy that was "right close to the Bible." Religion, he said, "means the love of God and the Brotherhood of Man" and in the UCAPAWA, "we are all brothers."[32]

PIAR brotherhood turned into a reunion of many of its national leaders—including Williams, DeBerry, Koger, Chappell, Don West, A. L. Campbell, W. L. Blackstone, and Zella Whitfield—at an institute in St. Louis in early May. Attended by over one hundred preachers, the sessions included new lessons attuned to wartime politics, including one from DeBerry called "Hitlerism and True Religion"; "The 'Four Freedoms' in the South" by Williams; "Racism and True Religion" by Owen Whitfield; "Plantation Oppression and True

Religion" by West; and "The People and True Religion" by Zella Whitfield. This was the first time the whole PIAR arsenal of activists had assembled together, and it proved to be a powerful event. At a closing meeting, called the "Upper chamber" (a reference to the place where the Apostles received the power of the Holy Spirit on Pentecost [Acts 1:13]), the preachers of applied religion renewed their vow to fight fascism abroad and in the South.[33]

The Bootheel MAWC locals strained that sense of unity by pushing for an unauthorized strike later that spring. While Whitfield was busy in Memphis, local activists met with C. L. R. James, a famous black scholar and anti-Stalinist communist who was in the area to cover the January lynching of Cleo Wright in nearby Sikeston for *Labor Action*, the newspaper of the Socialist Workers Party, a leading critic of the CP. James encouraged their plans to strike for higher cotton-chopping wages. The UCAPAWA did not support their wish to strike, because it had joined the CIO pledge to the Roosevelt administration not to disrupt the war effort with work stoppages. In defiance of their union's no-strike pledge, cotton farmers in the Bootheel went ahead with a wildcat strike in June. Henderson, a CP member, was furious that a Trotskyite like James had broken the ranks of the UCAPAWA at a time when the union was backing the war effort of the United States and the Soviet Union against the Nazis. He declared the strike illegal, threatened to throw anyone who joined it out of the union, and promised Bootheel planters that he would help police identify and arrest its leaders. The strike caught Whitfield in an awkward position. His union bosses clearly valued the no-strike pledge and their sectarian affiliations more than they did grassroots militancy, but it was difficult for Whitfield not to support the locals he had helped create. Deploying a now tried and tested tactic, Whitfield played both sides. While he stopped stirring up workers in Memphis, Whitfield assured a May meeting in St. Louis of CIO activists sympathetic to the wildcat strike that "we will win our wage scale." Once it was clear that the rebellious locals would go ahead with their strike, Whitfield defied Henderson by backing the wildcat choppers, who did win their wage scale. The victory was the first in the nation for rank-and-file unionists since the no-strike pledge. Determined to reassert his authority, Henderson punished the strikers by placing their local on probation until all of its members signed oaths affirming their loyalty to the UCAPAWA. Seeing Henderson's demands as a humiliating form of submission after a victory, most of these proud black choppers refused and left the union. Suddenly exposed, Whitfield had little choice but to fall into line with Henderson, but the affair had damaged his relationship with the UCAPAWA.[34]

Whitfield redoubled his work that autumn by orienting his organizing around the PIAR mission. He had been reelected to his post as a UCAPAWA vice-president, but not without opposition due to the wildcat strike. "Old whit

he was elected," he informed Williams, "in spite of all of the evidence and
liars that piled up against" him, led mainly by CP members who questioned
his loyalty. Now back in Memphis, Whitfield informed Williams that he was
"all set to do what ever you suggest [and] I know that you would want me
to do some things as I see fit." Applied religion was foremost in his mind,
especially after the recent difficulties with Henderson: "YES I am in the best
place to be ASST DIRECTOR than ever before." "We have lots of preachers
of the common people in OUR union here, who work in plants and preach
on sunday," he reported, and "I will train these and have them go out and
train others and set up institutes." The prospect of applied religion made his
work for the UCAPAWA seem more promising; he could still preach what he
wanted within the confines of his official union role. "I spoke to a group last
night of a bout 100 men and women in our UCAPAWA class," he explained
to Williams, "and I mentioned your and my work." When Whitfield told the
workers about the PIAR "charts," he recounted, "you should have heard the
people yell": "BRING EM! THATS WHAT WE NEED." He wrote straight
away to Zella in St. Louis, asking her to bring the charts, so that "I will have
[them] on the wall, and go to town."[35] Zella joined him that Thanksgiving
and together they held institutes under the guise of the UCAPAWA with
groups of workers from four different plants. Zella thrived in these meetings. "You know her," Whitfield told Williams, "she has the chance she has

Figure 7. Owen Whitfield preaching the applied religion in the 1940s. Source:
Folder 9, Box 5, Williams Papers, Reuther Library, Wayne State University.

been waiting for a long time. some big preachers are going to catch hell." If only the sponsors of the PIAR "could see how the common preachers and common people respond to what they call these 'GOSPLE FEASTS' and how they rush up and shake hands and give thanks, and invite me to come to their churches."[36] Their fear now dissipated as they seized collective power. "I don't think you will ever be arrested in memphis again," Whitfield assured Williams, "because the CIO is taking this town by storm."[37]

Whitfield's enthusiasm for the PIAR barely covered his uneasiness with the UCAPAWA. Not long after writing to Williams, Whitfield penned a plaintive letter to Fannie Cook, an ally in St. Louis who had helped buy the Cropperville land in Missouri. Still angry that he had been forced to choose between his Missouri followers and the official UCAPAWA line, he told Cook that he "reserved the right to stick with our people in" the Bootheel whatever his role as a union leader. Whitfield detested Donald Henderson after the events of the summer. Whitfield told Cook how Henderson ordered him to get his family "the hell out of St. Louis," where they had lived since 1939. Whitfield responded angrily that he would not be told where to reside, "so the Whitfields remain where they are until I say move." The truth was that Whitfield felt like his talents were not being used very well. When he was sent to organize a large cotton compress plant south of Memphis that the UCAPAWA had failed to unionize in 1940, Whitfield suspected that they dispatched him on a fool's errand. The UCAPAWA "sends me down here," he told Williams in December 1942, "and puts 'THE DEAD CAT' in my hands and if I dont make good then I will be considered NO-GOOD as an organizer." He explained to Cook that certain UCAPAWA leaders who were obsessed with sectarian politics "thought that I would be LOW down enough to go and destroy all of the possibilities of organizing negroes in the south. They knew I possess such power. But," he continued, "I am sure you know old Whit well enough to know I would not do such a dirty thing as that, THEY WERE ALL RONG." Cook encouraged Whitfield to stay the course. "When you bother about how the Cropperville families will live, you are being the pastor to your people," she wrote, "but when you go out and organize unions and train other men to head them, you are being a leader for your people." Putting the choice in biblical terms, Cook concluded, "You must think the situation through and decide whether you want to be a Moses or a minister."[38]

Whitfield still wanted to be a Moses. Despite misgivings, he could not deny the powerful effect of the PIAR relationship with the UCAPAWA in Memphis. By the end of 1942 the CIO boasted 15,000 members in over fifty plants, most of which were organized by the UCAPAWA.[39] Moreover, the federal government and the NWLB had acknowledged the standing of the

CIO by recognizing it in negotiations with the Crump machine. Its influence would only grow. By the end of the war, the CIO had the strength of 32,500 members in 117 different local plants. Even the city's newspaper of record, the *Commercial Appeal*, changed its tune by comparing Nathan Bedford Forrest to Adolph Hitler, suggesting that Nazi generals may have studied the Confederate's career. Although Crump was still central to Democratic Party politics in the city and the state, he was more susceptible than ever to protests from African Americans and trade unions. The *Chicago Defender* wrote how local blacks, thanks to the labor movement there, had begun to refuse the "crumbs from Crump."[40] PIAR members no doubt saw this transformation in Memphis as the product of their hard work since August 1940.

II

PIAR success in the River City meant that Williams was not in Indiana long before activists from elsewhere came looking for him. In May 1942 Williams had accepted an invitation from Detroit-based Presbyterian minister Henry D. Jones to spend a month working in his Dodge Christian Community House, a center for social activism that ran educational programs with the United Auto Workers (UAW). Williams had impressed Jones when he spoke in the Motor City in February 1941. After Williams returned to Evansville, Jones convinced the Church Extension Committee of the Detroit Presbytery to offer him a six-month trial position as the "Presbyterian Minister to Labor." The offer included a salary and expense account of up to $2,500 from the committee's World Emergency Fund. Although Williams had not forgotten how the Presbyterian Church (USA) had ousted him from his Paris ministry, this was an offer he could not refuse. Williams relished the opportunity to launch the PIAR in a northern industrial city, and the money was good. He accepted with a start date in December 1942. This would give him a few more months in Evansville to coordinate PIAR events across the South, and spend time with Joyce, who planned to remain in Indiana to run the PIAR and care for the girls.[41]

Detroit needed Williams's message of unity. The coming of war transformed the Motor City from a depressed city to a boomtown as automotive factories and other industrial plants converted their assembly lines to build airplanes and tanks. The shift brought migrants by the thousands looking for well-paying jobs. Many of these migrants came from the South, and many of them were African Americans. Before the outbreak of war, Detroit's manufacturers employed a very limited number of African Americans. Leading the way was Ford Motor Company with a workforce that was 12 percent black by 1940.

While the UAW and other CIO unions had won important victories in the late 1930s, race problems, exacerbated by the presence of southern migrants, continued to bedevil organized labor on the shop floors and in the neighborhoods. In 1941 alone, whites struck Curtis Aircraft, Hudson Motors, and Packard Motors in protest against the hiring or upgrading of black workers. Although Detroit was a sprawling city, the scale of the immigration created a housing crisis in African American neighborhoods like Paradise Valley. Among Detroit's white workers, racism, fueled by religious demagogues, spawned hate strikes. In the summer of 1942, over 25,000 white Packard workers refused to work alongside newly promoted black workers, shouting statements like, "I'd rather see Hitler or Hirohito win than work on an assembly line with a Negro." Despite fair employment policies from the federal government, the employment of African Americans continued to lag. In one 1942 survey, for example, 119 of 197 Detroit manufacturers admitted having no black employees.[42] Although the task ahead was massive, the prospect of establishing a northern front for applied religion in the Arsenal of Democracy thrilled Williams, who spent the latter part of 1942 thinking and writing about how to best reach transplanted southern preachers in Detroit.[43]

The Detroit Presbytery recruited Williams because of worries over the city's "migrant problem." Church leaders and other liberals fretted that culturally backward southerners might disturb war production if not properly educated and assimilated. "I think there is an ample basis for the fear that the religious groups which are now enjoying the largest increase in membership," one church leader wrote, "are the more or less fanatical sects which the larger denominations have not accepted as 'regular.'" Pentecostal-Holiness "sects" like the Church of God in Christ, the Pillar of Fire, the Assembly of God, and others devolved spiritual power directly to ordinary believers that the established denominations rebuked, in Detroit as in the South. As one writer claimed, these migrants embraced "the Protestant principle to its *reductio ad absurdum*" by giving "every man who can read, or who can recite biblical phrases, an authority and religious status as impressive as that of the Pope."[44]

With few ideas about how to reach these "impossiblist . . . holy rollers," the Presbyterian Church Extension Committee wanted Williams to preach tolerance "to Detroit's increasing thousands of ex-rural, ex-southern population which is predominantly anti-Negro, anti-Jews, anti-Yankee, anti-union." While he accepted the premise of the so-called migrant problem, Williams did not necessarily accept the verdict about the hopelessness of "new sect" worship. He certainly considered aspects of southern culture and many of its practitioners "vicious and primitive." But this "new population," one PIAR statement read, "constitutes a sort of No Man's Land, providing at once a headache for the unions, liberal churchmen, [and] social workers." And as symbolized by the hate strikes, right-wingers seemed to have a running start in preaching to these migrants. Since the 1930s Detroit had been home to legendary preachers of vitriol who spread messages of intolerance in the city and regionally via radio: Father Charles Coughlin and his League of the Little Flower; Reverend Gerald L. K. Smith, friend of Huey Long and leader of the Committee of One Million and the America First Party; Gerald B. Winrod of the anti-Semitic Christian Temple; and the Texan J. Frank Norris, a Baptist known as the "Texas Cyclone." In the early 1940s, Detroit offered "fertile soil for the seeds of American fascism" sown by such preachers: "Hate the Jew. Hate the Negro. Hate the foreignborn. Amen." "The industrial capital of the United Nations is Detroit," Williams surmised, where "the weapons are forged for the greatest military struggle of all history . . . to destroy the prophets of the New Slavery" of fascism. "All the hopes of free people are centered on these weapons and the men and women who make them." Yet, the hearts and minds of the city's workers were "where fascist and anti-fascist meet" and it remained to be seen whether they would become "an army" of hate or of justice.[45]

Williams's first goal was to bring together interested "representative leaders from the mass ecstatic religious groups" to adopt basic democratic positions on "racism, anti-Semitism, Ku Kluxism, organized labor, etc."[46] The task was urgent since the "500,000 uncritical ex-rural people who have come to Detroit within the last 19 months provide fertile soil for all who would sow [the] 'Divide and Conquer' seed of hate." His ministry aimed to expose the demagogues who spread fascism in America "under guise of religion." Second, Williams sought to convert the "natural leaders" of these migrants, their "work-a-day" preachers, to the teachings of applied religion because the "mass religious phenomenon" of southern migrants "contains a very definite democratic dynamic."[47] He knew this from experience. The groups that leading Christians in Detroit loathed were the same ones that had given PIAR activists the warmest welcome in the rural South. According to Williams, the leaders of these churches possessed the power to be "a great unifying force— if they preach, in the same simple Fundamentalist language, the dynamic social message of the Bible" that applied religion represented.[48] Otherwise, the new-sect churches contained enough "dynamite . . . to blow institutional religion with its Wall Street investments into primordial stardust."[49]

Williams's ally Henry Jones put him in touch with sympathetic local preachers. One of the first he met was Reverend Charles Hill of the Hartford Avenue Baptist Church. Hill, an African American, had a reputation for his resistance to Henry Ford in the 1920s, long before the UAW set out

Lloyd Jones, ex-southern evangelist, addressing a group of pastors and church workers. He is president of Local No. 2 UAW-CIO. Detroit.

Rev. Caleb Thompson, shop preacher and pastor meets a group each week. Detroit.

An Institute of share-cropper preachers, St. Louis.

Claude Williams with a group of Institute Leaders. St. Louis.

An Institute leader talking with cotton choppers in the field. Photo by Essary, Memphis.

Inter-racial group at The People's Church. Rev. Virgil Vanderberg. Detroit.

Figure 8. The People's Institute of Applied Religion across New Deal America: Memphis, St. Louis, and Detroit. Source: Folder 1, Box 19, Williams Papers, Reuther Library, Wayne State University.

to organize black workers, and was involved with the Detroit Council of the NNC, whose members played a key role in organizing black autoworkers. Hill's assistant pastor was John Miles, whom Williams had originally met in Tennessee. The three formed a fast bond. Together they created a new interracial, working-class congregation called the People's Church, the only interracial church in Detroit.[50] The PIAR also spread its gospel onto the shop floors. In support of this mission, Jones hosted applied religion classes at the Dodge House for preachers, who would in turn enter auto plants and other factories to preach to migrant workers. Williams believed this focus was crucial because industrialists had recruited and employed many of the two thousand workaday preachers as chaplains and moral officers to keep their workers beholden to quiescent company unions. By the summer of 1943 Williams was working on sermon outlines with a number of shop-floor preachers who had converted to applied religion and who now preached it to their congregations.[51]

To complement this grassroots organizing, Williams also waged a national publicity campaign to champion the PIAR cause. In February 1943 the New York Sponsoring Committee of the PIAR, a group established with the help of Cedric Belfrage and Harry Ward, hosted a musical event in the Community Church Auditorium to raise funds for Williams's Detroit ministry. The evening featured a number of works by composer Earl Robinson, as well as performances by Josh White, Huddie Ledbetter (Leadbelly), and the American People's Chorus, a group that popularized folk songs among activists of the Left. Many of these performers had worked closely with Lee Hays and the Almanac Singers, who carried with them the stories of the "singing preacher."[52] While in the city, Williams arranged a roundtable session at the New York Public Library entitled "What Shall We Do About the South and Detroit as Danger Spots to a Democracy at War?" Williams argued "that the interests of all people irrespective of race, color, or creed demanded the destruction of Hitlerism at home and abroad."[53]

Williams's work with the PIAR, supported by advocates in New York and elsewhere, convinced the Church Extension Committee in Detroit to renew his contract for another year, until May 31, 1944. They agreed to fund his ministry with a total grant of $5,000. Moreover, the committee included, at the urging of Henry Jones, a pledge to provide Williams with additional funding of $2,400 in the year 1944–45 and $1,200 in the year 1945–46 as he worked to establish the PIAR on a basis of self-sufficiency. Williams rejoiced by moving his family to Detroit. Joyce agreed on the condition that they had a decent house to live in. He quickly put a down payment on a home in the Highland Park neighborhood, and Joyce and the girls joined him later that summer.[54]

Now in Detroit for a longer stay, Williams published a work in the spring of 1943 that went on the offensive against fascists and liberals alike in the Motor City. The pamphlet, "The Hell-Brewers of Detroit," charted the activities of a dozen reactionary church groups and also criticized the liberal church minority for "speaking in terms of general abstractions." The more he reached out to southern migrants in Detroit, the more Williams believed there was a hidden power in southern religious culture that was waiting to be used by a righteous remnant, the "saving remnant" that would "reclaim and reconstruct the Bible Way of Righteousness." Williams's experience with the "natural leader" who "speaks the language of his people" showed him that the rural preacher often possessed "uncanny wisdom." In "Hell-Brewers," Williams publicly rejected the modern idea of progress that many Detroit liberals used to define southern migrants as a problem. Yes, these people needed help, Williams concluded, but they also had more power to expand democracy than many of the liberals who dismissed them as "rednecks."[55]

A. L. Campbell personified the redemptive potential of the white rural preacher. Campbell, a Free Will Baptist minister from rural Arkansas and one-time member of the Ku Klux Klan, first encountered applied religion when local planters sent him to a meeting as a spy. Hearing Williams's message at a March 1941 institute in St. Louis, however, Campbell began to rethink the meaning of the gospel and ended up coming home with a set of PIAR charts. He soon found himself without a home or a pulpit. In the two years that followed, Campbell continued to hold applied religion institutes while his family slept in a tent alongside the banks of the Arkansas River. His frequent reports to Williams in Detroit told of sustained success, including a series of big meetings in Helena, Arkansas, in the spring of 1943.[56] Williams argued in "Hell-Brewers" that unless the churches and unions reached more preachers like Campbell, the "dynamite" tensions between Detroit's workers would soon explode. As an article in *Life Magazine* surmised, the supposed Arsenal of Democracy "can either blow up Hitler or it can blow up the U.S."[57]

On the morning of June 21, 1943, Detroit detonated. That morning Williams walked outside of his "dollar-a-day" hotel near the shanty neighborhood of Paradise Valley to find "bedlam" in the streets. He ran to a pay phone and called Reverend Hill, who explained that the previous day a confrontation in Belle Isle had ignited a citywide riot. Williams later pieced the details together from eyewitness accounts: thousands of people had flocked across the bridge to Belle Isle to get relief from the heat; tempers flared and a few fights broke out in the overcrowded park; then rumors spread that whites had thrown a black woman and child off the Belle Isle bridge, leading to the riot the following morning. His fears seemingly come true, Williams and others called for an urgent meeting at the Lucy Thurman Young Women's Christian Association (YWCA) building, an African American community center. Members of the Detroit Council of Churches, who had initially planned to meet in a white-only neighborhood, joined the meeting at the YWCA at the urging of Henry Jones, who argued that racial separation in response to a racial crisis was neither right nor productive. The mayor, who joined the impromptu conference of religious leaders, followed their advice by declaring a state of emergency and appealing for calm in a radio broadcast. Eventually the rioting stopped, but not before three days of conflict wrecked large parts of the city, resulted in the loss of over one million man-hours of war production, injured over seven hundred people, and claimed thirty-four lives.[58]

Since Williams had been warning of such a conflagration for months, reporters sought him out in the aftermath of the riot. White and black "ex-rural people," Williams told them, represent "a mass protest against things economically and culturally unattainable." Until democratic religious leaders reached these people, he predicted, more riots would occur, because hate groups would appeal to their frustration with simple yet effective slogans like "The Jews He-brews Trouble." The PIAR remained the best way to reach Detroit's workers, he argued, because only it offered the theological basis for creating unity.[59] Until PIAR could beat back the ministers of division, he predicted more trouble to come.

In the weeks that followed, Williams expressed this view in a series of newspaper articles that established him as an authority on the causes of racial violence in the city. "In the Babel that is Detroit," he wrote in July, "with its unexampled confusion of tongues in the pulpit" and volatile mix of races and ethnicities, "it would be most surprising if the enemy powers did not take advantage of their unrivaled opportunity for widening and deepening the disruption." There were biblical examples of this tactic. One of his PIAR lessons showed how it was "the priests of false religion who first used the Babel-Tower story." His interpretation of this parable from Genesis explained how the people united by shedding their individualism and agreeing to build a city as a labor of love. But their lords, who turned out to be false prophets, smashed this unity "in the name of . . . religion" and dispersed the people across the earth, dividing them by language, race, and ethnicity. As Williams preached it, Detroit was a modern-day Babel: a place to build unity to defeat fascism. "The Carpenter of Nazareth," he concluded, "would have helped to build the tower" of unity, and today workers had the potential to "return to the word of God" for "the true religion that could be found in the ideals of the labor movement."[60]

The PIAR accomplishments among southern workers elsewhere gave Williams the confidence to make such bold claims. The UCAPAWA leadership hoped that the PIAR could replicate the success of the Memphis campaign in Winston-Salem, North Carolina, where Whitfield, Koger (who now worked for the UCAPAWA's Tobacco Workers Organizing Committee [TWOC]), and William DeBerry launched an organizing drive in late 1942. Williams supported their efforts by helping to run a weeklong applied institute before he moved from Evansville to Detroit that winter. The R. J. Reynolds Company employed thirteen thousand people in twenty plants around the town, the majority of whom were African Americans. Again, the PIAR activists made measured but impressive gains. By the spring of 1943, the trio had helped organize a Citizens' Committee to register black voters in Jim Crow North Carolina and put forward a black candidate, Reverend Edward Gholson, for the city's Board of Aldermen. Gholson, a preacher who joined the PIAR, represented a new brand of local leader who favored the union movement as a base for racial and economic justice. Although Gholson lost by a landslide, the electoral contest itself marked the emergence of a public civil rights challenge to the white board.[61]

Whitfield led the union campaign from the pulpit. At the Mt. Pisga Holiness Church he urged tobacco workers to elect the CIO in the upcoming NWLB election. "Whitfield did not follow his usual way of lashing, lambasting, and accusing the management of industries," an FBI informant present noted, "but he argued the urgent need of . . . allowing the C.I.O. to become their bargaining agent." When the AFL and Reynolds colluded to try to block the UCAPAWA from winning the NWLB ballot that summer, Whitfield got more vocal. At Mt. Calvary Holiness Church, he spoke to 350 African American tobacco workers in the weeks before their vote. His speech applied the four freedoms that President Roosevelt had talked about in his 1941 State of the Union address—freedom of speech, of worship, from want, and from fear—to the union struggle. Civil rights and economic rights, Whitfield told these workers, were attainable through unions, and the CIO was the only union calling for both. "The company is virtually a slave pen," he declared, and "the C.I.O. has come to put an end to that." While the workers had been eating beans and cornbread, Whitfield explained in his customary way, there had been "some chicken and western stake back in the [employer's] kitchen . . . and we are going to eat some of that stake and chicken also." "The crowd burst fourth in uncontrollable applause," noted the FBI agent.[62]

A TWOC flier issued in the run-up to a September NWLB hearing reinforced this distinct union culture. One side of the flier advertised daily meetings for Reynolds plant workers, with separate times for workers in different parts of the plant and on different shifts.[63] These meetings empowered local leaders like Theodosia Simpson of Reynolds Plant 65, who told her coworkers that while local billboards touted "Camels lead the world," the union would soon announce that the "UCAPAWA-CIO leads Reynolds."[64] The flier's reverse side, titled, "Jesus and the People," showed the influence of the PIAR activists. "While it is not the policy of the T.W.O.C. to use the Bible as an instrument for organization, we feel we should quote you the scriptures to stave off anti-union propaganda" by "so-called . . . preachers in the plant," it read. The careful wording suggested that the PIAR influence was not universally embraced; union leaders like Frank Hargrove were reluctant to admit the centrality of faith in workers' lives. But what followed left no ambiguity. From August 9 to 11 the PIAR hosted a "Righteousness, Justice, Freedom" through "Organization" meeting at the Holy Trinity Baptist Church, where preachers compared the struggle in Winston-Salem to how Jesus, the "First Organizer," led the "oppressed multitudes" in his lifetime.[65] When the NWLB finally held the election on union representation in December, the TWOC won a landslide victory, and four months later the unionized tobacco workers negotiated their first ever contract with Reynolds. It included new seniority rights, maternity leave, and a new grievance procedure backed by the NWLB. The police chief of Winston-Salem admitted to the FBI that "it would have been impossible for the CIO organizers to gain as much influence as they did

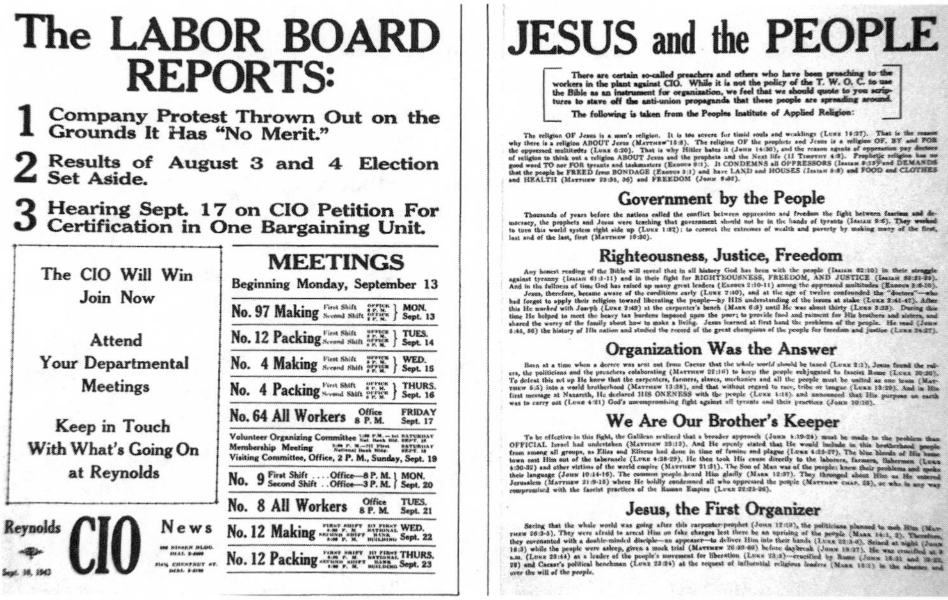

The LABOR BOARD REPORTS:

1 Company Protest Thrown Out on the Grounds It Has "No Merit."

2 Results of August 3 and 4 Election Set Aside.

3 Hearing Sept. 17 on CIO Petition For Certification in One Bargaining Unit.

The CIO Will Win
Join Now

Attend
Your Departmental
Meetings

Keep in Touch
With What's Going On
at Reynolds

MEETINGS
Beginning Monday, September 13

No. 97 Making	First Shift / Second Shift	MON. Sept. 13
No. 12 Packing	First Shift / Second Shift	TUES. Sept. 14
No. 4 Making	First Shift / Second Shift	WED. Sept. 15
No. 4 Packing	First Shift / Second Shift	THURS. Sept. 16
No. 64 All Workers	Office 8 P. M.	FRIDAY Sept. 17
Volunteer Organizing Committee		SATURDAY
Membership Meeting		SATURDAY
Visiting Committee, Office, 2 P. M., Sunday, Sept. 19		
No. 9	First Shift . . . . Office—8 P. M. / Second Shift . . Office—3 P. M.	MON. Sept. 20
No. 8 All Workers	Office 8 P. M.	TUES. Sept. 21
No. 12 Making	First Shift / Second Shift	WED. Sept. 22
No. 12 Packing	First Shift / Second Shift	THURS. Sept. 23

Reynolds CIO News
Sept. 16, 1943

JESUS and the PEOPLE

There are certain so-called preachers and others who have been preaching to the workers in the plant against CIO. While it is not the policy of the T. W. O. C. to use the Bible as an instrument for organization, we feel that we should quote to you scriptures to stave off the anti-union propaganda that these people are spreading around.

The following is taken from the Peoples Institute of Applied Religion:

The religion OF Jesus is a man's religion. It is too severe for timid souls and weaklings (Luke 14:27). That is the reason why there is a religion ABOUT Jesus (Matthew 15:8). The religion OF the prophets and Jesus is a religion OF, BY and FOR the oppressed multitudes (Luke 6:20). That is why Hitler hates it (John 14:30), and the reason agents of oppression pay doctors of religion to think out a religion ABOUT Jesus and the prophets and the Next life (II Timothy 4:3). Prophetic religion has no good word TO nor FOR tyrants and taskmasters (Exodus 3:1). It CONDEMNS all OPPRESSORS (Isaiah 3:15) and DEMANDS that the people be FREED from BONDAGE (Exodus 3:1) and have LAND and HOUSES (Isaiah 5:8) and FOOD and CLOTHES and HEALTH (Matthew 25:35, 36) and FREEDOM (John 8:32).

Government by the People

Thousands of years before the nations called the conflict between oppression and freedom the fight between fascism and democracy, the prophets and Jesus were teaching that government should not be in the hands of tyrants (Isaiah 9:6). They worked to turn this world system right side up (Luke 1:52); to correct the extremes of wealth and poverty by making many of the first, last and of the last, first (Matthew 19:30).

Righteousness, Justice, Freedom

Any honest reading of the Bible will reveal that in all history God has been with the people (Isaiah 62:10) in their struggle against tyranny (Isaiah 61:1-11) and in their fight for RIGHTEOUSNESS, FREEDOM, AND JUSTICE (Isaiah 53:21-23). And in the fullness of time God has raised up many great leaders (Exodus 2:10-11) among the oppressed multitudes (Exodus 3:6-10).

Jesus, therefore, became aware of the conditions early (Luke 2:40), and at the age of twelve confounded the "doctors"—who had forgot to apply their religion toward liberating the people—by HIS understanding of the issues at stake (Luke 2:41-47). After this He *worked* with Joseph (Luke 2:49) at the carpenter's bench (Mark 6:3) until He was about thirty (Luke 3:23). During this time He helped to meet the heavy tax burdens imposed upon the poor; to provide food and raiment for His brothers and sisters, and shared the worry of the family about how to make a living. Jesus learned at first hand the problems of the people. He read (John 5:45, 56) the history of His nation and studied the record of the great champions of the people for freedom and justice (Luke 24:27).

Organization Was the Answer

Born at a time when a decree was sent out from Caesar that the *whole world* should be taxed (Luke 2:1), Jesus found the rulers, the politicians and the preachers colaborating (Matthew 22:16) to keep the people subjugated to fascist Rome (Luke 20:20). To defeat this set up He knew that the carpenters, farmers, slaves, mechanics and all the people must be united as one team (Matthew 5:5) into a world brotherhood (Matthew 13:38), and that without regard to race, tribe or tongue (Luke 13:29). And in His first message at Nazareth, He declared HIS ONENESS with the people (Luke 4:18) and announced that His purpose on earth was to carry out (Luke 4:21) God's uncompromising fight against all tyrants and their practices (John 10:10).

We Are Our Brother's Keeper

To be effective in this fight, the Galilean realized that a broader approach (John 4:19-24) must be made to the problem than OFFICIAL Israel had undertaken (Matthew 23:13). And He openly stated that He would include in this brotherhood people from among all groups, as Elias and Eliseus had done in time of famine and plague (Luke 4:25-27). The blue bloods of His home town cast Him out of the tabernacle (Luke 4:28-29). He then took His cause directly to the laborers, farmers, fishermen (Luke 4:30-32) and other victims of the world empire (Matthew 21:31). The Son of Man was of the people: knew their problems and spoke their language (John 10:14-16). The common people heard Him gladly (Mark 12:37). They thronged about Him as He entered Jerusalem (Matthew 21:9-15) where He boldly condemned all who oppressed the people (Matthew chap. 23), or who in any way compromised with the fascist practices of the Roman Empire (Luke 22:25-26).

Jesus, the First Organizer

Seeing that the whole world was going after this carpenter-prophet (John 12:19), the politicians planned to mob Him (Matthew 26:3-5). They were afraid to arrest Him on fake charges lest there be an uprising of the people (Mark 14:1, 2). Therefore, they covenanted with a double-minded disciple—an appeaser—to deliver Him into their hands (Luke 22:3-6). Seized at night (John 18:3) while the people were asleep, given a mock trial (Matthew 26:59-68) before daybreak (John 18:27). He was crucified at 9 a.m. (Luke 23:44) as a leader of the people's movement for liberation (Luke 23:5)—crucified by Rome (John 18:31 and 19:23, 28) and Caesar's political henchman (Luke 23:24) at the request of influential religious *leaders* (Mark 15:1) in the absence and over the will of the *people*.

Figure 9. The People's Institute of Applied Religion led CIO organizing efforts in Winston-Salem, North Carolina. Source: Folder 2, Box 3, Williams Papers, Reuther Library, Wayne State University.

through the churches had it not been for the help of the Negro ministers."
Many of those ministers now preached applied religion.[66]

Before the battle was even won in Winston-Salem, however, the UCA-
PAWA sent Whitfield and Koger to spearhead organizing campaigns in
Suffolk, Virginia, and Charleston, South Carolina. In Suffolk in early 1943,
Whitfield and Koger battled the Planters Peanut Company, not by going
to the plant and incurring the wrath of local police, but by showing up at
the workers' favorite lunch places. Having gained the trust of the workers,
Whitfield then enlisted their preachers. Once he had the support of at least
three ministers, he would hold PIAR meetings. In Suffolk, this strategy got
enough union cards signed to force the NWLB to intervene, hold an election
on union recognition, and declare the UCAPAWA the new bargaining agent
of the peanut workers.[67] By the time of the election, however, the UCAPAWA
had again sent Whitfield someplace else—this time Charleston, where he
fought not only against the American Tobacco Company but also the AFL's
Tobacco Workers International Union (TWIU). The TWIU was notorious
in the late 1930s for gaining the trust of some black workers but then largely
ignoring them or isolating them in segregated locals after they had voted for
TWIU representation.[68] With yet another challenge awaiting him, Whitfield
hardly had time to take a breath.

In the days leading up to the contested union election in Charleston,
both unions parked sound trucks outside the plant with speakers arguing
their cases. While TWIU officials broadcast prepared statements, Whitfield
played "boogie woogie" records from his truck and, between songs, gave
short talks about religion and the CIO. The music proved contagious; a few
workers began to dance and eventually many more joined them. When the
police arrived, they did not know what to do, so they just cordoned off the
street as workers frolicked to the piano-based blues that Whitfield spun as
their disc jockey. Later that day the police ordered both unions to turn off
their broadcasts. By then, however, the message had gotten through to the
workers: they voted overwhelmingly for UCAPAWA representation.[69] While
local people were responsible for winning these gains, Whitfield provided
inspiration for them to expand and sustain their demands.

Yet Whitfield was not satisfied as a roving union organizer. He was used
to working closely with a local community, but the UCAPAWA wanted him
to establish union beachheads that could be developed by others. Whitfield
struggled to enjoy work that he never actually saw come to fruition. In March
1943, for example, he complained to Fannie Cook that "just as soon as I gets
[started] at WINSTON-SALEM and gets the ball rooling so they can handle
things, they pulled me out and sends me here to help brother KOGER with

7,000 planter's peanut workers. And I am getting them organized at the rate of 40 per day, and will have an NLRB election on the 12th of APRIL, and I feel sure of winning it." These victories were bittersweet for Whitfield, because he was always by then on his way somewhere else. "All I do down here is organize them (or get them to join the union)," he complained, "then the white man (from new york or some place) takes over the handling of them."[70]

As the tensions of the previous summer reemerged, Whitfield increasingly blamed the white leaders of the UCAPAWA for the problems he perceived. He complained to Cook that union leaders never asked him for strategic advice. "THEY FORGETS THAT I AM ONE OF THESE PEOPLE, AND KNOW WHAT TO DO WITH AND ABOUT THEM," he exclaimed. Whitfield's anger only grew that summer when he visited the UCAPAWA headquarters in Philadelphia, where he was appalled to see expensive office equipment and an all-white secretarial staff. He wondered why the union's lily-white office clerks should have it so much easier than the workers, many of them African Americans, who fought for living wages, not to mention organizers like himself who struggled to pay travel expenses let alone acquire a working typewriter.[71] By late 1943 Whitfield had lost all confidence in Henderson's leadership style. But, as Claude Williams would later explain, "you didn't work with Don Henderson, you worked for him."[72] Whitfield did not like working for anyone but himself.

Separation from his family also weighed on Whitfield. During his long absences, Zella had relocated with the children to Cropperville in the Bootheel to lead the camp's UCAPAWA local. Owen viewed their marriage as a partnership of activists by the 1940s, referring to her as "the little radical," a name that reflected her importance to both the UCAPAWA and the PIAR.[73] While the couple considered themselves a working pair, their separation allowed Zella to grow as a leader. During a brief reunion at a PIAR institute in St. Louis in May 1943, both Owen and Zella gave speeches, but Zella stole the show by stressing the importance of love in religious and working-class activism. "Please, Lord, draw us together in that love that only you can understand," she told a rapt audience, because love would lead to "understanding of each other, black and white, all together."[74] Since Owen was to leave for South Carolina soon after the St. Louis institute, Zella felt both exhilarated to be at the heart of PIAR activities but also depressed about losing her husband to the organizing road. "I guess," she confided to Cook, "I'll remain a married widow for the rest of my life."[75]

The strain of separation and struggle caught up with the family in late 1943. Zella's health failed that winter, mainly due to exhaustion caused by taking sole care of a large family (the Whitfields still had six children under the age of twelve, the youngest born in 1941) as well as a union local and a food garden. Owen wrote to Claude from Charleston to explain that "the mental physical strain is breaking down my wife's health" and that he had lost twenty pounds himself. "Most of us organizer have lost their family," Whitfield stated, "but I don't intend to loose mine."[76] No doubt recalling how his mother had died young from overwork, Owen left the East Coast to rejoin Zella at Cropperville. Thereafter, no one heard from him for months. Williams tried several times to contact Whitfield but received no reply. "I put it lightly when I say that I am deeply troubled at not hearing from you," Williams wrote in February 1944. "I sincerely hope that all is well and that there is no break in our personal friendship or your interest in the work of the Institute."[77]

Whitfield finally replied to inform Williams that Zella was not well. "I guess I will be here from now on," he wrote. "My wife's health is not so good and I cant do my work outside of this state. . . . [I]t is not safe for me to go to work a thousand miles from home." He intended to "live and work in this state to be near her" and "the small children." He applied to the UCAPAWA for a transfer to Missouri but was denied, so he left the union. "If I do any kind of work like organizing or teaching," he told Williams, "it must be close enough to home."[78]

Whitfield's next step was to rededicate himself to the cause of agricultural workers, whom he believed had been neglected by the UCAPAWA and the federal government's wartime programs. "After four years of constant travel contacting people of many races, and peoples of all statuses and all walks of life, from highest executive to the vagabond of the roads," Whitfield wrote, "I have taken many days out from work and isolated myself to give thorough study to the present condition of the soil tillers." Looking at the larger picture, he decided to return to his union roots and help those who "have no soil to till" but wanted to "get off relief . . . and earn a living by the sweat of their brow, as God said do."[79] He restarted his letter-writing campaign to federal officials and was rewarded when the FSA agreed to provide loans to the residents of Cropperville to participate in the Food for Victory program. As part of the bargain, Whitfield moved to Cropperville "for keep this time" to "direct the garden and feed program," as well as to "personally produce 15 acres of cotton on the outside as a cash crop to pay off our loan."[80]

Out of the UCAPAWA fold, Whitfield looked more and more to the PIAR for support. He arranged with Williams to preach applied religion full time in Missouri and took the official position of codirector of the organization. "I am very happy and so is the madam to be free to carry on P.I.A.R. work this year because in my oppinion it is the only organization in america today that

realy gets to the roots of the cause of the suffering of the people, as well as it
reaches the hearts of the Grass Root People, where all els has failed including
trade unions." "I know what it means to carry the true gospel," Whitfield assured Williams, "because all powers that be are against it but the carpenter's
son the peoples leader said 'it shall not prevail.'" He even offered to hit the
road with Zella to raise money for the PIAR "if one or both of us could get
before groups" to speak.[81]

Whitfield and Williams both remained certain that their ministry worked
best when applied to the everyday struggles of life and that taking orders
from labor unions made them less effective. As Williams would later claim,
"the working class preacher has been spurned by progressives because he is
religious" and "labor unions have refused to organize his people because they
could not pay dues." The PIAR cared less about NLRB status or dues-paying
membership; it instead castigated "rocking-chair reds" who "dismiss religion" in favor of partisan politics. To Whitfield, the PIAR's characterization
of sectarians on the left epitomized his frustration with both H. L. Mitchell
and Donald Henderson, who each used religion tactically rather than out
of conviction. These leaders failed to see how religion constituted the core
of activism. "No one can be a good trade unionist," Whitfield affirmed to
Williams, "until he is realy Educated and anchored in the FACT that the
Brotherhood of Man is the only salvation for the Common People." "The
madam and I dedicate the rest of our days," Whitfield concluded, "to the end
that the children of the common people will have a more free and a happyer
world than we have today."[82]

III

Whitfield's move was timely since Williams was busy steering the PIAR into
the biggest fight of its existence in Detroit. Williams made the Packard Motor
plant, a site of racist hate strikes in 1942, a primary target in late 1943 when
he enlisted Virgil Vanderburg to preach the applied religion to his coworkers,
many of whom belonged to J. Frank Norris's right-wing Baptist church. By
early 1944 Vanderburg, a key African American "work-a-day" preacher, had
organized more than forty preachers at the plant to provide twenty "noon
hour" religious meetings each week. These meetings attracted more preachers
to the PIAR, such as Reverend Robert Hill, a popular minister in the Church
of God in Christ, the leading black Pentecostal denomination in the United
States. When Hill started preaching applied religion, Vanderburg recounted,
"the faces of the Temple Baptist workers and their stooges colored up into a
million hues." Hill's testimony, in turn, got a white preacher in the audience
to admit, "Brother Hill spoke the truth today." Using the Packard campaign

as a model, Vanderburg and Williams recruited Francis Downing, a white Catholic layman, to become part of an applied religion "squadron" that included an interracial octet. The squadron entered shop floors and storefront churches to preach and sing the PIAR gospel.[83] "O Brother," Williams later recalled, "You should have heard [them] sing, 'Were You There When They Crucified My Lord.'" Their "arresting harmonies" helped John Miles convert many "captive" preachers in Ford's River Rouge plant and at a half dozen other large factories.[84] The People's Church was growing too, from 50 members at its initial meeting to an average of 150 weekly congregants who themselves spoke to hundreds more listeners on shop floors, in local churches, and in community centers during the week. The PIAR was becoming a conspicuous force in wartime Detroit.[85]

Looking to consolidate these gains, Williams planned to hold a People's Congress of Applied Religion in Detroit in the summer of 1944. The congress would feature "shop preachers and southern tenant farmer preachers, Negro, White, labor and liberal clergy." "The very promising program," he informed his financial backers in the Detroit Presbytery, would demonstrate how "members of all religious groups will be united in the stand for 'a world founded on economic justice, racial brotherhood, religious freedom, and political equality.'"[86] Williams enlisted the Whitfields, Koger, DeBerry, Campbell, and other southern PIAR activists, such as Theodosia Simpson of Winston-Salem, to speak alongside theologians, preachers, and union activists from northern cities, such as Alva Taylor and Lloyd Jones, a former Pentecostal evangelist who was the president of a Detroit UAW local. Perhaps more important, the congress had the support of national CIO leaders. Kermit Eby, the CIO's director of education, assured Williams that the "CIO share your interest." "We propose," Eby declared, "that all people of our country must work together to create a world free from unemployment and war."[87]

The PIAR congress was meant to be confrontational. Williams told Owen Whitfield, the keynote speaker of the congress, "to pull off the gloves and put on brass knucks. Tell what you thought your religion was. Tell the conditions you were in and the experiences you had when you thought religion only preparing to die. Tell what you have come to see religion is. Tell what it has done for the people down there. . . . We want you to speak about Dixie."[88] In other words, he wanted Whitfield to talk as a sharecropper and rural preacher, not as an experienced organizer of factory workers. Presumably, Whitfield did not need this kind of instruction since he had used his rural experience to reach urban, industrial, and even government audiences since the late 1930s.[89]

Whitfield's speech, "A Sharecropper Discovers True Religion in the Peoples' Fight," did just what Williams had asked. Before an audience of 208 delegates from twenty-five states, he talked about how southerners had more religious devotion than northerners and thus more potential to bring true democracy. The speech, according to an FBI agent in the audience, was "dynamicly delivered" and "applause greeted many of Whitfield's statements" as he discussed ending the poll tax, expanding the PIAR in the South, and helping the CIO to bury Memphis's "Boss Crump" for good.[90]

Williams used his platform at the congress to comment on the fight in Detroit. He argued that the big denominations did not really live up to the teachings of Jesus if they did not support labor causes. Other speakers echoed this line. R. J. Thomas, the president of the UAW, used his speech to attack unsupportive churches. "I don't care if they walk up this aisle every Sunday," he thundered, if ministers "preach the righteousness of inequality" then "they

Figure 10. The People's Institute of Applied Religion Congress in 1944 challenged racial division in Detroit. This flyer was produced after the Detroit congress. Source: Folder 7, Box 19, Williams Papers, Reuther Library, Wayne State University.

do not really believe in the brotherhood of man." The overarching theme of the congress was that mainstream Christianity was "more concerned with building itself than with building a good society."[91] Williams's rough sense of ecumenical politics frustrated long-time allies like Henry Jones, who began to wonder if Williams suffered from hubris. "Just at the time we need to push through a request for $4000 [Williams] comes out to call his church a puppet," Jones complained. "I spent 7 years gaining the confidence of this Presbytery," he reminded Williams, whom he scolded for lashing out without first consulting "your friends" or considering "the long term gains that might be made."[92]

The congress brought Claude Williams and the PIAR new attention, as did the publication that summer of Cedric Belfrage's latest version of Williams's biography, *A Faith to Free the People*. Compared to the feeble sales of the first two editions, the success of the book this time around testified to how far Williams had come since his crises of 1939. The cover featured glowing quotes from leading labor activists and public intellectuals, including Lillian Smith, Carey McWilliams, and William H. Levitt, the educational director of the CIO-UAW, who hoped "to see the day when this book will be on the shelves of every local union library throughout the country."[93] Labor union leaders had shunned Williams when the book was first published in 1940; now they embraced him. Remarkably, Williams had brought himself back from defeat once again without compromising his core ideals. As the *New York Times* noted, "many respectable people still look down the nose at Claude Williams. They still call him a Communist. He says in reply, 'I am a fellow-traveler with the Man Who went to the Cross.'"[94]

Williams's fame in some circles gained him infamy in others. Reverend Gerald L. K. Smith, a Disciples of Christ minister who had been close to Louisiana's Huey Long and the "Share Our Wealth" campaign in the 1930s, led a fresh fight to discredit Williams. A public supporter of pro-Nazi and white supremacist groups, Smith had moved to Detroit in the hopes of building a political career. After Williams blamed him as one of the instigators behind the June 1943 riot, Smith studied Williams's activities with an obsessive zeal. As early as July 1943, Smith had lobbied the Detroit Presbytery to fire him. Claiming to be the leader of 123,000 Detroit Christians, Smith demanded to know how the "liberal wing of the church can stomach this Williams," and threatened to inform its members how "their money is being spent" to support this radical unless the presbytery cut ties with him.[95] Reading closely, Smith explained that *A Faith to Free the People* contained "63 different pages" of "Communistic, obscene, or atheistic" ideas and that Williams's "Hell-Brewers" pamphlet had nine inaccuracies about conservative church groups.[96]

Presbytery leaders dismissed Smith's complaints at first. William Molbon of St. John's Presbyterian Church said that Smith's letters were "a great waste of money and time." Not to be ignored, Smith enlisted his political allies in the America First movement, most importantly North Dakota's Republican senator Gerald Nye, who leaked a confidential six-page memorandum from the House Un-American Activities Committee (HUAC) on Williams's associations with left-wing leaders. As Jones had warned, Williams's activities led a conservative faction within the presbytery to try to revoke his funding. The attempt failed, however, because Williams still had sympathetic allies on the presbytery's War Emergency Board. "It's safe to assume that the closer you get to the Communist Party, the more Claude likes it," one Detroit church leader concluded, "but our regular churches have failed their responsibilities to the war-workers so completely that I don't see how we can be too critical."[97] But the ranks of the ambivalent were growing. For every staunch defender of Williams, many other church leaders worried about the damage that pressure from Smith and Nye could inflict on the presbytery.[98]

While Detroit liberals wrung their hands about Williams's relationship with communists, CP leaders dismissed him as a maverick who could not be fully trusted. As the FBI would later discover from an informant, the CP offered Williams $10,000 during the war but "wanted to attach strings." Williams refused the money, it was claimed, because he did not want to compromise the independence of the PIAR. Nevertheless, HUAC in 1944 labeled the PIAR "one of the most vicious Communist organizations ever set up in this country."[99]

The Whitfields returned home from Detroit energized by the congress. They introduced the PIAR to several Bootheel churches. Owen explained that news of the congress "is making hell raises out of all the rest of us Sharecropper preachers," Zella in particular.[100] "She is receiving lots of fan-Mail from the People that attended the Congress," Owen informed Claude. "I think she is getting a little swelled headed (smile)."[101] Compared to earlier years, when Zella had performed the hard day-to-day work running Cropperville and its UCAPAWA local, she now felt liberated by her public PIAR persona. She expressed this sense of delayed empowerment to a close friend who was perhaps the person best placed to understand it: Joyce Williams. "Rev Joyce [Williams] + Rev [Zella] Whitfield," she boasted to Joyce, "have work to do yet and we realy are the guys that can do it. Just wait until we hich up together. we are going to make Rev Claude and Owen shamed of themselves (smile)."[102]

This letter epitomized the supportive correspondence between Joyce and Zella in the last half of 1944. Zella praised Joyce for her work and declared that "if there is any extra honor to bestowed on any one of us its you who deserve it." "You are the one that have suffered the most among our gang for this cause," she explained to Joyce, "and I just worship you for it." "Of course we owe Claude every thing to," Zella admitted, but he, like Owen, "was made for this cause."[103] Zella was particularly concerned about Joyce's health and expressed joy over her recovery. "You don't know how happy it makes me to see you up again and able to keep Claude in the traces! ha You sure looks fine and old Claude just looks at you and grin and think devilment," she wrote. Zella eagerly sought to carry forward the PIAR work but joked with Joyce, in a way that only good friends can joke, that she was suffering because "Owen haven't had time to get his breath since he's been home." This meant, Zella explained, that I "haven't had no love and no nothing for a week."[104]

The PIAR undertook a frenzy of activity that winter. The Whitfields were busy setting up PIAR institutes in the Bootheel at the same time as they organized cotton pickers to take advantage of local labor shortages to push for higher wages. "Uncle Sam has took all [the bosses'] Labor," Owen explained to Williams, "so we are making him pay like hell."[105] Meanwhile, Williams was shuttling through Detroit, Chicago, Pittsburgh, and Philadelphia to start a simultaneous program called "Mobilize for Brotherhood—And Mean It," a campaign to broaden the PIAR by asking people to sign pledges to work toward the "defeat of all fascist forces; for racial brotherhood; against anti-Semitism; the poll tax; . . . and for unobstructed labor union organization."[106] At the same time, Harry Koger moved to Little Rock to take charge of institute activities there and in Arkansas generally.[107] Keen to encourage PIAR growth at the regional level, Williams advised Koger, Whitfield, and DeBerry to establish local southern PIAR councils that would mirror the work of the July 1944 congress. Membership in the councils, Williams explained to Koger, "is eligible only to workers, churchmen and others who are progressive." Williams admitted that developing these councils would, in addition to helping the PIAR, finally allow him to "get revenge on the STFU by really organizing in Arkansas."[108]

The establishment of PIAR councils in Indianapolis, Little Rock, St. Louis, Detroit, and Chicago in the first two months of 1945 reflected the regional success and coordination of the applied religion activists. In Little Rock in February, Koger welcomed over two hundred delegates to the council's first meeting. The St. Louis council meeting that month was a similar success. Whitfield hosted it in the headquarters of the St. Louis Industrial Union Council, a consortium of the city's CIO leaders, with the help of Elsie Newell Johnson, the sister of Zilphia Mae Horton of the Highlander Folk School. Similar council meetings in Chicago and Detroit followed, while a new council was established in New York.[109]

At the Little Rock meeting, Williams ordained new ministers as PIAR activists, but he rambled on too long, cutting into Whitfield's allotted speaking time. When Williams finished, he whispered for his old friend to "be as brief as possible." Whitfield glared back at Williams and told him in a loud voice, "I didn't say a word when you were talking and I want you to keep quiet!" The audience gasped. After all, as Williams recounted, this was Arkansas, where a black man never contradicted a white man in public. Whitfield barreled ahead. He proceeded to lecture the gathering for forty minutes, vigorously poking his pointer stick at the PIAR chart "Religion and the Common People," until there "wasn't a dry eye" in the audience because, Williams explained, people were "realizing the dynamic of their religion for the first time."[110] The Whitfields returned to the Bootheel set to continue the PIAR's southern advance.

But in their fast-moving efforts to extend the PIAR, the Whitfields got stuck in past animosity. In an April organizing tour in Mississippi County, they paid a visit to the Delmo communities near Wyatt, where they learned that the FSA was planning to auction all of its projects for private sale. The main achievement from the roadside demonstration, the Delmo Homes, faced liquidation. During the war, the FSA had come under attack by southern conservatives, and the enactment of Public Law 76 made it illegal for the federal government to use funds to improve the living conditions of farm workers. Now at the war's end, the government looked to eviscerate the FSA's legacy and clear the way for the restructuring of the southern agricultural economy around corporate farms and casual wage labor. Bureaucrats in Washington decided the quickest way to do so would be to auction the government land from under the clients who lived on it and force them to adapt to modern farming.[111]

Holed up at Cropperville all winter, the Whitfields were slow to respond to these developments. The STFU was not. H. L. Mitchell and Reverend David Burgess, a white Congregational minister, led an early effort to defend the residents of Delmo by organizing all six hundred families in an attempt to purchase their homes themselves with the help of a range of liberal allies, including NAACP leaders and the department store magnate Marshall Field Jr.[112]

The Whitfields arrived at the Wyatt project in the middle of the STFU's effort to put together a bid. When they learned that Mitchell was involved, the Whitfields panicked and preached for hours, not about applied religion, but to "blast the hell out of [H. L. Mitchell] and his STFU." The Whitfields returned to Wyatt several times that summer to explain that Mitchell was not to be trusted. The families in the South Wyatt project agreed, withdrawing support from the STFU plan and giving money to the Whitfields, who claimed to have a plan to keep these farmers independent of both large landowners and the STFU.[113] The couple left confident that their efforts had achieved a great victory.

Back in Detroit, Williams worked to establish the city's PIAR council as a force independent of him. Under the leadership of Shelton Tappes, an African American leader of the city's NNC and treasurer of Ford Local 600; Ellsworth Smith of the Detroit Council of Churches; and Sam Sage of the Wayne County CIO, the Detroit council brought together dozens of local religious, labor, and civil rights leaders who together represented thousands of union members and believers. Their cumulative efforts had bettered the working conditions of white and black workers as they collectively demonstrated the PIAR mission of interracial brotherhood in the Motor City.[114]

Perhaps Williams sensed that his local enemies were getting bolder. The PIAR campaigns had gone far beyond what the presbytery had hired him to do. Williams was no longer helping southern migrants adapt in a new environment; he was trying to radically restructure that environment. During 1944 he had stepped up his attacks on the city's leading liberals, as well as its right-wing preachers, by accusing them all of building an arsenal with no democracy. Why, Williams asked a crowd of PIAR supporters, had Detroiters created a segregated city where whites could not venture "West of God" and blacks could not move "East of God"? Now, in February 1945, the church board responsible for Williams's employment informed him that it would discontinue his funding on May 31. "Will [the church] fire an Industrial Chaplain for taking seriously and doing too well what he was employed to do?" he asked Henry Jones. It would.[115]

Williams decided that "it is time to come in to the open and really fight" his true enemies. He announced that the PIAR would host two "revivals" in the summer of 1945, one in Chicago and one in Detroit. He requested that Owen and Zella Whitfield come to preach the revival sermons. Claude "says to tell you that he wants the sermons Biblical and Revival, and for you to arrive fresh as you can because he may want you to preach the night you arrive!" Joyce Williams informed the Whitfields.[116] The call to preach up north threatened to distract from their fight against the STFU's plans for Delmo, but they agreed anyway. "When you say the word," Owen replied, "Here we come."[117]

The Whitfields joined Williams and a roster of other PIAR activists for thirteen nights of revival meetings in Detroit at the end of July and eleven nights in Chicago at the end of August. "R-E-V-I-V-A-L of TRUE RELIGION!" read the announcement for the Detroit gathering. "Save Yourselves! from this Crooked Generation! . . . BIBLE SERMONS on Housing, Health, Jobs, Elections, Reconversion, Collective Bargaining—Brotherhood! Hear the Gospel to the Poor." The *Chicago Defender* described the meeting in the Windy City as a "new technique for reaching the masses." Amid the familiar hymns, ecstatic worship, and call-and-response of an evangelical

Figure 11. "R-E-V-I-V-A-L of TRUE RELIGION!" The 1945 People's Institute of Applied Religion Revival in Detroit. Source: Folder 3, Box 19, Williams Papers, Reuther Library, Wayne State University.

revival, Whitfield, Don West, and Virgil Vanderburg inveighed not about "the salvation of the soul," but "instead, with the same rousing spirit that always brings a response from the faithful, these parsons assailed Gerald L. K. Smith, anti-labor practices in industry and racial quotas in Christian schools." The PIAR evangelists not only replicated the sound and feel of a Pentecostal-Holiness revival but based their sermons on the same scripture as well. Fliers announcing the revival backed up the PIAR claims with citations from the New Testament books of Acts and Luke.[118]

Upon his return to Cropperville from the Chicago revival, Owen reported to Claude that "the Delmo Home situation is still hanging Fire, but we still hope to win."[119] They would not. While they did manage to raise $2,700 from the residents of the South Wyatt project and claimed to have raised $25,000 altogether, there is no evidence that they ever entered into serious negotiations to purchase the homes. Whitfield had prided himself since the 1930s on not taking sides in sectarian battles between unions and different "isms," but in this case he let his personal animosity and distrust lead the people of South Wyatt astray. The STFU, with the help of several wealthy, liberal backers, created a Delmo Housing Corporation and successfully purchased eight of the Delmo communities and then resold them to the residents on low-interest, long-term mortgages. Only the people of South Wyatt were left out. The Whitfields had not raised enough money to back their alternative plan, and a local alfalfa mill bought the land as a result. Owen Whitfield blamed Mitchell for sabotaging him, saying that "if the planters gets the Projects the STFU don't get the credit, but that will be alright so long as the St Louis group or the Cio don't get it." While this charge may have had truth in it, the Whitfields had also failed to prioritize what was best for the rural people they claimed to represent. In their effort to expand the reach of applied religion, they instead preached a message based on petty divisions and in the process wrecked the lives of dozens of families who had to move away from their homes.[120]

Williams, meanwhile, was also in serious combat in Detroit. That autumn he took a contingent of PIAR activists to picket a meeting of Gerald L. K. Smith's Christian Youth for America. The keynote speaker was Kenneth Goff, an inveterate anticommunist, who used passages from Belfrage's *A Faith to Free the People* to argue that Williams and his followers favored free love, miscegenation, and abortion. With applied religion activists loudly disputing these claims at the doors, Goff incited the audience to visit the PIAR office as cries of "Let's get that bastard" rose from the Christian Youth members in the hall.[121] The applied religion preachers had "been raising hell," Williams assured Whitfield, and planned "another real assault on that fascist."[122]

The Detroit PIAR council retaliated by circulating a petition among the city's ministers that demanded Smith be barred from holding fundraisers for his America First Party at local schools. Asked to comment on the PIAR's opposition to him, Smith said, "[I am] honored to be opposed by Williams and his crew of communists, pro-communists, and radical stooges." Williams's campaign was partially effective. Detroit city officials prevented Smith from raising money at an upcoming appearance at North High School, but they allowed the event to go on. Inside the school on September 27, Smith spoke in front of a hundred people, while outside several hundred PIAR, CIO, and other civil rights activists formed a picket line "around his meeting . . . that just didn't stop." About a thousand onlookers took in the scene. Described by Smith-friendly newspapers as a "riot" and criticized by liberals who thought it best to just ignore Smith, Williams hailed it as a victory. The lesson of Germany, he reasoned, had been that silence bred complicity in the spread of fascism. Now that Nazi Germany had been defeated on the battlefield, Williams declared that the PIAR could not stand by and let Smith declare America a "White, Christian, Nation."[123] By aligning an opposition of unions, preachers, and civil rights activists, the PIAR successfully discredited (and even converted a few) profascist groups in Detroit, and in the process gave real voice to the causes of religious fellowship and racial unity.

Yet, less obvious enemies were growing stronger after the end of the war. Williams noted a developing "cleavage" in the UAW as the preacher Homer Martin allied with groups whose "first line is also fanatical opposition to the Soviet Union, Communists, [and] fellow travelers."[124] One such group was the Association of Catholic Trade Unionists (ACTU). Hated by followers of Father Charles Coughlin for their support of unions and token black membership, the ACTU pioneered a form of militant anticommunist liberalism to combat leftist leaders who fostered "domineering or irresponsible leadership" in unions. It began as an educational organization to help the Catholic Church retain working-class male members. Near the end of the war, the ACTU changed its policy by developing a Catholic "caucus-within-a-caucus" in trade unions that could then make pragmatic alliances with socialists and other anticommunist union members.[125]

The growing anticommunist alliance proved very effective at stopping the progress of the PIAR in Detroit. A big part of Williams's effort to take the fight to his foes was PIAR's decision to back two candidates in the 1945 municipal elections: Richard Frankensteen for mayor and Reverend Charles Hill for city councilman. "The real purpose of [PIAR] revival meetings," a confidential informant told the FBI, "was to campaign in behalf" of Hill and Frankensteen. The FBI made the obvious sound clandestine; the PIAR did not hide its support for Hill, a Baptist preacher, long-time ally of Williams, and applied religion stalwart. Williams thought they had a chance with support from the PIAR, the CIO's Political Action Committee, and the NNC. But the election campaign was ugly and rife with charges of communism. Both candidates lost. Mary Lou Koger, the daughter of Harry Koger and a union organizer herself, told Williams that she had a "sick feeling in my stomach when I read of Frankensteen's defeat as mayor," and asked Claude whether the result was due to disunity among workers. Williams believed it was. Not much later, Walter Reuther, backed by the faction of Catholics and socialists, took over the UAW leadership. The work that the PIAR had done to connect people across denominations, races, and workplaces thereafter diminished as the new political climate of postwar America altered the parameters of political dissent, civil rights, and religious belief.[126]

With so much at stake, Williams's own thunderous speeches on religion increasingly drew sharp dichotomies between true and false religion, and thus increasingly paralleled some of the demagogues he sought to counteract. Indeed, one of these demagogues, Father Coughlin, had said during the Depression in Detroit, "Let us have a Christian Front! Not a 'front' to throttle, enslave and destroy America, but one to PRESERVE America as one of the last frontiers of human liberty! Outside of practical Christianity in the United States, all is darkness. . . . On the one side stand the unrelenting rocks of greedy industrial capitalism. On the other, billowing swells of mistreated workers are being gradually rolled up into a Communist sea. Without AP-PLIED CHRISTIANITY there can be no charity on one side, and peace on the other."[127] Save for a few minor points, this quote could have come from Williams in 1945. Parallel to the invective by ministers he opposed, Williams's increasingly militant rhetoric left little room for differences of opinion, and thus frightened some allies away from the PIAR rather than unifying them.

Williams chose the transitional moment of December 1945 to assemble the leading members of the PIAR in New York. In this four-day meeting, they would take stock of where they had gone and where they would venture in the postwar era. Whitfield could not attend but sent his annual report to be read into the minutes. Despite the disappointment over the Delmo Homes debacle, he reported that he and Zella had organized nine Bootheel PIAR groups. At one meeting in Butler County, Whitfield wrote, they enacted the PIAR "worker's communion." The ritual featured real wine (most pastors disdained drinking alcohol) and a makeshift cross (of benches) set up outdoors. At the start, Whitfield explained, the invited pastors sang in a "modified voice" with "their Eyes and Ears cocked like a bunch of Jackasses at a Jackass Convention." Once Whitfield assembled the cross, however, "you could feel their Knees Knocking." "I pointed out that we had no intention to change their Religeon, and each one was asked to get his Bible and turn to the Book of Timothy, 4:1–8 and Timothy 3:16," and they read: "I have fought a good fight, I have finished my course, I have kept the faith: Henceforth there is laid up for me a crown of righteousness, which the Lord, the righteous judge, shall give me at that day: and not to me only, but unto all them also that love his appearing"; "all scripture is given by inspiration of God, and is profitable for doctrine, for reproof, for correction, for instruction in righteousness" (2 Tim. 4:7–8, 3:16). "Then the fun started," Whitfield wrote. "One sister screamed out loud, 'GLORY TO GOD I have been smitten with the Truth,' and an old mid-wife said Aman, right between the eyes." When it came time to drink communion wine, preachers who had "preached Hellfire and Brimstone to anyone who dared to drink anything stronger than CoaCola" suddenly opted to drink the wine at the foot of the makeshift cross. "There is a deep inspiration, and great awakening" here, Whitfield concluded.[128]

After relating Whitfield's report to his PIAR colleagues in New York, Williams stopped the meeting to comment on what had just been read. He had recently seen a clipping from the *St. Louis Post-Dispatch* that told about Whitfield's work for the PIAR at Cropperville, and believed that Whitfield had been too modest in his report. Whitfield's account, he said, "really is literature" that reflected "the dynamic in the native leadership of the country." Summarizing the clipping, Williams described how Whitfield "merged religion and unionism as joint forces for the brotherhood of man" and linked "religion with everyday strife as shown in the new words to the old religious songs they sing," like the hymn "Old Time Religion." He then sang, in his sonorous southern cadence, a few lines that he hoped would carry them on in the postwar era: "Give me that old time religion / It's good enough for me. / It will end religious hatred. / It will end all persecution. / It will help us work together. / It will help exalt the people." "When that song is sung through the sharecropper areas of the South," Williams concluded, "it gets across a message with the emotional appeal which is necessary for social action."[129] Whitfield's work demonstrated that in order to move America forward, the PIAR now had to look back, and take the fight to Dixie.

Conclusion
Clods of Southern Earth

PIAR leaders believed democracy could flourish in postwar America now that working people had defeated fascism abroad. At the board meeting in New York in late 1945, they discussed how to make this vision a reality. After discussing Whitfield's report, Williams ceded the floor to Don West, the Georgian poet. West congratulated the group on its northern wartime achievements but pointed out that the South was the true "seat of world reaction" where forces "are doing more to stymie the progress of the world than any other part of the world today since we defeated fascism." The southern activist, West explained, "does not belong in New York," because the "roots of the problem" remained southern, and they "are sinking down and becoming stronger" and we "must not go away and leave them there to grow." The preachers of applied religion had to go South to confront the wells of "Ku Kluxism" that "poison the rest of the U.S.," West said, because "if we are going to nip anything in the bud, we have to go there to the roots."[1]

Claude and Joyce Williams agreed. They announced to their friends and coworkers that they would soon return to the South. They considered moving to Atlanta, the engine of New South modernization, but after discussing the options with colleagues Harry Koger, Alva Taylor, and Virginia Durr, they decided to relocate to Birmingham, Alabama. Taylor welcomed the Williamses' "coming south." He explained that Birmingham "will be best from an industrial standpoint," and there would be plenty of work to do since, "unions there, even CIO, are said to be rather cautious." Claude Williams later explained that these allies convinced him that Birmingham would become the main battleground for "progressive democratic action" because "the way Birmingham goes, so goes Alabama; the way Alabama goes, so goes the South; and the way the South goes, so goes the nation."[2]

I

The Williamses' move that summer coincided with the start of a massive CIO organizing campaign called "Operation Dixie." Beginning in May 1946, the union budgeted a million dollars for 250 organizers to unionize large southern industries. The CIO targeted the South as the number one economic problem facing the nation's workers, because its industries remained hostile to unions and permitted unequal wages, often due to racial and gender discrimination. Harry Koger, William DeBerry, and other PIAR activists who still worked as organizers for the UCAPAWA were all redeployed around the region as part of the "big drive in the South," as DeBerry called it.[3] Once again, the Williamses hoped to position the PIAR at the forefront of industrial union activism.

Still, Claude Williams could not leave New York without a bang. "So," Whitfield inquired in January 1946, "Claud going to hook up a white and Negro couple Eh? That ought to bring him about $25 in NY. It would bring him a thousand down here (kukluxers) ha." Williams confirmed the rumor: he would officiate the marriage of a white Unitarian minister from Norfolk, Virginia, to an African American United Service Organization worker at Harlem's Abyssinian Baptist Church. Thereafter, the couple would remain in New York to do "some real work" for the city's PIAR council. Whitfield jokingly predicted that "the Sun-of-a-Gun Winks at the Bride at the end of the ceremony" and advised Joyce to "attend all of the Weddings that that Bird have anything to do with." The radical act was a serious one, however. The *Chicago Defender* reported that "public rebuke of the Southern minister was so hot" that newspapers would not print the story.[4]

With the wedding as just one example, the New York PIAR council represented a new core of activism within the organization. It hosted a Youth Congress of Applied Religion in early 1946 aimed at "binding the youth of the world together without regard to sect, sex, race, caste, or color [for] the realization of democratic principles and ideals of our Judaeo-Christian heritage." The PIAR could also boast growing councils in Baltimore (led by Winifred Chappell), Chicago, and Detroit. The South, however, would remain the frontline.[5]

Already in the trenches, Owen Whitfield looked to do his part in Missouri. Since Owen left full-time work for the UCAPAWA in early 1944, the Whitfields had lived on income from the PIAR and what they could reap from their farm. Now that the PIAR was without Presbyterian funding, they

needed a new source of income. In early 1946 Whitfield found a new sponsor, the United Negro and Allied Veterans of America, a lobbying group for
black soldiers just returned from the war. Although not a veteran himself,
Owen Whitfield organized several well-attended meetings in southeast Missouri, Kansas, and northern Arkansas as its regional director.[6] In these travels
Whitfield made even more promising contact with the St. Louis council of
the NNC. After the war, Revels Cayton, a West Coast trade unionist, communist, and grandson of Reconstruction-era black senator Hiram Revels
of Mississippi, led a revival of the civil rights and labor federation. NNC
councils that had diminished in size and stature since the 1930s took off
again, including the one in St. Louis, whose leaders amassed two hundred
dues-paying members as well as many other allies. Whitfield offered to "work
up and down the [Mississippi] River" so long as he would be able to see his
family in Cropperville once a week. He started as a full-time organizer for the
NNC in September 1946, earning a monthly wage of $150 for a three-month
trial period. The NNC agreed to pay half of his salary, while the CP paid the
other half.[7] To St. Louis NNC activist Nathan Oser, Whitfield's reputation
spoke for itself. Oser reported to the NNC office in New York that Whitfield
knew the local area "better than any of us," and "doesn't need me or anyone
else to tell him where to go and what to do."[8] Organizers like Whitfield, Oser
explained, were required now more than ever.

Only a few weeks before Whitfield joined the NNC, William Howard, a
black veteran, had been murdered in St. Louis by William Niggemann, a
white, off-duty policeman. When NNC members tried to organize a protest
campaign in response, they ran into resistance. One black attorney suggested
the NNC should "teach the Negro people . . . to behave properly," while another commentator lamented that other attorneys—black and white—"do
not recognize a lynching in their own back yards." Oser concluded, "If we
had had Whitfield, it would have been so much better!"[9]

The NNC needed Whitfield to take the offensive, and Whitfield needed
the NNC to get back on his feet. He made his first speech on behalf of the
NNC in late September at a meeting sponsored by the William Howard
Committee. According to an FBI informant, Whitfield told the audience that
although he was a preacher, he had "ceased to pray and is now commencing
to fight." The struggle was hard, he said, because African Americans were
not united. Perhaps drawing on his past experience as a black nationalist,
Whitfield pledged to "labor for unity among the Negro because in unity
there is strength."[10]

He looked to build that unity behind the election campaign of William
Massingale, a black Democrat who ran for the Missouri state legislature

in 1946. Massingale, a St. Louis resident, veteran of World War I, and CIO member since 1936, embodied the kind of progressive black politician that the NNC believed to be crucial in the fight to bring rights to blacks in Missouri. But they needed to convince voters from the Eleventh District of St. Louis, previously won by white candidates, to vote for a black man. Whitfield crafted campaign appeals and literature for Massingale aimed at St. Louis blacks. One pamphlet read, "It is time to stop being suckers for the politicians. . . . We must vote for THE MAN, NOT THE PARTY." As a Democratic candidate, NNC members explained, Massingale would fight for better housing, fair employment, and antilynching laws. Thanks in no small part to Whitfield and the NNC, Massingale won.[11]

Whitfield's resurgence did not stop there. Not long after Massingale's victory, the William Howard Campaign successfully pressured the St. Louis police department to remove officer Niggemann from the force.[12] Whitfield and the NNC celebrated these successes at a mass meeting (featuring Fannie Cook, a long-time Whitfield ally, and Massingale) to protest "jim-crowism and discrimination" and to demand the creation of a state Fair Employment Practices Commission (FEPC).[13]

Despite this impressive and growing list of achievements, Whitfield decided to leave St. Louis at the end of his three-month trial period in January 1947. His name was conspicuously absent from this list of speakers at follow-up meetings about the proposed FEPC in Missouri. By this point working for money more than anything else, Whitfield took his wages and returned to Cropperville, much to the chagrin of other black activists who felt he had not lived up to his iconic reputation. These young people wanted more, but Whitfield could not give it.[14] He would spend most of 1947 with his family in Cropperville, where his contact with activist allies was limited to a two-week visit by Cedric Belfrage, who was gathering material for a proposed biography about him.[15]

Efforts by Claude Williams to get started again in Birmingham were equally rocky. He and Joyce had bought a small farm in Fungo Hollow near the town of Alabaster, Alabama, but discovered that the social climate there was not hospitable. No fewer than seven informants reported Williams's every move to the FBI while he worked out of an office on Third Street in Birmingham that was shared with allies from the SCHW and the SNYC, both suspected of communist loyalties. One informant concluded that Williams believed "all people should be mixed up" and preached "perverted brotherhood" to "gullible people" who do not realize they were working for a "Communist transmission Belt."[16] Williams and his family may have wished they had been part of a "transmission belt," because money was incredibly scarce. More serious, however, was the pervasiveness of anticommunist vigilance in the postwar

South. "I am not a Communist," he declared, "but I think Red-baiting comes in the same category as Negro-baiting, Jew-baiting, and labor baiting." Thus, Williams saw how the emerging Cold War might begin as a crusade against communists and then engulf all activists for democratic justice. "Fascism, defeated on the military front," he contended, "is seeking to organize on a non-military level and accomplish what it failed to do with the sword."[17]

Moving back South brought Williams into closer contact with Don West, who used his pen to fight against the kind of fascism Williams described. While working for the PIAR during the war, West had served as a school principal and resident poet in the tiny Georgia town of Lula. In 1946 he published a remarkable collection of poetry called *Clods of Southern Earth* that reflected both the fear and optimism of postwar Dixie. West toured the South reading his poetry with the support of the PIAR, which helped distribute fourteen thousand copies of the book. West hoped his collection of "people's poetry" would inspire a "deep faith in love" in working people, whose anxieties seemed to have risen since the end of the war. The poems focused upon the dignity and struggles of millhands, miners, and share-croppers who rose up despite terrible conditions and odds.[18] In the final section, called "No Lonesome Road," West included a short poem entitled, "For Claude Williams":

> Oh, he who clambers through the stars
> And plants his toe on highland peak
> Shall not again be satisfied
> To tramp the level waters seek.
>
> For he who tastes life deep and hard
> Shall not trip lightly on its rim,
> But surging strong against its barbs
> There'll be no quiet peace for him. . . .

For West, Williams personified the southern leader who had over the past decade seen glimpses of this more democratic world and whose faith bade him to seek it no matter the hardship. West knew that Williams would not accept "quiet peace" but would rather brave the "barbs" to live "deep and hard" in his search for a democratic world. Unlike his 1930s poems that endorsed the ideology of communism, however, West had intentionally replaced "the c-word" with "agitator" in *Clods*. Fearing the alienation of liberal allies dur-ing "Operation Dixie," West sought to retain an aggressive stance without the pejorative communist label.[19]

But if West hoped this new rhetoric would keep the PIAR at the forefront, he and Williams would turn "cynical" by 1947. With former allies fearful of associating too closely with "reds," PIAR leaders painfully watched as the

CIO (especially Van Bittner, the head of Operation Dixie), churches, and liberal southern groups like the SCHW backed away from their campaigns. With frustration, Williams noted how liberals "promised support and LIED" to him, concluding that they "paid lip service" but did not follow through with assistance. The sense of ostracism came at the same time as the federal government passed restrictive legislation like the Taft-Hartley Act of 1947, which forced unions to purge communists or lose protection under national labor law. PIAR activists found it harder and harder to reach for the stars of West's verse.[20]

As the Cold War emerged in America, Williams received an offer to travel to Yugoslavia during the summer of 1947 to see behind the "Iron Curtain" for himself. Unable to work on behalf of the PIAR because his car was broken, Williams accepted. The idea for the trip had started at a New York dinner where Yugoslavia's ambassador invited a group of American clergy to study religious tolerance in his country. Williams had heard about the trial and imprisonment for war crimes of Catholic archbishop Aloysius Stepinac and the subsequent protests by the pope and American Catholics. This must have made him think about the dangerous potential of anticommunist persecution in the United States, particularly the new forms of anticommunism he had witnessed among Catholics in Detroit. Williams was also aware of the rule of Josip Broz Tito, the resistance leader during the wartime occupation who helped to oust the Nazi government and to establish the current Yugoslavian state. Car or no car, this was another offer Williams could not refuse.[21]

With six other Protestant clergy, Williams traveled to Yugoslavia in August for a two-week tour. The delegation tried to deflect potential criticism by bringing their own interpreter and dictating their own itinerary. They traveled widely in the multinational state—to Serbia, Croatia, Slovenia, and Bosnia—without restriction, and talked with people of all faiths. Visiting the archbishop at Lepoglava Prison, the delegation found Stepinac healthy and in reasonable conditions. They also talked with Jews about Nazi atrocities and Tito's efforts to rebuild war-torn synagogues. The group even met Marshal Tito himself at his summer home in Bled. Williams talked with Tito several times over a two-day period. The two got on well, aided by their mutual affinity for pipe smoking. Tito gave the preacher one of his own as a souvenir.[22]

The delegation wrote a report of their experience that contradicted hostile American press accounts about Yugoslavia. To remind the American public why Stepinac was in jail, they wrote that his conviction "was based on nearly a thousand photographs and documents submitted to the court [and] the testimony of many witnesses" that showed his "serious collaboration" with the Nazi occupation and complicity with their "racial program" that mass murdered Jews as well as forced Orthodox Serbians to convert to Catholicism.[23] Williams wrote that the workers he encountered had high hopes and common dreams for Yugoslavia. "For once in my life," he concluded, "I have seen religion being applied."[24]

Williams "hit the ground running" when he got back to Birmingham. With a newly purchased big-top style revival tent in tow, Williams set out with Bob Silverman, a musicology student from New York, for the PIAR's first southern postwar tour. They drove first to Don West's summer camp in northern Georgia, then into Tennessee, where they made stops at Chattanooga, Highlander Folk School, Auburntown, and Williams's hometown of Greenfield, and then through Kentucky and Missouri to Arkansas, where they retrieved Williams's repaired car before going back home to Birmingham. Williams admitted that these meetings consisted of "small groups" and that the PIAR "team" included only Silverman, himself, Joyce, and their daughter Claudera. In September, Williams took another tour, this time with Cedric Belfrage, which ended in Missouri's Bootheel. "Peoples' leaders from neighboring counties attended" a two-day camp meeting in Cropperville, where they "sang here-and-now religious songs and listened to the simple down-to-earth messages of PIAR speakers," including Whitfield, A. L. Campbell, E. L. Hughes (a leader in the 1939 roadside demonstration), the photographer George Straus, and Zella Whitfield, who "spoke for the women." Claude Williams "used PIAR charts to document the world picture and the peoples' task in light of the Scriptures." Cropperville made a fitting place for the event, the PIAR leaders reckoned, because it was "a colony of poor but free people symbolizing by its very existence the advance made by the struggle in the past dozen years in the South." Before returning to Birmingham, Williams drove to the North Wyatt Delmo project, where residents celebrated the fact that they now lived "in standards of decency and freedom previously unknown."[25] The positive reception must have heartened Whitfield, whose intervention in 1945 had proved so disastrous for the South Wyatt Delmo community.

These tent meetings would be the last time Owen Whitfield and Claude Williams preached together. Williams's subsequent trips into Tennessee, North Carolina, and Texas to assist Food, Tobacco, Agricultural, and Allied Workers (FTA, as the UCAPAWA was renamed in 1944) union campaigns proved disappointing. In Winston-Salem, he tried to help Mary Lou Koger, Harry's daughter, with a strike, but white workers continued to cross the picket line. In Texas, Joyce and Claude met up with Harry Koger but failed to stop the erosion of FTA union gains due to the importation of Mexican laborers whom factory owners paid "cut-throat" wages.[26] Desperate for funding, Williams went to Detroit in January 1948 to raise money. At the

People's Church, he directed a play he had written that compared the HUAC to the "Roman Activities Committee" that persecuted the early Christians and crucified Jesus.[27] Williams believed that the PIAR had a big role to play in progressive politics, especially with a presidential election looming. Williams attended the Progressive Party convention in Philadelphia that summer, where Henry Wallace received the party's nomination to run for the presidency, and thereafter helped organize a campaign event for Wallace in Birmingham. Police Commissioner Eugene "Bull" Connor prevented Wallace from addressing his intended audience, however, with carefully orchestrated violence. In the end, Wallace had to give his speech over the radio. "We shall prosper together in love and understanding, or perish in hatred and ignorance," he said. Williams agreed with this analysis but despaired that the event had been so easily stymied.[28]

The intensity of anticommunist pressure from HUAC and other groups meant difficult days for the PIAR. Wallace's resounding defeat in November 1948 closed off any real space that might have existed for progressive politics. The following March, the PIAR's national leaders met in Brooklyn to formally dissolve the organization because of financial problems and political attacks. Unconcerned about maintaining the institution for its own sake, they did away with the PIAR rather than make the compromises that might ensure its survival. They pledged, however, to continue working in a loose fellowship they called the "way of righteousness." The informal affiliation was based on Williams's understanding of the Bible, which provided evidence, he argued, of a revolutionary underground movement of oppressed people that was around in the days of the Old Testament prophets and resurfaced again with Jesus and the disciples. He believed that the applied religion group was the latest part of this historic spiritual movement. In addition to embarking on a book-length explanation of this theological theory called the "Bible Way of Righteousness," Williams continued to issue occasional PIAR bulletins.[29]

But to add personal injury to professional decline in 1949, the Presbyterian Church revoked the disability pension Williams had received since 1935. The presbytery claimed that if he was well enough to work on behalf of the PIAR and to own a farm, then Williams was not disabled. Only contemporary politics could explain this arbitrary decision, since the church itself had hired Williams to work on its behalf in Detroit and had no problem with his pension then. Williams begged them for five months to reinstate it; "I am in need," he explained. The church refused.[30]

Out of options, Williams wrote an open letter to President Harry S. Truman in late 1950. Lamenting the passage by Congress of the Subversive Activity Control Act, which required the registration of organizations deemed to be communistic by the attorney general and gave the government the power to intern their members, Williams's letter epitomized both his anguish and dark sense of humor. "In light of certain legislation . . . and of its implications to the religious freedoms and civil liberties of our country . . . I, Claude C. Williams, as a colonist of the Kingdom of Heaven wish to register as a representative of a foreign power." As a member of the "Way of Righteousness" and with the "weapon" of "love," Williams petitioned the president to oppose the anticommunist bill put forth by the "agents of Mammon within your government" who seek to "misuse" it to suppress those of the "way" who have labored for the "Kingdom of God."[31] Truman did veto the act, but Congress overrode his veto. The bill that became known as the McCarran Act would usher in restrictions on free speech, assembly, and the press that would kill the work of many labor and civil rights activists.[32]

The letter earned Williams fresh media attention that brought him a handful of new supporters. In 1950 Marion Davidson and other Williams allies in New York created the Claude Williams Committee to publicize his career, issue circular letters with his latest thoughts, and raise money to support him and Joyce in Alabama. This group of younger activists kept him connected to contemporary issues and, most importantly, regularly sent him modest checks.[33]

Whitfield, by contrast, did not have the luxury of white liberal supporters during the Cold War. Rather, he had to work hard, whether in the fields or in surrounding churches, to raise enough money to feed his family. He returned to his previous career as a local minister and farmer. Whitfield bought a truck to haul and sell firewood, much like his own father had done during his childhood. "It is tough," he explained to Fannie Cook, "but we gets by somehow and are very happy together, sharing our sweets and bitters." Whitfield's institutional allies—the FTA, PIAR, and NNC—had either disbanded or cut back their operations. For a while he wrote articles for Cedric Belfrage's progressive newspaper, *The National Guardian*, under the pseudonym "Cotton-Patch Charlie." The articles were full of Whitfield's humor but offered little political punch. In 1948 Whitfield spoke at a rally for the Civil Rights Congress (an organization created after the NNC's demise), saying that people had become "sullen and afraid," and that the church "was not leading the people out of their misery." He called for grassroots organizers to band together like they had in the Depression years, arguing that there was "nothing to lose because [we] have nothing."[34] But with New Deal programs like the FSA now closed and HUAC on the offensive, Washington was no longer a receptive place for local movements looking for government help. In January 1949 Cook and the CRS handed over control of Cropperville to a board of residents appointed by Whitfield. The following year, claiming the need for better schooling for the four children who remained at home, the Whitfields moved to Du Quoin, Illinois, a small town near Cairo, where Owen became the pastor of the St. Paul Baptist Church.[35]

Whitfield's pessimism and retreat no doubt also stemmed from harassment by the FBI, whose agents continued to follow him and question anyone he met. The FBI kept track of the family in Illinois, where agents pestered their new neighbors.[36] Hoping to quash further persecution, Whitfield agreed to an interview in December 1952.

Sitting down with agents in Springfield, Illinois, Owen Whitfield admitted someone had asked him to join the CP in 1940 and had mailed in a membership card for him, and thereafter he had attended a couple of meetings. But Whitfield, who was now in his late fifties, also explained how he resented the leaders of the CP, who, much like the STFU, tried to take credit for his work with sharecroppers and the roadside demonstration. He said that since 1939 he had worked for CIO unions like the UCAPAWA and then the FTA because he was committed to union organizing (and preaching the applied

Figure 12. Owen and Zella Whitfield celebrating their fiftieth wedding anniversary in 1963. Source: Folder 4, NP57, TAM 143, Belfrage Papers, Tamiment Library, New York University.

religion), but explained that he had not concerned himself with the policies of communists, as his defiance of Donald Henderson proved.[37]

From then on in the interview, Whitfield carefully played the role of the humble black preacher unaware of the "evil" character of communists. He explained to the FBI agents how after the war "I began to realize what the CP was, how it was trying to injure the United States" and later he learned that all FTA "officials were Communists." His last contact with the CP came in 1948 when he agreed to attend a weeklong communist school in Chicago but claimed he did so only for the $50 payment. Similarly, Whitfield explained how he disassociated himself with the PIAR when he heard on the radio that it was on the attorney general's list of subversive organizations. Whitfield's story convinced the FBI of his innocence. The agents were aware that in 1949 the CP had cut itself off from Whitfield because of "his inability to adequately handle the Party's work." By acting as the naïve and foolish "good darkey," as Whitfield called it, he played into the preconceived racial prejudices of the white FBI agents. This interview, and the fact that multiple informants reported he had no associations beyond Du Quoin, led the FBI to cancel the "security flash" on Whitfield and close his file in March 1953.[38]

Whitfield withdrew peacefully; Williams chose to fight but ended up in a similar place. The U.S. government responded to Williams's plea to register as a "foreign agent" by deeming him a high-security risk. While the FBI reported that Joyce Williams had managed to pay off the mortgage on their farm, the couple had trouble raising money beyond what the Claude Williams Committee sent them. They continued to try to help people, however, by collecting clothing for the poor. The Williamses also made plans to build a chapel on the grounds of their farm.[39] But by 1953 their plans came to naught; Claude only had $7.35 in the PIAR bank account and, as one informant claimed, "Subject has lost most of his fervor and that his life has more or less degenerated into a struggle to earn a livelihood."[40]

Being considered a risk to national security not only affected Williams's health and finances but also led mainstream Christians to cast him out. A Methodist minister from Vermont exemplified the attack against Williams in a 1953 book, *Apostles of Discord*, that admitted the PIAR had been "reasonably successful" but concluded Williams's "lack of discretion" had "seriously delayed the work of Protestantism among trade unions" because he encouraged "party-liners" and "deluded idealists."[41] This book and other media reports about Williams encouraged the Presbyterian Church to summon their former labor minister back to Detroit on charges of heresy. Williams was technically still a member of the Detroit Presbytery, and church elders like Louis Konjathy wanted to hold him accountable for what they considered his strange application of Christian belief. In January 1954, Williams, with assistance from Cedric Belfrage, headed back to Detroit to face his Presbyterian accusers.[42]

"I feel," Williams told the panel of judges, "that my entire life as a minister, the last forty years, is at stake." For hours on end, the panel of ministers interrogated Williams on statements and writings he had made that suggested his beliefs contradicted the "basic teachings and beliefs of the Presbyterian Church, U.S.A." They criticized him, for example, for giving up his ordination vow confirming the "Scriptures of the Old and New Testaments to Be the Word of God" when he had suggested that not every word of the Bible was written by God and specifically that the writings of Paul contradicted the importance of Jesus as the "Son of Man."[43] As one of Williams's lawyers would later write, the charge of preaching doctrines against the church was valid; Williams had challenged Presbyterian denominational orthodoxies since the 1920s. Williams saw the church's doctrine as a living one that had to follow the inspiration of Christ's teaching; to him, the truth of the gospel trumped the rules of the church. Williams reminded the judges that they knew his views when they offered him the job of labor minister in 1942. They also knew that he had taken the job on the condition that he would not end up defending himself against the presbytery like he had been forced to do in Paris, Arkansas.[44]

The presbytery nonetheless wanted to make an example of him in the political climate of 1954. The real charge, according to Williams and his allies, was not heresy but communism. The panel therefore tried to enter into evidence anticommunist propaganda like "100 Things You Should Know about Communism," which listed Williams as a fraudulent preacher who really worked for a party that promoted "Godless atheism." He admitted, as he had done in 1938, to holding CP membership for four months in 1937 but stated he had "never been recognized as a trustworthy person by Communist people officially." He said that CP leaders were aware that "I have never been directed by any organized group or any ideological group. When we were [in Detroit] it was during the war against fascism," Williams explained, and "we did not ask 'What are your political views?'" Instead, they fought to defeat "American fascists" at home in a struggle that may have paralleled the "Communist Party line." But that was a line that many others followed too, including people in the federal government and "all of us in the war effort." As the trial wore on, Claude, sensing defeat, read a letter from Joyce into the transcript. She asked her husband, "Are they sure it's the Constitution of the U.S.A. Church they are defending or 'One Hundred Things You Should Know?'" Offering an answer to her own question, Joyce concluded that "I would like to tell them not to go to H——, but to stay in the nice one they are making for themselves and others."[45]

Williams was defrocked on the "technical grounds" of heresy but found not guilty on the charge of communist subversion. Despite protests from his few remaining Presbyterian allies, the Synod of Michigan and then the General Assembly in Los Angeles affirmed the decision in what one chief executive officer of the United Presbyterian Church would later admit was "one of the worst things that the Presbyterian Church has ever done."[46] Williams, ordained as a minister in 1921, became a casualty of the church's own cold war in the spring of 1955.

But just when Williams's religious vision seemed completely marginal to American society, a new church-based movement for civil rights broke through as the U.S. Supreme Court's 1954 *Brown v. Board of Education* ruling and then the 1955–56 Montgomery bus boycott rocked the South in general and Alabama in particular. As outspoken proponents of black protest, the Williamses attracted the attention of a renewed Ku Klux Klan. They refused to back down. As one FBI informant stated, Claude "unhesitatingly starts conversations with people he does not know, discussing religion [and] current events and frequently states his feelings," which often caused controversy. On one such occasion, Williams got a reply in the form of a punch in the face from a white neighbor at the market. The violence escalated. Already the recipients of several death threats, the Williams family awoke in the middle of the night in 1957 to find a cross burning in their yard. And although the cause was never discovered, the family's house would burn down twice in the decade that followed, ultimately forcing the couple to live in a trailer home on their farm.[47]

Claude and Joyce Williams feared for their lives but also knew that the renewed intimidation meant that civil rights activists of a new generation had threatened the status quo in the Cold War South. It was no coincidence, for example, that the cross burning on the Williamses' property occurred around the same time that Birmingham whites rallied to protest the deployment of federal troops to help integrate Central High School in Little Rock, Arkansas. What really got Claude Williams riled up was the 1962 jailing of Birmingham reverends Fred Shuttlesworth and J. S. Phifer on an old charge of disorderly conduct for having integrated buses in 1958—a pretext not so far removed from his 1935 arrest on barratry charges. Williams knew first hand the value of support during times like this and appealed to his fellow clergy to help the civil rights preachers; he was rebuffed with excuses. If "pastors here can't do or say anything about this case" then "they themselves are only in the outer court of the same jail," Williams declared, and they served only as a "decorated guard to protect the status quo and give it respectability." A year later in his "Letter From a Birmingham Jail," Martin Luther King Jr. would make a similar argument "to dear fellow clergymen" about how those who chose not to protest evil were complicit in it. In 1962 national pressure from King's Southern Christian Leadership Conference helped free Shuttlesworth and Phifer on bail, an early victory in Birmingham, which would become a central battlefield for the civil rights movement in 1963.[48]

The Claude Williams Committee helped get him in touch with young activists involved in the struggle. In September 1961 James Aronson, Richard Mofford, and Willard Uphaus organized a benefit event for Williams in New York. The "tribute to Claude Williams" featured testimonials to the preacher as well as updates from him on conditions in the South. Pete Seeger entertained the audience with folk songs. "I'm one of these Yankees that got an education from the South," he explained in his tribute. "I learned music, but I learned a lot else . . . from Rev. Claude Williams, who has organized sharecroppers and done all kinds of brave things." Seeger implored others to contribute money so that Williams could keep going. "The South needs him, America needs him, the world needs him, in that job!" Seeger later encouraged Williams to write an article that explained the origins of well-known folk songs like "We Shall Not Be Moved" and "Roll the Union On." "Claude," Seeger explained, "it is very important that you do this. Every new generation that comes along must learn what the previous generations have done to fight for freedom." He pointed out that many of the songs he was singing, "I got from you." The problem was that the current generation "had never heard your name, had never heard of the UCAPAWA, or the STFU for that matter."[49]

Williams sought to change that generational ignorance. Throughout the early 1960s the Williamses got involved in Alabama civil rights struggles and offered their home as a way station for movement activists. Their main effort revolved around black voting rights. Alongside their ally Asbury Howard, a nationally known African American civil rights activist and organizer in Alabama for the International Union of Mine, Mill, and Smelter Workers, the Williamses helped organize and run the Bessemer Voters League. The league encouraged countywide voter registration and held classes to help train African Americans how to answer questions asked by white Alabama registrars under the Jim Crow "understanding clause," which had been de-signed in the 1890s as an easy way to rule blacks ineligible to vote. Due in part to the league's efforts from 1961 to 1964, registered black voters in the county increased from three hundred to six thousand. Later, the league ran a program called "Become a Leader as You Lead," which supported the call for Black Power by training local black workers to demand access to previously lily-white jobs.[50]

Claude and Joyce also educated white northern civil rights volunteers and sought to reform their "clipped Yankee approach." As Williams told Sally Belfrage, Cedric's daughter, whom he had baptized in a kitchen sink as a child, white students needed "to learn the rural cadence. Listen to a man's problems, [and] don't anticipate him with the answers." To educate these new activists, Williams traveled to Greenwood, Mississippi, during the Freedom Summer project in 1964 to address hundreds of civil rights workers in a mass meeting. "I have fought for 40 years, seen the inside of the best jails in Dixie, been flogged by some of the best Christians," he told them, "but in all this time I have never been so encouraged as I am seeing you people giving everything for the future that will come." In the years that followed Williams spoke in Alabama and Mississippi at "Freedom Revivals" and at meetings of an array of civil rights organizations. By the late 1960s and early 1970s, the Williamses even worked with a revived CP club in Alabama in the hopes that they could reach white "New Left" activists who Claude felt had become too sectarian and dismissive of the movement of the Depression years. During this period, the Williams home became "a refuge, a research center, a clearing house for exchange of ideas, an informal conference center, a training school

Figure 13. Claude and Joyce Williams in the 1970s. Source: Folder 2, Box 5, Belfrage Papers.

for all leaders." Far more important, however, was the opportunity to learn directly from Claude and Joyce Williams, who gave young people access to a complex history that was already all but lost to them. Increasingly, young historians, including Donald Grubbs, William Cobb, Louis Cantor, and Mark Naison, paid them visits to get first-hand testimonies about the history the Williamses had helped to create.[51]

For Williams the 1960s was both a "wonderful time" and a "terrible time." On the one hand, Williams returned to Detroit in 1965 to be reordained as a minister, this time in the Baptist Church. His old friend and ally Charles Hill had invited Claude and Joyce to his Hartford Avenue Baptist Church for the service. While Williams claimed that he "had no inclination to go naked just because the Presbyterians disrobed me" and that "I don't in my old age feel the need for the protection of that cloth," he still found in Hill's gesture an important moment of redemption.[52]

But in the midst all of this activity, Williams lost Owen Whitfield. After four years in Du Quoin, the Whitfields moved to Cape Girardeau, Missouri, where Owen continued to preach until 1961 when the family moved to Mounds, Illinois. The Whitfields lived there until Owen's death in August 1965.[53] "I was shocked to hear of Whit's death," Williams confided to Cedric Belfrage in the 1970s, "and grieved that I did not know of it at the time, and probably for years after it."[54] At a small memorial service, the Missouri State Conference of the NAACP honored the "grandfather of street demonstrations" at their 1965 convention in Cape Girardeau.[55] Aside from this local ceremony and obituaries in several newspapers, including the *New York Times*, Whitfield passed rather inconspicuously from the world.[56] When historian Louis Cantor contacted Williams in the mid-1960s about his research on the 1939 roadside demonstration, Williams was delighted. "I am interested that the Whitfield(s) get full credit for this historic work in which they were the sole movers. . . . We were close personal friends of the Whitfields," Williams declared, "and colleagues with them" in the struggle. Williams remembered Whitfield as "the most effective union organizer, the most effective speaker that I've ever seen or heard."[57]

Claude Williams outlived Owen Whitfield by fourteen years. He died in late June 1979, three years after Joyce had passed. His funeral was held at the Sixteenth Street Baptist Church in Birmingham, a sacred site in the struggle for civil rights. Bruce Maxwell, a student organizer who had worked with the Williamses in the 1960s, said in his eulogy that to him Williams sometimes seemed "almost a myth" in all that he accomplished. To this statement, Williams might have replied that he was not a myth but merely a man who, as Don West once wrote, "tastes life deep and hard."[58]

II

What kind of faith did Williams and Whitfield share? In their lives, they came to reject the dominant institutional iterations of Christian religion. They instead sought to "apply" religion, which suggested to some a pernicious manipulation of Christianity. But doubt, criticism, and analysis led them not to atheism but rather to a stronger faith galvanized by experience. Both preachers saw Christianity as a subject embedded in human history, as something conceived and interpreted by people who lived in the world, and they embraced it as a very real, powerful force. But Williams and Whitfield also knew that the power of religion was subject to the ways that people interpreted it. While the established churches tried to harness faith to the status quo and breakaway "new sect" churches looked to access religious power themselves, these two prophets worked on a way to give ordinary believers direct access to the spiritual knowledge that would enable them to make the Kingdom of God on earth. As Williams once explained, the process began with people loving the brothers and sisters they could see, before learning to love what they could not see. Theirs was a faith in the power of human love, work, and justice to attain all of what God had already provided in this world.[59]

This practical approach meant that Williams and Whitfield understood religion in terms of the struggles of workers. Experiences with socialists and communists, federal and state government officials, other religious thinkers, and rural and urban laborers provided them with a multitude of contexts with which to make sense of how race, class, gender, and culture were inextricably linked in earthly struggles for power. In their battle to defeat Jim Crow, Whitfield and Williams learned that the main battleground was in the heads and hands of the common people, whether they worked in cotton fields or factories or migrated between the two. No one had a better understanding of the contours of economic and social inequality than these workers. The way to convince them to fight was to communicate in a way that spoke to both the realism of their experience and the idealism of their hope. Applying the Marxist concept of dialectical materialism, for example, Williams thought about how "the Son of Man reasoned from the ground up . . . from the physical to the spiritual."[60] For Whitfield, there was no greater demonstration of faith than the expectation that hard work would make a difference. Whitfield and Williams successfully reached all types of workers, rural and urban, farm and factory, because they based their spiritual message on the dignity of labor as a devotion to God that earned them the right to demand justice. Elite attempts to strip people of the benefits of their work were contrary to Christian promise; the defense of the working class, both in and out of unions, was a moral obligation, a religious duty.

The partnership between Whitfield and Williams provided an answer to the biggest obstacle to workers' empowerment in America: race. Both men grew up on opposite sides of the color line in the South, but managed, through their faith in God and in humanity, to come together as activists. They argued that others should have more faith in ordinary people to overcome their received prejudices, as both of them had done. Williams stressed that liberals and others should not dismiss poor whites as "rednecks" but rather understand the social and political constraints that made them embrace Jim Crow: "Let [a white man] be out there sawing wood with a Negro and they'll like each other, talk and laugh, drink out of the same jug—but let another white man come along and the situation changes, because the man thinks the other white man believes what he is supposed to believe."[61] Williams, a former believer in white supremacy, knew this dynamic all too well.

Whitfield learned this lesson from his own relationship to black nationalism. He understood how hard it was for African Americans to trust white people. It would not happen overnight. Zella Whitfield liked to tell a story about a time her father was putting a new roof on their house. When called for dinner, his foot scaffold broke loose and he began to fall. Just as he began to tumble through the air, however, his brother hollered, "Look out! You're falling on a white woman!" Well, Zella explained, her father turned right around in mid-air and went back up onto the roof. This story, Williams would later recall, painted "a profound picture of 400 years of terror."[62] Both Williams and Whitfield found a personal solution to the social and psychological trauma that was the legacy of American racism. Neither man believed that working-class whites or blacks in the South needed to abolish their cultural heritage. Rather, the two preachers believed that southerners needed to transform that heritage. Understanding Whitfield's progress as a thinker and activist in this way provides us with greater historical insight into the activism of so many rural black churches in the 1960s civil rights movement. Both Whitfield and Williams saw beauty in forms of marginalized cultures that others dismissed as primitive or backward. These despised cultures, just like despised people, represented the "saving remnant," the raw ingredients for a movement to make the South and then the nation anew.

Williams and Whitfield could have realized nothing of this vision without the contributions of women who devoted themselves to the working-class gospel. Female activists, intellectuals, and preachers served as central pillars in every group Claude and Owen led, whether the New Era School, the STFU, Commonwealth College, Cropperville, or the PIAR. None stood taller or stronger than Joyce and Zella, whose own careers proved remarkable at a time when most women did not participate fully in public life, let alone stand to lead labor unions and preach against Jim Crow. Although Claude and Owen did not totally escape the dominant gender roles in society, they did respect women as equals in the struggle to make the world a more democratic place. The loyalty of comrades such as Winifred Chappell, Fannie Cook, Hattie Walls, Charlotte Moskowitz, Theodosia Simpson, and numerous others who led STFU and UCAPAWA locals provided testimony to the power of applied religion to challenge inequalities of gender, as well as race and class.

Far from a stable or singular ideology, these ideas were constantly reassessed by Whitfield and Williams to blaze a path for activists who shared their belief in a more democratic nation. Williams once suggested that preachers should take the Bible and underline in red pencil "all worthy passages" and in black pencil all passages that would "defeat or confuse."[63] Sure of the destination but not the route, their experience shaped and reshaped their teachings. Whitfield did this by reworking and retelling allegorical parables that translated actual events into folk wisdom laden with common sense. In the 1940s, for example, he retold the history of Missouri organizing campaigns by omitting the vital STFU efforts that supported his activism. Many times he took sole credit for victories that others helped create, including giving Williams little credit for his conversion to a working-class gospel. While partly a product of robust self-regard, these distortions were also part of a creative process of building politically usable collective memories. Artistic inaccuracy had its benefits, as Williams would later admit: "Over the years I've long since learned that to be exclusively right is to be wholly wrong."[64]

Some, of course, argued that neither Williams nor Whitfield ever learned this lesson. Always ready to sacrifice personal alliances in pursuit of the pure path, both men accumulated an impressive roster of enemies in their lives that included conservatives, liberals, communists, socialists, and the U.S. government. Dismissed often as fanatics, heretics, zealots, stooges, or worse, both men acted in fidelity to their own ideals and convictions, even if it meant expulsion, arrest, or the vulnerability of their families. What they called faith could look like rampant hubris, a fact that constantly troubled and ultimately limited their careers.

That faith, which allowed Whitfield and Williams to see the divine in the despised and downcast, and to make others see it too, also proved the pair's most powerful asset. Indeed, Cedric Belfrage's recollection about Williams also applied to Whitfield: "His magnificently earthy sense of humor which was never far below the surface" showed his "love for ordinary people," which allowed him to combat a "hypocritical world" and act "on his convictions, wherever they may lead."[65] And according to Williams, Whitfield's "pro-foundness and his realism" were the traits that made him so effective as an activist. "It was," he said, "shocking to all middle-class persons who come in contact with him and was devastating to the opposition."[66] Their attempts to empower ordinary people to fight for social and economic justice and claim the redemptive, democratic promises of the American political tradition should give us pause. The pathogenic, divisive aspects of American life that Williams and Whitfield fought against, at great odds and with terrible risks, are still around us: inequality, poverty, and the reactionary interpretation of evangelical Christianity. Both preachers realized that moral protest movements in American history are usually unfinished ones. As far as epitaphs go, Whitfield supplied the best one in his November 1945 report to the PIAR when he cited 2 Timothy 4:7: "I have fought a good fight, I have finished my course, I have kept the faith."

Notes

Introduction: Brothers in the Fight for Freedom

1. Claude Williams, "Diary: Record," 19, Folder 2, Box 16, Williams Papers, Wayne State University.

2. Owen Whitfield quoted in Belfrage, "Cotton-Patch Moses," 97.

3. "Brothers in the Fight for Freedom," PIAR pamphlet, n.d. [1944], 11, Folder, 1, Box 19, Williams Papers.

4. In recent years historians have paid more attention to the role of religious institutions in social movements, including labor unions, but not necessarily religious ideas and beliefs. For the best examples, see Honey, *Southern Labor and Black Civil Rights*, 71; Korstad, *Civil Rights Unionism*, 30–31; Craig, *Religion and Radical Politics*, 130–73; Fannin, *Labor's Promised Land*, 288–300; Woodruff, *American Congo*, 4–7; De Jong, *A Different Day*, 53–54; Gilmore, *Defying Dixie*, 4–7, 15–24; Kelley, *Hammer and Hoe*, 228–31; and Rolinson, *Grassroots Garveyism*, 21–23, 192–96. Charles Payne's *I've Got the Light of Freedom* does this for the later period. Most scholars of the New Deal era, by contrast, have focused on the conservative or reactionary religious thought of preachers like Father Charles Coughlin or Reverend Gerald L. K. Smith. See, for example, Jeansonne, *Gerald L. K. Smith*; and Brinkley, *Voices of Protest*.

5. This study builds on excellent recent scholarship on social movements in the South and the urban North. See Korstad, *Civil Rights Unionism*; Phillips, *AlabamaNorth*; Woodruff, *American Congo*; De Jong, *A Different Day*; Honey, *Southern Labor and Black Civil Rights*; Sullivan, *Days of Hope*; Gilmore, *Defying Dixie*; and Kelley, *Hammer and Hoe*.

6. Belfrage, *South of God*, 116.

7. Accounts such as Korstad, *Civil Rights Unionism*; Gilmore, *Defying Dixie*; Kelley, *Hammer and Hoe*; Sullivan, *Days of Hope*; and Honey, *Southern Labor and Black Civil Rights*, all touch on how southerners interpreted unionism and politics through the traditional inheritance and collective memory that gave meaning to their lives, but none of them focus on religion as the basis of that inheritance. One important exception, although it deals more with religion than social activism, is Harvey, *Freedom's Coming*. See also Roll, *Spirit of Rebellion*.

8. For examples of excellent studies that focus on movements of either blacks or whites, see Green, *Grass-Roots Socialism*; Rolinson, *Grassroots Garveyism*; Kelley, *Hammer and Hoe*; Gilmore, *Defying Dixie*; and Anthony Dunbar, *Against the Grain*.

9. Few historians have credited this aspect of southern Christianity after 1900, especially among whites. See Creech, *Righteous Indignation*, xxvii–xxviii; Harvey, *Redeeming the South*, 86–88, 206–26; and Chappell, *A Stone of Hope*.

10. We support Timothy Tyson's case for biography: "The thing that makes any biography worth writing or worth reading . . . is the way that a single human life can speak to the transformation of the world and to our battle against determinism and disdain" (Tyson, "Robert F. Williams and the Promise of Southern Biography," 38–52, quote p. 51). This study is deeply indebted to earlier work on Williams and Whitfield, including Anthony Dunbar, *Against the Grain*; Grubbs, *Cry from the Cotton*; Cantor, *A Prologue to the Protest Movement*; Lorence, *A Hard Journey*; Craig, *Religion and Radical Politics*; Harvey, *Freedom's Coming*; Mark Naison's articles and manuscripts; and, most important, Cedric Belfrage's body of research and writing.

11. This book contributes to the scholarship on the long civil rights movement by cutting across a range of historical categories. It also reveals a neglected chronology of events that places new emphasis on the activism of the 1930s and 1940s as the culmination of movements building since the late nineteenth century, and shows the limits of discussing this period as a "seedbed" for the later Civil Rights Movement. Jacquelyn Hall wrote that historians must "make ourselves heard without reducing history to formulaic mantras" by showing both "individual agency" and the "hidden history of institutions." This book responds to her call for "novel forms of storytelling [that] convey what it means to have lived through an undefeated but unfinished revolution." See Hall, "The Long Civil Rights Movement," 1262–63.

Chapter 1: Southern Strivings

1. Manuscript pages II 11–12, Folder 2, Box 26, Belfrage Papers, Tamiment Library, New York University.

2. Note 71, Folder 2, Box 26, Belfrage Papers.

3. "Owen Hones Whitfield," July 5, 1917, Registration Card, Poinsett County, Arkansas Draft Board, Roll 1530571, accessed on www.ancestry.com; "Reverend Owen H. Whitfield, with aliases," report made at St. Louis, Mo., October 19, 1942, File 100-1194, FBI Records—1083786; "Deaths: Rev. Owen H. Whitfield," August 11, 1965, Folder 11, Box 26, Belfrage Papers; "Rev. Owen Whitfield, Led Sharecroppers' '39 Protest," *New York Times*, August 13, 1965.

4. "Owen Hones Whitfield," July 5, 1917, Registration Card, Poinsett County, Arkansas Draft Board, Roll 1530571, accessed on www.ancestry.com.

5. U.S. Bureau of the Census, Manuscript Census Schedules, 1900 ("Jane Whitfield," Fourth Beat, Aberdeen precincts, Monroe County, Mississippi); 1870 ("Thomas Whitfield," Township 14, Monroe County, Mississippi); Owen Whitfield, "Birth Data," report made at Springfield, Ill., January 30, 1953, File 100-36331-53, FBI Records—1083786.

6. Jacqueline Jones, *Labor of Love, Labor of Sorrow*, 86–88; Woodward, *Origins of the New South*, 264–72.

7. Jacqueline Jones, *Labor of Love, Labor of Sorrow,* 79–109; Rosengarten, *All God's Dangers,* 8–15.

8. Foner, *A Short History of Reconstruction,* 104–47; Hahn, *A Nation under Our Feet,* 242–43.

9. Hahn, *A Nation under Our Feet,* 275–76, 288–89.

10. McMillen, *Dark Journey,* 1–32, 38–48 (Vardaman quote p. 43).

11. Schweninger, *Black Property Owners in the South,* 143–237.

12. McMillen, *Dark Journey,* 111–16; Schweninger, *Black Property Owners in the South,* 161–66; Sitton and Conrad, *Freedom Colonies,* 3–4, 61–62; Note 71, Folder 2, Box 26, Belfrage Papers (quote).

13. Schweninger, *Black Property Owners in the South,* 162–66; Sitton and Conrad, *Freedom Colonies,* 4–28.

14. James Cobb, *The Most Southern Place on Earth,* 69–124; Notes 70a and 71, Folder 2, Box 26, Belfrage Papers.

15. McMillen, *Dark Journey,* 232.

16. Vardaman quoted in McMillen, *Dark Journey,* 224; Litwack, *Trouble in Mind,* 206–16.

17. Manuscript pages II 2–3, Folder 2, Box 26, Belfrage Papers (quotes).

18. On the two-ness of African American life, see Du Bois, *The Souls of Black Folk.*

19. Manuscript pages II 3–4, Folder 2, Box 26, Belfrage Papers; Jacqueline Jones, *Labor of Love, Labor of Sorrow,* 102 (quotes).

20. Note 71, Folder 2, Box 26, Belfrage Papers (quotes).

21. Note 70a, Folder 2, Box 26, Belfrage Papers; Litwack, *Trouble in Mind,* 10–11, 208–9.

22. Manuscript pages II 3–5 and Note 70a, Folder 2, Box 26, Belfrage Papers; McMillen, *Dark Journey,* 142.

23. Note 141, Folder 4, Box 26, Belfrage Papers.

24. Woodruff, *American Congo,* 8–37.

25. Manuscript pages II 7–9, Note 71, both in Folder 2, and Note 141, Folder 4, all in Box 26, Belfrage Papers; Gellman and Roll, "Owen Whitfield," 306–7.

26. Manuscript page II 10 (quote) and Note 83a, both in Folder 2, Box 26, Belfrage Papers.

27. Note 144, Folder 4, Box 26, Belfrage Papers (quote); Schultz, *The Rural Face of White Supremacy,* 43–44, 52–53.

28. Ritterhouse, *Growing Up Jim Crow,* 205–10.

29. Manuscript pages II 11–12 (quotes), Folder 2, Box 26, Belfrage Papers.

30. Note 74 and Manuscript page II 12, both in Folder 2, Box 26, Belfrage Papers.

31. Manuscript page II 11, Folder 2, Box 26, Belfrage Papers; McMillen, *Dark Journey,* 72–83 (quote p. 72).

32. "Fourth Annual Exhibit and Commencement, 1905–6," and G. W. Cable to Wallace Battle, March 23, 1912, both in Folder 844, Okolona Papers, The General Education Board Archives.

33. McMillen, *Dark Journey,* 94.

34. Wallace Battle to Robert C. Ogden, June 6, 1904 (first quote), Trustees and friends of Okolona Industrial College to General Education Board, April 14, 1911 (last quote), and G. W. Cable to Wallace Battle, March 23, 1912, all in Folder 844, Okolona Papers; Charles H. Wilson, *Education for Negroes in Mississippi since 1910,* 458–59.

35. Royal Raymond to Wallace Buttrick, January 31, 1906 (first quote), and LeRoy Percy

to Mark Denman, August 22, 1912 (final quotes), both in Folder 844, Okolona Papers; McMillen, *Dark Journey,* 72 (second quote), 89–94.

36. Trustees and friends of Okolona Industrial College to General Education Board, April 14, 1911, Folder 844, Okolona Papers (quotes).

37. Royal Raymond to Wallace Buttrick, January 31, 1906, Folder 844, Okolona Papers (quote).

38. Note 76, Folder 2, Box 26, Belfrage Papers.

39. Note 70, Folder 2, Box 26, Belfrage Papers; Jacqueline Jones, *Labor of Love, Labor of Sorrow,* 90.

40. Notes 76–80, Folder 2, Box 26, Belfrage Papers.

41. Notes 80, 81 (quotes), and 82, all in Folder 2, Box 26, Belfrage Papers.

42. Notes 82 and 83, Folder 2, and Note 146, Folder 4, all in Box 26, and "W's Children," Folder 8, Box 25, all Belfrage Papers.

43. Note 146, Folder 4, Box 26, Belfrage Papers; Woodruff, *American Congo,* 47–50, 59 (final quote).

44. Note 146, Folder 4, Box 26, Belfrage Papers; U.S. Bureau of the Census, *Statistical Abstract of the United States: 1919,* 158–61, 574.

45. Note 146, Folder 4, Box 26, Belfrage Papers (quote); Woodruff, "African American Struggles for Citizenship," 36–37.

46. Note 146, Folder 4, Box 26, Belfrage Papers; Woodruff, *American Congo,* 80–91 (quote p. 86).

47. Note 146, Folder 4, Box 26, Belfrage Papers; Grim, "African American Landlords in the Rural South," 405 (quote); Sitton and Conrad, *Freedom Colonies,* 61–64.

48. Foner, *A Short History of Reconstruction,* 104–79.

49. Foner, *A Short History of Reconstruction,* 117, 146.

50. Belfrage, *Let My People Go,* 8 (quotes); Foner, *A Short History of Reconstruction,* 184–98; Lester, *Up From the Mudsills of Hell,* 75.

51. Belfrage, *Let My People Go,* 6–7.

52. Belfrage, *Let My People Go,* 5–7 (quotes p. 7).

53. Belfrage, *Let My People Go,* 9; Boles, *The Great Revival,* 135, 159–63; Morrow, "Cumberland Presbyterian Theology," 203–05 (first quote p. 204, second quote p. 205); "Cumberland Presbyterian Church," in Hill, *Encyclopedia of Religion in the South,* 188–89.

54. Morrow, "Cumberland Presbyterian Theology," 220 (quote).

55. Belfrage, *Let My People Go,* 9–10.

56. Belfrage, *Let My People Go,* 10–11; Lester, *Up From the Mudsills of Hell,* 18–29.

57. Lester, *Up From the Mudsills of Hell,* 27–33 (planter quote p. 33); Belfrage, *Let My People Go,* 8.

58. Lester, *Up From the Mudsills of Hell,* 59–238.

59. Waldrep, *Night Riders,* 63–139.

60. Vanderwood, *Night Riders of Reelfoot Lake,* vi, 15–59; Lester, *Up From the Mudsills of Hell,* 217–31.

61. Belfrage, *Let My People Go,* 15–16 (quote p. 16).

62. Belfrage, *Let My People Go,* 14–17 (quote p. 16).

63. Belfrage, *Let My People Go,* 18–20.

64. John B. Wilson, *Maneuver and Firepower,* 98; Striffler and Moberg, *Banana Wars.*

65. Williams to M. L. Gillespie, November 9, 1933, Folder 5, Box 1, Williams Papers, Wayne State University.

66. Belfrage, *Let My People Go,* 22.

67. "Claude Clossey Williams, Cumberland Presbyterian Licentiate, 1921–1923."

68. Claude Williams, Bethel College Transcript, Folder 1, Box 1, Williams Papers; "History of Bethel College"; David E. Harrell, Jr., "Tennessee," in Hill, *Religion in the Southern States,* 305.

69. Belfrage, *Let My People Go,* 25–27; Carpenter, *Revive Us Again,* 43–49.

70. Belfrage, *Let My People Go,* 26–27; Craig, *Religion and Radical Politics,* 145; Claude Williams and Joyce King, May 16, 1922, Carroll County, Tennessee State Marriages, 1780–2002, accessed on www.ancestry.com.

71. Belfrage, *Let My People Go,* 25–30; Claude Williams, Bethel College Transcript, Folder 1, Box 1, Williams Papers.

72. "Claude Clossey Williams, Cumberland Presbyterian Licentiate, 1921–1923" (all quotes).

73. Williams quoted in Naison, "Claude and Joyce Williams," 39.

74. Belfrage, *Let My People Go,* 28–30; "Claude Clossey Williams, Cumberland Presbyterian Licentiate, 1921–1923" (quote).

75. Belfrage, *Let My People Go,* 30–32; Naison, "Claude and Joyce Williams," 39 (last quote); Claude Williams, "A Minister's Choice," n.d. [1940s] (first two quotes), Folder 3, Box 23, Williams Papers.

76. Naison, "Claude and Joyce Williams," 39 (first quote); Belfrage, *Let My People Go,* 41 (third quote), 48–49 (second and fourth quotes).

77. Belfrage, *Let My People Go,* 39 (quotes); "Claude Clossey Williams, Cumberland Presbyterian Licentiate, 1921–1923"; Glass, *Strangers in Zion,* 1–6, 26–27; Carpenter, *Revive Us Again,* 3–12, 124–25.

78. Belfrage, *Let My People Go,* 35–37.

79. Naison, "Claude and Joyce Williams," 40; Belfrage, *Let My People Go,* 39–40.

80. James O. Duffey, Moody Bible Institute, Chicago, to Thomas E. Bryant, Lebanon, Tennessee, August 31, 1927, Folder 1, Box 1, Williams Papers; Carpenter, *Revive Us Again,* 17–18; Glass, *Strangers in Zion,* 35–36 (quote), 57–58; "History of Moody Bible Institute."

81. Craig, *Religion and Radical Politics,* 145; Belfrage, *Let My People Go,* 52.

82. Fosdick, *The Modern Use of the Bible,* 3 (first quote), 110 (second quote), 196 (third and fourth quotes), 201–3 (fifth quote p. 201), and 268 (sixth quote).

83. Belfrage, *Let My People Go,* 52–53; Fosdick, *The Modern Use of the Bible,* 167 (final quote).

84. Anthony Dunbar, *Against the Grain,* 28–29 (first quote); Kloppenberg, *Uncertain Victory,* 207–8; Belfrage, *Let My People Go,* 54–55 (third quote); Egerton, *Speak Now against the Day,* 26 (second quote), 77–78.

85. Belfrage, *Let My People Go,* 54–55 (final quotes); Troy and Williams, "People's Institute of Applied Religion," 47; Craig, *Religion and Radical Politics,* 145 (first quote).

86. Belfrage, *Let My People Go,* 38, 55–56; U.S. Bureau of the Census, Manuscript Census Schedules, 1930 ("Claude C. Williams," Watertown City, District 16, Wilson County, Tennessee).

87. Anthony Dunbar, *Against the Grain,* 28–31; Lorence, *A Hard Journey,* 19–22; Martin,

Howard Kester and the Struggle for Social Justice in the South, 1–86; Naison, "Claude and Joyce Williams," 40 (final quote); Twelve Southerners, *I'll Take My Stand,* xli–lii (first four quotes p. xlii).

88. Martin, *Howard Kester and the Struggle for Social Justice in the South,* 17–40; Adams with Horton, *Unearthing Seeds of Fire,* 7–16.

89. Anthony Dunbar, *Against the Grain,* 33 (Kester quote); Belfrage, *Let My People Go,* 72–74.

90. Belfrage, *Let My People Go,* 56 (second quote), 64 (fourth quote); Williams to Robert Snyder, 1975 (first and third quotes), Folder 12, Box 15, Williams Papers.

91. Belfrage, *Let My People Go,* 75–80 (quote p. 77); Naison, "Claude and Joyce Williams," 41.

92. A. S. Hulit, Charleston, Missouri, to Governor A. M. Hyde, Jefferson City, December 16, 1922 (quote), Folder 106, Hyde Papers, WHMC, University of Missouri, Columbia; Roll, *Spirit of Rebellion,* 11–62.

93. Roll, *Spirit of Rebellion,* 52–62.

94. All quotations from the *Sikeston Standard*: "Negro Farmers Being Intimidated," January 12, 1923 (final quote); "What Class Shall Run Southeast Missouri," January 19, 1923 (first quote); "Editorial," January 19, 1923 (second and third quotes).

95. Marcus Garvey speech, January 1924, quoted in Wintz, *African American Political Thought, 1890–1930,* 234.

96. "U.N.I.A., Nearing the Greatest World Conference of Race, Calls upon Negroes Everywhere to Rise Up and Be Men," *Negro World,* April 27, 1929 (quotes).

97. Hill and Bair, *The Marcus Garvey and Universal Negro Improvement Association Papers,* 7:986–96; and Rolinson, *Grassroots Garveyism,* 197–99.

98. Rolinson, *Grassroots Garveyism,* 8, 47; Whitfield family, oral history, November 14, 1982, Audio Cassette "Tom," Side A, Box 107, Oral History 500, Tamiment Library, New York University.

99. "Thousands of Negroes Driven from a Missouri Town in America," *Negro World,* March 10, 1923.

100. Royal Raymond to Wallace Buttrick, January 31, 1906, Folder 844, Okolona Papers.

101. Garvey quoted in Burkett, *Garveyism as a Religious Movement,* 49 (quote), 59.

102. "Wyatt, Mo.," *Negro World,* December 8, 1928.

103. Whitfield family, oral history, November 14, 1982, Audio Cassette "Tom," Side A, Box 107, Oral History 500.

104. Burkett, *Garveyism as a Religious Movement,* 5–33.

105. Whitfield family, oral history, November 14, 1982, Audio Cassette "Tom," Side A, Box 107, Oral History 500.

106. Harvey, *Freedom's Coming,* 114–20, 142; Giggie, *After Redemption,* 180.

107. Note 146, Folder 4, Box 26, Belfrage Papers; Whitfield family, oral history, November 14, 1982, Audio Cassette "Tom," Side A, Box 107, Oral History 500; "Proceedings of Fourth International Convention," *Negro World,* August 16, 1924 (quote).

108. Note 147, Folder 8, Box 25, and Note 146, Folder 4, Box 26, both in Belfrage Papers.

109. Note 146 (quote), and Manuscript page VI 3, both in Folder 4, Box 26, Belfrage Papers; U.S. Bureau of the Census, *Statistical Abstract of the United States: 1926,* 635.

110. "Flood May Be Blessing in Disguise," *New Madrid Weekly Record,* May 6, 1927.

111. Note 158, Folder 8, Box 25, Belfrage Papers; Roll, *Spirit of Rebellion,* 71–75; Spencer, "Contested Terrain," 170–81; Rolinson, *Grassroots Garveyism,* 181–82.

112. Note 146, Folder 4, Box 26, Belfrage Papers.

113. Tindall, *The Emergence of the New South,* 354–72; Note 147, Folder 8, Box 25, Belfrage Papers.

114. Roll, *Spirit of Rebellion,* 75–81; Note 146, Folder 4, Box 26, and Note 147, Folder 8, Box 25, both in Belfrage Papers.

115. Bright, "Farm Wage Workers in Four Southeast Missouri Cotton-Producing Counties," 204–5; "The Church," Project Notes, 1 (quote), 11–12, Report File on the Southeast Missouri Study, 1937, Entry 52, FHA Records, NARA, Great Lakes.

116. Giggie, *After Redemption,* 166.

117. Church listings, Folder 6915, Reel 262, Folder 6941, Reel 263, Folder 13980, Reel 459, and Folder 16197, Reel 528, all in Works Progress Administration—Historical Records Survey, C3551, WHMC, Columbia; Harvey, *Freedom's Coming,* 142–48.

118. "The Church," Project Notes, 12, Report File on the Southeast Missouri Study, 1937, Entry 52, FHA Records, NARA, Great Lakes.

119. Note 146, Folder 4, Box 26, and Note 147, Folder 8, Box 25, both in Belfrage Papers.

120. "Reverend Owen H. Whitfield," FBI report made at St. Louis, Mo., October 19, 1942, File 100-1194, FBI Records—1083786.

121. Note 146, Folder 4, Box 26, Belfrage Papers; Roll, *Spirit of Rebellion,* 75–95.

122. Note 147, Folder 8, Box 25, Belfrage Papers; Wright, *Old South, New South,* 228–32.

123. Owen Whitfield quoted in Naison, "Claude Williams Talks about Owen Whitfield," 24.

124. Evanzz, *The Messenger,* 108–10 (quote p. 108); Gallicchio, *The African American Encounter with Japan and China,* 95–101; Allen, "Waiting for Tojo," 18–22.

125. "Sikeston among Towns Organized by Negro 'Benevolent' Order," Folder 20, Box FC 3.1, Clippings Collection, 1871–2001, KL; "OAPMOTW," *Charleston Spokesman,* August 18, 1934; "Local Negro Organizer in Court Battle," *Charleston Enterprise-Courier,* August 23, 1934.

126. "Sikeston among Towns Organized by Negro 'Benevolent' Order," Folder 20, Box FC 3.1, Clippings Collection, KL (first quote), Southeast Missouri State University; "OAPMOTW," *Charleston Spokesman,* August 18, 1934; "Local Negro Organizer in Court Battle," *Charleston Enterprise-Courier,* August 23, 1934; Owen Whitfield quoted in *St. Louis Post-Dispatch,* March 6, 1942 (second, third, and fourth quotes).

127. Roll, *Spirit of Rebellion,* 90–95; Whitfield quoted in *St. Louis Post-Dispatch,* March 6, 1942; Note 143, Folder 8, Box 26, Belfrage Papers; H. L. Mitchell to David Burgess, n.d. [1945], Reel 31, STFU Papers.

128. Note 146, Folder 4, Box 26, Belfrage Papers.

129. Note 146, Folder 4, Box 26, Belfrage Papers; U.S. Bureau of the Census, *Fifteenth Census of the United States,* 1380.

130. Grubbs, *Cry from the Cotton,* 47, 84–86, 94–95; Fannin, *Labor's Promised Land,* 94–112.

131. Roll, *Spirit of Rebellion,* 95–102.

132. John Handcox to H. L. Mitchell, September 16, 1936, Reel 3, STFU Papers; Whitfield quoted in Naison, "Black Agrarian Radicalism in the Great Depression," 58–59 (quote p. 59).

Chapter 2: Seeking the Kingdom of God

1. Belfrage, *Let My People Go,* 78–85 (quote p.78).

2. Claude Williams, "Diary: Sketches from the Paris Pastorate," 1–2 (first and second quotes), Folder 1, and Willard Uphaus, "A Foul Miscarriage of Justice," 1 (final quote), Folder 5, both in Box 16, Williams Papers, Wayne State University.

3. Claude Williams, "Open Forum: A Congenial Discussion of the Amusement Problem," n.d. [1932], *Paris Express,* Folder 8, Box 16, Williams Papers.

4. Bevis, "Rocky Point," 78–97.

5. Williams, "Diary: Sketches," 4 (quotes), Folder 1, and Uphaus, "A Foul Miscarriage of Justice," 1–2, Folder 5, both in Box 16, Williams Papers.

6. Norman Thomas to Williams, September 22, 1931, Folder 2, and The Fellowship of Reconciliation to Williams, February 17, 1932, Folder 3, both in Box 1, Williams Papers.

7. Williams, "Diary: Sketches," 3 (first quote), Folder 1, Box 16, Williams Papers; Belfrage, *Let My People Go,* 94 (second quote); Davis, "Not Marriage at All, but Simple Harlotry," 1137–38.

8. Belfrage, *Let My People Go,* 91 (first three quotes); Claude Williams, "Open Forum: A Congenial Discussion of the Marriage Problem," n.d. [1932], *Paris Express,* Folder 8, Box 16, and M. L. Gillespie to Williams, July 28, 1932 (final quote), Folder 4, Box 1, both in Williams Papers.

9. Miners' quotes in Uphaus, "A Foul Miscarriage of Justice," 8–10, Folder 5, Box 16, Williams Papers.

10. Warren Wilson quoted in Gillespie to Williams, September 26, 1932, Folder 4, Box 1, Williams Papers.

11. Uphaus, "A Foul Miscarriage of Justice," 8–11, Folder 5, and Williams, "Open Forum: New Battle Fronts," and "Open Forum: Do You Know," n.d. [1932–33], *Paris Express,* both in Folder 8, all in Box 16, Williams Papers; Belfrage, *Let My People Go,* 151–55.

12. Fred Arthur Bailey, "That Which God Hath Put Asunder: White Baptists, Black Aliens, and the Southern Social Order, 1890–1920," in Feldman, *Politics and Religion in the White South,* 12.

13. Williams to Alva Taylor, October 7, 1932, Folder 4, Box 1, Williams Papers.

14. Green, *Grass-Roots Socialism,* 193–96, 283–86, 291 (quote p. 284); Fred Dunbar, "Coal Mining Strikes"; Dubofsky and Van Tine, *John L. Lewis,* 108–9.

15. Howard Kester to Williams, February 16, 1932 (quotes), Folder 3, Box 1, Williams Papers; Adams with Horton, *Unearthing Seeds of Fire,* 25–53; oral history interview with Don West, January 22, 1975, interview E-0016, Southern Oral History Collection, Wilson Library, University of North Carolina.

16. Williams, "Diary: Sketches," 5–6, Folder 1, and Uphaus, "A Foul Miscarriage of Justice," 3–4, Folder 5, both in Box 16, Williams Papers.

17. William Cobb, *Radical Education in the Rural South,* 42–109; Cunningham and Friesen, *Red Dust and Broadsides,* 112–13, 129; Belfrage, *A Faith to Free the People,* 92–94; Lorence, *A Hard Journey,* 26, 30, 63; Williams, "Diary: Record of Activities," Folder 2, Box 16, Williams Papers; "1932 Presidential Election Results, Arkansas."

18. Williams to Taylor, October 31, 1932, and Taylor to Williams, November 5, 1932 (quotes), both in Folder 4, Box 1, Williams Papers; Belfrage, *Let My People Go,* 122–23.

19. W. A. Gilbert to Williams, November 11, 1932, Folder 4, Box 1, and "A Proletarian

Church in Arkansas," *Economic Justice*, December 1932, Folder 6, Box 16, both in Williams Papers.

20. Williams to Taylor, October 31, 1932, Folder 4, Box 1, Williams Papers.

21. "The Proletarian Church and Labor Temple," 2, Folder 6, Box 16, Williams Papers.

22. "The Proletarian Church and Labor Temple," 5 (first and second quotes), and "A Proletarian Church in Arkansas," *Economic Justice*, December 1932, both in Folder 6, Box 16, Williams Papers.

23. Belfrage, *South of God*, 116.

24. Fosdick, *The Modern Use of the Bible*, 196.

25. Williams to Taylor, October 7, 1932, Folder 4, Box 1, Williams Papers.

26. M. L. Gillespie to Williams, November 17, 1932, Folder 4, Box 1, Williams Papers.

27. David Fowler to Claude Williams, December 21, 1932 (all quotes), Folder 25, Box 98.2, UMW Papers, Pennsylvania State University; "David Fowler," *Muskogee Phoenix*, January 30, 1970; Egerton, *Speak Now against the Day*, 72–73.

28. David Fowler to R. F. White, December 21, 1932 (first and second quotes), Folder 14, Box 16, Williams Papers; Fowler to Lewis, December 28, 1932 (third quote), Folder 25, Box 98.2, UMW Papers.

29. Belfrage, *Let My People Go*, 162–67.

30. Claude Speegle, "Annual Report of the State Mine Inspector," 1930, Folder 13, and Williams, "Diary: Sketches," 6, Folder 1, both in Box 16, Williams Papers.

31. Williams, "Diary: Sketches," 7, Folder 1, Box 16, Williams Papers.

32. Williams, "Diary Sketches," 8, Folder 1, Box 16, Williams Papers.

33. Williams, "Diary: Sketches," 7–8 (quote p. 8), Folder 1, Box 16, Williams Papers.

34. Williams, "Diary: Sketches," 8–9, Folder 1, Box 16, Williams Papers.

35. Fowler to John Lewis, August 14, 1932 (quote), Folder 9, Box 98.2, UMW Papers; "1932 Presidential Election Results, Arkansas."

36. Committee of 12, "Report on Autonomy Movement," November 17, 1933, and "Report of Miner's Convention Held in Fort Smith," November 29, 1933, both in Folder 14, and Signed Autonomy Declarations by Union Locals, Folder 15, all in Box 16, Williams Papers.

37. Official Ballot, UMWA election held March 27, 1934, Folder 15, National Recovery Administration, Divisional Labor Board #4 (Kansas City), Case 11, Decision 8, January 4, 1934, Folder 13, and National Recovery Administration, Divisional Labor Board #4, Case 252, Decision 204, September 18, 1934, Folder 15, all in Box 16, Williams Papers.

38. Dubofsky and Van Tine, *John L. Lewis*, 131–36; Alinsky, *John L. Lewis*, 65–72.

39. Fowler, G. E. Mikel, and John Saxton, to all District 21 members, April 26, 1933, Folder 17, Box 98.2, UMW Papers (second quote); David Fowler to the "Few Misinformed Delegates," December 8, 1933, Folder 14, "Organizational Structure to Strengthen the Autonomy Movement and Supplementary Notes," n.d. [1933], Folder 13, and Williams, "Diary: Sketches," 9 (first quote), Folder 1, all in Box 16, Williams Papers.

40. NRA Divisional Labor Board #4, March 7, 1934 (first quote), Folder 28, Box 98.2, UMW Papers; David Fowler to Bert Loudermilk, March 5, 1934, and Fred Howell to UMW District 21 members, March 22, 1934 (final quote), both in Folder 15, Box 16, Williams Papers.

41. Williams to Helen Ridick Wilson, Emergency Relief Director, September 10, 1933 (first quote), Gillespie to Williams, September 29, 1933 (second quote), and Williams to Gillespie, November 9, 1933 (final quotes), all in Folder 5, Box 1, Williams Papers.

42. Williams to Gillespie, November 9, 1933, Folder 5, Box 1, Williams Papers.

43. Uphaus, "A Foul Miscarriage of Justice," 3–5, Folder 5, and Williams, "Diary: Sketches," 10–11, Folder 1, both in Box 16, Williams Papers; Anthony Dunbar, *Against the Grain,* 30–32, 70.

44. Williams to Warren Wilson, April 20, 1934, Folder 6, Box 1, Williams Papers.

45. Belfrage, *South of God,* 149–50 (fourth quote); "Religion: Church v. Council," *Time Magazine,* June 6, 1932; M. L. Gillespie quoted in Warren Wilson to Williams, September 26, 1932 (first quote), Folder 4, Gillespie to Williams, January 31, 1933, and Wilson to Williams, November 13, 1933 (second quote), both in Folder 5, and Wilson to Williams, April 24, 1934 (third quote), Folder 6, all in Box 1, Williams Papers.

46. Uphaus, "A Foul Miscarriage of Justice," 4–6, Folder 5, and Williams, "Diary: Sketches," 11–12, Folder 1, both in Box 16, and Williams to Roy E. Burt, April 27, 1934 (quote), Folder 6, Box 1, Williams Papers.

47. Williams to Roy E. Burt, Chicago, April 27, 1934 (quotes), Folder 6, Sherwood Gates, NRLF, to Williams, May 2, 1934, James Meyers, Federal Council of the Churches of Christ in America, to Williams, May 10, 1934, and Gates to Williams, May 24, 1934, all in Folder 7, and Ward H. Rodgers to Reinhold Niebuhr, New York, August 28, 1934, Folder 9, all in Box 1, Williams Papers; Anthony Dunbar, *Against the Grain,* 70–71.

48. Williams, "Diary: Sketches," 12–14, Folder 1, Box 16, and Williams to Sherwood Gates, May 28, 1934 (quote), Folder 7, Box 1, both in Williams Papers.

49. H. L. Mitchell to the Judicial Commission of Arkansas Synod Presbyterian Church, July 3, 1934, Mitchell Papers, Reel 1, *Green Rising.*

50. Myles Horton to Warren H. Wilson, August 8, 1934, Folder 9, Box 1, Williams Papers.

51. Gates to Williams, June 8, 1934, Folder 8, Box 1, Williams Papers.

52. Armin Shuman, ILD, to Williams, June 9, 1934 and June 20, 1934 (quote), both in Folder 8, Box 1, Williams Papers.

53. Willard Uphaus to Williams, August 4, 1934, Folder 9, Box 1, Williams Papers; Uphaus, *Commitment,* 42–50.

54. Warren Wilson to Williams, September 4, 1934, Folder 10, Box 1, Williams Papers.

55. "1912 Presidential Election Results, Arkansas," and "1928 Presidential Election Results, Arkansas."

56. Egerton, *Speak Now against the Day,* 124; Abram Nightingale to John Schroeder, August 10, 1934, and Horton to Warren Wilson, August 8, 1934, both in Folder 9, Box 1, Williams Papers.

57. Norman Thomas to Williams, September 11, 1934, Folder 10, Box 1, Williams Papers.

58. Anthony Dunbar, *Against the Grain,* 89–91 (quote p. 91).

59. Williams to H. L. Mitchell and Ward Rogers, September 14, 1934 (quotes), Unknown to Reinhold Niebuhr, September 15, 1934, both in Folder 10, and Dr. John F. Smith to Whomever it May Concern, June 9, 1934, Folder 8, all in Box 1, Williams Papers.

60. H. L. Mitchell to Howard Kester, December 18, 1934 (first and second quotes), Kester Papers, Reel 59, STFU Papers; Mitchell to Norman Thomas, December 18, 1934 (final quotes), Mitchell Papers, Reel 1, *Green Rising.*

61. Williams to H. L. Mitchell and Ward Rogers, September 14, 1934, State of Arkansas, eviction notice, September 8, 1934, and Unknown to Reinhold Niebuhr, September 15, 1934, all in Folder 10, Box 1, Williams Papers; Mitchell, *Mean Things Happening in this Land,* 1–45.

62. Williams to Myles Horton, August 7, 1934, Folder 31, Box 29, Highlander Records.

63. Claude C. Williams to Myles and Group, Monteagle, Tennessee, n.d. [1934], Folder 31, Box 29, Highlander Records, Wisconsin Historical Society Archives.

64. Adams with Horton, *Unearthing Seeds of Fire,* 73.

65. Willens, *Lonesome Traveler,* 24–29 (quote p. 26).

66. Williams, "Diary: Record of Activities, October, 1934," 1–11 (quote p. 4), Folder 2, Box 16, and Ward Rodgers to Reinhold Niebuhr, September 15, 1934, Folder 10, Box 1, both in Williams Papers.

67. Williams to Walpole, August 29, 1934 (second quote), Folder 31, Box 29, Highlander Records; Williams, "Diary: Record," 10–11 (all other quotes), Folder 2, and "Large Number Attend Meet," undated news clipping [1934] (third quote), and "Conference on Economic Justice," November 9–11, 1934, both in Folder 9, all in Box 16, Williams Papers.

68. Williams, "Diary: Record," 11–14 (all other quotes p. 14, last quote p. 12), Folder 2, Box 16, Williams Papers.

69. Williams, "Diary: Record," 15–16, Folder 2, Box 16, Williams Papers.

70. Williams, "Diary: Record," 15–20 (quote p. 20), Folder 2, Box 16, and J. R. Cunningham to Julian Price Love, n.d. 1934, Folder 11, Box 1, both in Williams Papers.

71. Uphaus to Williams, October 17, 1934, Folder 10, Box 1, Williams Papers.

72. Williams, "Diary: Record," 19, Folder 2, Box 16, Williams Papers.

73. Williams, "Diary: Record," 20–24 (quotes pp. 21, 23, 19), Folder 2, Box 16, Williams Papers; Belfrage, *Let My People Go,* 188–97.

74. Williams, "Diary: Record," 24–26, Folder 2, Box 16, Williams Papers.

75. Belfrage, *Let My People Go,* 94.

76. Belfrage, *Let My People Go,* 197.

77. Mark Naison, "Initial Reflections on the Significance of Claude Williams's Life and Philosophy," June 15, 1972, Folder 14, Box 17, Williams Papers (quote).

78. Craig, *Religion and Radical Politics,* 157; Belfrage, *Let My People Go,* 202–4.

79. Williams, "Diary: Record," 26, Folder 2, Box 16, Williams Papers.

80. Mitchell, *Mean Things Happening in This Land,* 59–63 (quotes); Anthony Dunbar, *Against the Grain,* 91–93.

81. Williams, "Diary: Record," 26 (last quote), Folder 2, and Williams, "Diary," January 22, 1935 (first quote), Folder 1, both in Box 16, Williams Papers; Belfrage, *Let My People Go,* 204–7.

82. Williams, "Diary," January 24–26, 1935 (quote January 26), Folder 1, Box 16, Williams Papers.

83. Williams, "Diary," February 1, 1935, Folder 1, Box 16, Williams Papers.

84. Belfrage, *Let My People Go,* 207–9 (quote p. 208); Willens, *Lonesome Traveler,* 26.

85. Williams to Norman Thomas, February 10, 1935 (second, fourth, and fifth quotes), Mitchell Papers, Reel 1, *Green Rising;* Williams to Earl Browder, February 8, 1935 (third, sixth, and seventh quotes), Delo 3750, Reel 290, CP Files. The first and final quotes are identical in both letters.

86. Carl Wilcox, FERA, to Nels Anderson, FERA, February 15, 1935 (first quote), FERA, Arkansas, University of Arkansas Libraries; Workers of Arkansas to Hilda Smith, Washington, D.C., December 1934, and Opal Lee to Willard Uphaus, February 24, 1935, both in Folder 15, and Williams, "Diary," February 10, 1935 (final quote), Folder 1, all in Box 16, Williams Papers.

87. Williams, "Diary," February 11–13, 1935, Folder 1, Box 16, Williams Papers.

88. "The Circuit Rider," in Terkel, *Hard Times,* 329 (second quote); Claude Williams to John Gans, February 14, 1935, FERA, Arkansas; Williams, "Diary," February 13–17, 1935, Folder 1, Box 16, Williams Papers (first and third quotes).

89. Williams, "Diary," February 18, 1935, Folder 1, Box 16, Williams Papers (first and third quotes); Joyce Williams telegram to G. C. Edwards, February 18, 1935 (second quote), Folder 9, Box 9, Edwards Collection, Wayne State University; Stolberg, *Bridging the River of Hatred,* 42–45; Belfrage, *Let My People Go,* 211–16; "Claude C. Williams," FBI report made at Little Rock, Ark., August 1940, p. 8, File 100-36, FBI Records—1083802.

90. Stolberg, *Bridging the River of Hatred,* 45.

91. George Edwards Sr., handwritten notes on Fort Smith case, Folder 10, Box 9, Edwards Collection (first quotes); Samuel Teitelbaum to Willard Uphaus, February 25, 1935 (last quote), FERA, Arkansas; Carolyn LeMaster, "Civil and Social Rights Efforts of Arkansas Jewry," in Bauman and Kalin, *The Quiet Voices,* 101–3.

92. Williams, "Diary," see all entries for February 1935 (quote March 1), Folder 1, Box 16, Williams Papers; "Claude Williams Framed and Imprisoned," *Economic Justice,* February 1935, Reel 59, STFU Papers.

93. Williams to Kester, February 25, 1935, reprinted in Anthony Dunbar, *Against the Grain,* 72–73.

94. Mitchell to Thomas, February 25, 1935, Socialist Party Papers, Reel 59, STFU Papers.

95. Williams, "Diary," February 1935, Folder 1, Box 16, Williams Papers; Belfrage, *Let My People Go,* 232 (quote).

96. Williams, "Diary," March 11–26, 1935, Folder 1, Box 16, Williams Papers; Willard Uphaus to Lee Hays, November 19, 1979 (first quote), Folder "Correspondence: Willard Uphaus," Box 2, Hays Papers, Smithsonian Institution; John Herling to Howard Kester, February 25, 1935, Mitchell to Clarence Senior, March 16, 1935, Uphaus to Dear Friend, May 7, 1935 (second quote), Uphaus to Kester, July 12, 1935, all in Kester Papers, Reel 59, STFU Papers; *The Sharecropper's Voice,* September 1935, Reel 58, STFU Papers.

97. "New Era Schools of Social Action and Prophetic Religion," n.d. [1935], Folder 16, Box 17, Williams Papers; Belfrage, *Let My People Go,* 254 (quotes).

98. "New Era Schools of Social Action and Prophetic Religion," n.d. [1935], Folder 16, Box 17, Williams Papers (quotes).

99. Egerton, *Speak Now against the Day,* 170–71; "New Era Schools of Social Action and Prophetic Religion," n.d. [1935], Folder 16, Box 17, Williams Papers; Hays to Kester, February 1, 1936 (quote), Kester Papers, Reel 59, STFU Papers.

100. Dyson, "The Southern Tenant Farmers Union and Depression Politics," 235, 244; Belfrage, *Let My People Go,* 248–50; Anthony Dunbar, *Against the Grain,* 133; Williams to various Arkansas County Federations of Teachers, 1936, Folder 17, Box 17, Williams Papers.

101. Grubbs, *Cry from the Cotton,* 62–86; H. L. Mitchell to Howard Kester, November 11, 1935, Kester Papers, Reel 59, STFU Papers (quote).

102. Fannin, *Labor's Promised Land,* 287–300; "Ceremony of the Land," Third Annual Convention Proceedings, Muskogee, Oklahoma, 1937, Reel 4, STFU Papers (quotes).

103. Rodgers to Kester and Mitchell, March 16, 1935, and Lee Hays to Kester, August 7, 1935 (second quote), both in Kester Papers, Reel 59, STFU Papers; Mitchell quoted in Grubbs, *Cry from the Cotton,* 83 (first and third quotes). See also Kelley, *Hammer and Hoe,* 119, 159–75.

104. Handcox to Mitchell, June 1 and 8, 1936, Reel 2, STFU Papers; Belfrage, *Let My People Go,* 286 (quote).

105. Anthony Dunbar, *Against the Grain,* 128–29.

106. STFU Press Release, June 16, 1936, Reel 2, STFU Papers; "Farmers: Resurrection," *Time Magazine,* May 31, 1937 (first quote); Belfrage, *Let My People Go,* 266–73 (second quote p. 273).

107. "King Cotton's Slaves," March of Time newsreel, vol. 2, episode 8, August 7, 1936 (New York: HBO film archives).

108. Grubbs, *Cry from the Cotton,* 99–120 (Roosevelt quoted p. 108, first quote, and p. 116, second quote); William Cobb, "Southern Tenant Farmers' Union."

109. Uphaus to Mitchell, April 12 and June 27, 1936, Reel 2, STFU Papers; "Statistics of the Congressional Election of November 3, 1936," 2; "1936 Presidential Election Results, Arkansas."

110. Handcox to Mitchell, September 28, 1936 (first quote), Williams to C. C. Kirkpatrick, October 16, 1936 (second quote), and "Union Meetings," n.d. [1936], all Reel 3, STFU Papers; Mitchell to C. C. Kirkpatrick, October 14, 1936, Folder 27, Box 1, Williams Papers.

November 5, 1936

1. Naison, "Claude Williams Talks about Owen Whitfield," 24.

2. Adapted from Belfrage, *Let My People Go,* 311–15.

3. Hays quoted in Koppelman, *Sing Out, Warning! Sing Out, Love!* 63.

4. Belfrage, *Let My People Go,* 315.

5. Naison, "Claude Williams Talks about Owen Whitfield," 24; Gellman and Roll, "Owen Whitfield," 310.

Chapter 3: Prophets in the Storm

1. Versions of Whitfield's story are in Cantor, *A Prologue to the Protest Movement,* 31; Owen H. Whitfield, interview by Howard Emerson, March 1963, quoted in Emerson, "Sharecroppers' Strike, 1939," 38; and Belfrage, "Cotton-Patch Moses," 97 (quotes).

2. Belfrage, "Cotton-Patch Moses," 97.

3. Pinn, *Why, Lord?* 157; and Cox, *Fire from Heaven,* 114.

4. Minutes of National Executive Council Meeting, October 4, 1936, Williams to Mitchell, November 19, 1936 (second quote), and Williams to W. E. Thompson, November 25, 1936 (first quote), all Reel 3, STFU Papers; "New Era Schools," n.d. [November 1936], Folder 15, Box 17, Williams Papers, Wayne State University.

5. Williams to Douglas Cobb, et al, December 9, 1936, "New Era Schools," n.d. [November 1936], and Don Kobler, "The New Era Schools at Work in Little Rock," December 1936 (all quotes), all in Folder 15, Box 17, Williams Papers.

6. Kobler, "The New Era Schools at Work in Little Rock," December 1936 (quotes), Folder 15, Box 17, Williams Papers. Ironically it was a former student of Commonwealth College, Governor Orval Faubus, who would lead resistance to the integration of Central High School in 1957. See Reed, "Orval E. Faubus," 13–29.

7. Williams, "We Sang It First Like This," n.d., Folder "Claude Williams," Box 2, Hays Papers, Smithsonian Institution; Willens, *Lonesome Traveler,* 53–56, 62, 96 (first three quotes p. 53).

8. Williams to Donald Grubbs, n.d. [1960s], Folder 8, Box 12, Williams Papers.

9. Kobler, "The New Era Schools at Work in Little Rock," December 1936 (first quote), Mary Jones, Edmondson, Arkansas, to New Era Schools, December 22, 1936 (second quote), and Clayton Donald to New Era Schools, n.d. [1936] (final quote), all in Folder 15, Box 17, Williams Papers.

10. William Cobb, *Radical Education in the Rural South,* 173–77.

11. Honey, *Southern Labor and Black Civil Rights,* 93–144; Zieger, *The CIO,* 22–41, 78 (quote p. 78).

12. Kester to Roger Baldwin, January 8, 1937, Reel 4, STFU Papers.

13. William Cobb, *Radical Education in the Rural South,* 175–77.

14. Aron Levenstein to Sidney Hertzberg and Norman Thomas, January 19, 1937, and Kester to Baldwin, January 8, 1937, both Reel 4, STFU Papers; Anthony Dunbar, *Against the Grain,* 152 (quote).

15. Williams speech reprinted in *Proceedings of the Third Annual Convention of the STFU,* January 14–17, 1937, pp. 15–16, Reel 4, STFU Papers.

16. Whitfield speech reprinted in *Proceedings of the Third Annual Convention of the STFU,* January 14–17, 1937, p. 16, Reel 4, STFU Papers.

17. Levenstein to Hertzberg and Thomas, January 19, 1937 (quotes), and Kester to Baldwin, January 28, 1937, both Reel 4, STFU Papers.

18. Levenstein to Hertzberg and Thomas, January 19, 1937 (first, second, and fourth quotes), Williams to Jackson, January 23, 1937 (third and final quotes), both Reel 4, STFU Papers.

19. Levenstein to Hertzberg and Thomas, January 19, 1937 (first quote), and Williams to Jackson, January 23, 1937 (second and third quotes), both Reel 4, STFU Papers.

20. Whitfield quoted in "Report of the Working Division on Government Programs," Third Annual Convention of the STFU, January 1937, Reel 4, STFU Papers.

21. *Charleston Enterprise-Courier:* "Levy Blasted," January 28, 1937, and "Total Number Flood Refugees Reaches 8400," February 11, 1937.

22. Roll, *Spirit of Rebellion,* 103–11.

23. "Minutes of the *Refugees of STFU CC,*" February 15, 1937, Reel 4, STFU Papers.

24. "Minutes of the *Refugees of STFU CC,*" February 15, 1937, Reel 4, STFU Papers.

25. "Super Flood Drives Thousands of Union Members from Homes," *Sharecropper's Voice,* February 1937, Reel 58, STFU Papers.

26. Roll, *Spirit of Rebellion,* 106–11.

27. John Handcox to J. R. Butler, April 8, 1937 (first quote), and Owen Whitfield to J. R. Butler, June 15, 1937 (second quote), both Reel 4, STFU Papers.

28. "Claude Williams Tours East," n.d. [1937] (quotes), and "Rev Claude Williams to Give Talks Here," n.d. [1937], both in Folder 15, Box 17, Williams Papers.

29. "Commonwealth College Program (tentative)," n.d. [1937], Folder 21, Box 17, and Williams to Walter Bergman, April 2, 1937 (quotes), Folder 4, Box 2, both in Williams Papers.

30. Williams to Uphaus, April 20, 1937, Folder 21, Box 17, and McKinney to Williams, March 3, 1937 (first quote), Folder 3, Box 2, both in Williams Papers; Williams to Jackson, January 23, 1937 (final quotes), Reel 4, STFU Papers.

31. Mitchell to the National Executive Council, Socialist Party, February 2, 1937, and Kester to Baldwin, January 28, 1937 (second quote), both in Kester Papers, Reel 59, and Mitchell to Hertzberg, February 1, 1937 (first quote), Reel 4, all STFU Papers.

32. Minutes, NEC Meeting, June 18–20, 1937 (quote), Reel 4, and Kester to Uphaus, July 28, 1937, Kester Papers, Reel 59, both STFU Papers.

33. Grubbs, *Cry from the Cotton*, 163–70; Naison, "Claude and Joyce Williams," 45.

34. Roll, *Spirit of Rebellion*, 112; *Proceedings of the STFU Annual Convention*, February 25, 1938, Reel 7, STFU Papers.

35. W. M. Harvey, Wyatt, to Butler, August 20, 1937, Reel 5, STFU Papers.

36. Williams to Butler, September 8, 1937, Reel 5, STFU Papers; Williams quoted in Green, *Grass-Roots Socialism*, 428.

37. "Preaching," Folder 10, Box 26, Belfrage Papers (quotes); Zieger, *The CIO*, 83–85.

38. Cantor, *A Prologue to the Protest Movement*, 32

39. "Statement by Mrs. Whitfield" (quotes), Folder 28, Box 17, Williams Papers; Note 124, Folder 9, Box 26, Belfrage Papers, Tamiment Library, New York University; Whitfield family, oral history, November 14, 1982, Audio Cassette "Tom," Side A, Box 107, Oral History 500, Tamiment Library, New York University.

40. "Announce Reorganization," *Commonwealth College Fortnightly*, August 15, 1937, Folder 24, Box 17, Williams Papers; Hays, "Christmas at Commonwealth" (final quote), Folder "Clippings: Commonwealth College and Claude Williams," Box 3, Hays Papers.

41. Crist, "'Everybody on the Left Knew Her'" (first quote p. 34; second quote p. 52); "'Winnie' Discovers Big Plans at College," *Commonwealth College Fortnightly*, August 1, 1934, Folder 13, Box 3, Koch Papers, Wayne State University.

42. "Educational Program of Commonwealth College, 1937–38" (first quote), Folder 4, Box 1, Koch Papers; Williams to Butler, September 8, 1937, Reel 5, and Mitchell to Kester, September 1, 1937 (last quote), Kester Papers, Reel 59, both STFU Papers.

43. Grubbs, *Cry from the Cotton*, 168.

44. Mitchell to Kester, September 1, 1937 (quotes), Kester Papers, Reel 59, STFU Papers.

45. Grubbs, *Cry from the Cotton*, 66–69.

46. Mitchell to Thomas, Amberson, et al., September 26, 1937 (first eight quotes), Thomas to Mitchell, September 29, 1937 (ninth quote), and Kester to Thomas, November 6, 1937 (final quote), all Kester Papers, Reel 59, STFU Papers.

47. *Commonwealth College Fortnightly*, December 15, 1937 (first four quotes), Folder 24, Box 17, and Claude Williams, Delegate's Card, Second National Negro Congress, October 15–17, 1937, Folder 14, Box 22, both in Williams Papers; "Special Session, NEC," January 2, 1938, and "Special Committee," February 1938 (final quote), both Reel 7, STFU Papers.

48. Mertz, *New Deal Policy and Southern Rural Poverty*, 44; "Negro Sharecropper Who Made Trip to Washington," *Charleston Enterprise-Courier*, December 23, 1937 (quotes).

49. "Negro Sharecropper Who Made Trip to Washington," *Charleston Enterprise-Courier*, December 23, 1937 (quotes); Owen Whitfield to H. L. Mitchell, December 27, 1937, Reel 4, STFU Papers.

50. Whitfield to Roosevelt, January 5, 1938, quoted in Ogilvie, "The Development of the Southeast Missouri Lowlands," 288–89.

51. Federal Bureau of Investigation, *Memorandum for the Attorney General*, 22–23 (quotes) (hereafter FBI report); Roll, *Spirit of Rebellion*, 111–31.

52. Anthony Dunbar, *Against the Grain*, 165–68.

53. Whitfield to Mitchell, March 28, 1938 (first quote), and Whitfield to Mitchell, January 10, 1938 (second quote), both Reel 7, STFU Papers; Roll, *Spirit of Rebellion*, 115–25.

54. "La Forge Farms" (quote), Box 411, Entry 4A, Project Records, 1935–1940, FHA

Records, NARA, College Park; Chase, "From the Lower Depths," 109–11; Baldwin, *Poverty and Politics*, vii–ix, 194–214.

55. Stepenoff, *Thad Snow*, 81–82; Note 125, Folder 8, Box 26, Belfrage Papers; Whitfield to Mitchell, June 6, 1938, Reel 8, STFU Papers.

56. Mildred G. Freeman, "Ten Million Sharecroppers," *The Crisis*, December 1939, 367–68 (quote); Note 127, Folder 8, Box 26, Belfrage Papers.

57. "Special Meeting of the NEC," April 25, 1938 (quote), Reel 8, STFU Papers; Grubbs, *Cry from the Cotton*, 166–87.

58. "Proceedings of the STFU Annual Convention," February 25, 1938, Reel 7, STFU Papers.

59. "Minutes of the Executive Council Meeting," May 21–22, 1938, Reel 8, STFU Papers.

60. Williams to Tania, n.d. [1938], Folder 21 (first quote), and Winifred Chappell to Methodist Federation of Social Services, September 10, 1938, Folder 22 (second quote), both in Box 17, Williams Papers; "Whit and Mister Thad," Folder 10, Box 25, Belfrage Papers; William Cobb, *Radical Education in the Rural South*, 191; Williams to Mabel Fulks, n.d. [1970s], Folder 37, Box 2, Koch Papers.

61. Whitfield to John T. Clark, St. Louis Urban League, August 3, 1938 (first three quotes), Folder 15, Box 7, Cook Papers, Missouri History Museum Library and Research Center; Whitfield to Williams, August 9, 1938 (fourth quote), and Williams to Whitfield, August 12, 1938 (final quote), both in Folder 10, Box 2, Williams Papers.

62. "The Case of Claude Williams," Reel 9, STFU Papers; Grubbs, *Cry from the Cotton*, 173–74; Anthony Dunbar, *Against the Grain*, 170–75.

63. "A meeting was held," n.d. [August 1938] (all quotes), Reel 8, STFU Papers.

64. Butler to Williams, August 22, 1938 (first quote), Butler to Thomas, August 23, 1938, and Lovestone to Butler, August 31, 1938 (second quote), all Reel 8, STFU Papers; Anthony Dunbar, *Against the Grain*, 170–77; Williams to Whitfield, September 9, 1938 (final quote), Folder 10, Box 2, Williams Papers.

65. Williams to Mable Fulks, n.d. [1970s], Box 37, Folder 2, Koch Papers.

66. "The Case of Claude Williams," Reel 9, STFU Papers (all quotes); Anthony Dunbar, *Against the Grain*, 170–75.

67. "A Program for a United, Democratic and Effective STFU," November 1, 1938 (all quotes), Reel 9, STFU Papers; Anthony Dunbar, *Against the Grain*, 174–75; Williams to Cedric Belfrage, n.d. [late 1938], Folder 15, Box 12, Williams Papers.

68. Roll, *Spirit of Rebellion*, 128.

69. Roll, *Spirit of Rebellion*, 128–38.

70. Whitfield to Mitchell, December 1, 1938 (quote), Reel 9, STFU Papers; "Who's Who in Our Union," *UCAPAWA News*, July 1939; Cantor, *A Prologue to the Protest Movement*, 54–55.

71. Whitfield to Mitchell, December 30, 1938, Reel 9, and J. R. Butler to Whitfield, January 7, 1939, Reel 10, both STFU Papers.

72. Cantor, *A Prologue to the Protest Movement*, 50–52, 60–61.

73. "Sharecroppers, Ordered Evicted, to Camp on Road," *St. Louis Post-Dispatch*, January 8, 1939 (quotes); Cantor, *A Prologue to the Protest Movement*, 60–61.

74. Whitfield quoted in FBI Report, 23; Mitchell to Gardner Jackson, January 30, 1939, Gardner Jackson to Mitchell, February 1, 1939, and Mitchell to Gardner Jackson, February

3, 1939, all in Folder "Mitchell, H. L. 1938–1940," Box 49, Gardner Jackson Papers, FDR Library.

75. This story is retold in Emerson, "Sharecroppers' Strike, 1939," 56; Belfrage, "Cotton-Patch Moses," 101; and Note 105 (first quote), Folder 10, Box 26, Belfrage Papers; President Franklin D. Roosevelt to Secretary of Agriculture Henry Wallace, January 19, 1939 (last quote), Folder "Tenant Farming, 1939–1944," Box 1, Official File 1650, FDR Library.

76. "Police Put Head of Tenant Union Out of Missouri," *St. Louis Post-Dispatch,* January 15, 1939 (first and second quotes); Roll, *Spirit of Rebellion,* 132–59; Note 31 (third quote) and Note 39f, both in Folder 10, Box 26, Belfrage Papers; "Baptist Preacher Tells of Cotton Slaves in South," *New York Amsterdam News,* February 11, 1939 (fourth quote); Whitfield to Thurgood Marshall, January 24, 1939 (fifth quote), Folder "Southern Tenant Farmers Union, Jan–Dec, 1939," Container 406, Series C, NAACP Part 18; Whitfield to Mitchell, February 15, 1939 (sixth quote), Reel 10, STFU Papers.

77. Whitfield to Thurgood Marshall, January 24, 1939, Folder "Southern Tenant Farmers Union, Jan–Dec, 1939," Container 406, Series C, NAACP Part 18.

78. Roll, *Spirit of Rebellion,* 132–59; Whitfield to all locals in Missouri STFU, February 5, 1939 (quote), Reel 10, STFU Papers.

79. Whitfield to all STFU locals in Missouri, February 5, 1939 (quotes); and Whitfield to All STFU Officers and Members in Missouri, February 11, 1939, both Reel 10, STFU Papers.

80. Whitfield to All Locals and Members of the STFU, February 24, 1939 (final quotes), and Whitfield to F. R. Betton, February 27, 1939 (first quote), both Reel 10, STFU Papers.

81. "Butler, Mitchell Removed from UCAPAWA and CIO," *UCAPAWA News,* July 1939; Cantor, *A Prologue to the Protest Movement,* 121; J. F. Moore quoted in Roll, *Spirit of Rebellion,* 151.

82. Whitfield, "What Was Done at the Convention of the Missouri Agricultural Workers' Council," Spring 1939, Folder 3, Box 6, Cook Papers.

83. Cadle, "'Cropperville' from Refuge to Community," 39–43.

84. "Southern States Plan Drive in Joint Meeting at Memphis," *UCAPAWA News,* October 1939; "Sharecroppers Ask Uncle Sam for Benefits Due Them," *UCAPAWA News,* February 1940.

85. "Press Release," Governor Lloyd Stark, Jefferson City, December 29, 1939, Folder 1941, Stark Papers, WHMC, University of Missouri, St. Louis; "Stark Calls FSA Head to Discuss Sharecroppers," *Charleston Enterprise-Courier,* January 4, 1940.

86. Whitfield to Eleanor Roosevelt, January 2, 1940, Folder "We–Wh, 1940," Box 348, Eleanor Roosevelt Papers, FDR Library.

87. "Roadside Signs Cite Plight of Sharecroppers," *St. Louis Post-Dispatch,* January 8, 1940; "Sharecropper Handbill" (quotes), Folder 32, Snow Papers, WHMC, St. Louis.

88. "Press Release," Sharecroppers' Conference, January 7, 1940, Folder 1942, Stark Papers, WHMC; "Watch Whitfield," *Sikeston Herald,* January 11, 1940 (quote).

89. "Sharecroppers Ask Uncle Sam for Benefits Due Them," *UCAPAWA News,* February 1940; Note 105 (quotes), Folder 10, Box 26, Belfrage Papers; Whitfield family, oral history, November 14, 1982, Audio Cassette "Tom," Side A, Box 107, Oral History 500.

90. "Rev. Whitfield and Wife Visit 'First Lady,'" *Negro Star,* January 26, 1940.

91. Roosevelt, "My Day," January 19, 1940 (all quotes); Eleanor Roosevelt to Gardner

Jackson, February 27, 1940, Folder "UCAPAWA, National Sharecropper Week 1940," Box 73, Gardner Jackson Papers, FDR Library.

92. "Delegation Goes to Washington," *Negro Star,* February 2, 1940.

93. "The Rev. Whitfield Calls on Mrs. Roosevelt," *Sikeston Herald,* January 25, 1940 (first quote); "What's Whitfield Got," *Sikeston Herald,* January 25, 1940 (second quote).

94. "New FSA Plan for Semo Farmers Gets Under Way," *Charleston Enterprise-Courier,* March 7, 1940; Note 39e (quote), Folder 10, Box 26, Belfrage Papers; Roll, *Spirit of Rebellion,* 156–59.

95. Whitfield to F. R. Betton, Arkansas, April 1940, Reel 14, STFU Papers.

96. "First Lady Named for Aid to Negroes: La Guardia Also Honored for Distinguished Achievement for Better Race Relations," *New York Times,* February 12, 1940 (first quote); "The Sharecropper," *Chicago Defender,* March 9, 1940 (second quote); "Outstanding Negroes and Whites of 1939 Named," *Negro Star,* February 16, 1940; "Negro Congress Convenes Friday," *Chicago Defender,* April 27, 1940; "Editorial," *Sikeston Standard,* February 9, 1940 (last quote).

97. Note 105 (first quote), Folder 10, and Note 109 (final quote), Folder 11, both in Box 26, Belfrage Papers; Whitfield to Harviell Campers, n.d. [1940] (middle quotes), Folder 4, Box 6, Cook Papers.

98. "STFU Exposed by Croppers," *UCAPAWA News,* February 1940.

99. "2,500 At Missouri Meeting," *UCAPAWA News,* May-June 1940 (last quote); Whitfield quoted in Honey, *Southern Labor and Black Civil Rights,* 129 (first two quotes).

100. Williams to Mitchell, July 1976 (first three quotes), Folder 12, Box 4, Belfrage Papers; Kester to Williams, December 11, 1939 (final quote), Kester Papers, Reel 60, STFU Papers.

101. "STFU 'Purges' CIO," *The Commoner,* March 1939 (quote), Folder 17, Box 24, and Donald Henderson to Claude Williams, February 23, 1939, Folder 12, Box 2, both in Williams Papers.

102. Williams to Henderson, March 6, 1939, Folder 20, Box 16, Williams Papers.

103. William Cobb, *Radical Education in the Rural South,* 200–201; Williams to Cedric Belfrage, n.d. [late 1938] (first quote), Folder 15, Box 12, and Norman LeFever to Williams, May 23, 1939 (second quote), Folder 21, Box 17, both in Williams Papers.

104. Williams to Mabel Fulks, n.d. [1970s], Folder 37, Box 2, Koch Papers; William Cobb, *Radical Education in the Rural South,* 206–7.

105. "Author's Preface," in Belfrage, *A Faith to Free the People,* viii (quote); "Red Preacher," *The Times Literary Supplement,* April 20, 1940.

106. J. D. Riley to Williams, February 12, 1940, Folder 15, Box 2, Williams Papers.

107. Naison, "Claude and Joyce Williams," 46; "Claude Williams elected Honorary Director of College," *Commonwealth College Newsletter,* September 1939 (quote), Folder 23, Box 17, Williams Papers.

108. "To the Members of the Commonwealth College Association," August 1939, Folder 23, Box 17, Williams to Walter Morris, December 1, 1939 (first quote), Folder 13, Box 2, and "Mid-Western Leaders urge Extended and Intensified Program," *Economic Justice,* October 1939 (last quote), Folder 25, Box 22, all in Williams Papers; Honey, *Southern Labor and Black Civil Rights,* 214–15; Williams to Mabel Fulks, n.d. [1970s], Folder 37, Box 2, Koch Papers.

109. Ridpath, "Case of the Missouri Sharecroppers," 148 (quote); Hoyle Houser to Williams, January 10, 1939, Folder 12, Box 2, Williams Papers.

110. Naison, "Claude and Joyce Williams," 46 (quotes); Dan Genin, Certification of Graphic Artwork, September 15, 1929 [1939], Folder 1, Box 1, Williams Papers.

111. Samuel Teitelbaum to Williams, April 25, 1940 (quote), and Maurice Halperin to Williams, April 3, 1940, both in Folder 15, Box 2, Williams Papers.

112. "Purpose of the Institute," April 10, 1940 (quotes), Folder 16, Box 2, and Williams to Don West, March 26, 1940, Folder 21, Box 15, both in Williams Papers.

113. Williams to A. Philip Randolph, March 28, 1940, Folder 15, Box 2, Williams Papers.

114. "First Lady to Address Human Welfare Parley," *Chicago Defender,* April 13, 1940; Egerton, *Speak Now against the Day,* 185–97.

115. Claude Williams, interview by the Memphis Police Department, August 2, 1941, File 100-507, FBI Records—1083802; "News of the Month," *UCAPAWA News,* April 1940.

116. Vernon G. Olson to Williams, May 27, 1940 (quotes), Folder 15, Box 2, Williams Papers; "East Texas Elects New Officers," *UCAPAWA News,* May–June 1940; "Claude C. Williams, et al, Un-American Activities," November 2, 1940, Little Rock Office, File 100-36, FBI Records—1083802.

April 27, 1940

1. "Negro Congress Convenes Friday," *Chicago Defender,* April 27, 1940.

2. "Address of Rev. Owen H. Whitfield before the Third National Negro Congress, Washington, D.C.," April 27, 1940, Folder "National Negro Congress, 1940–1944," Reel 16, NAACP Part 18.

3. "Address of Rev. Owen H. Whitfield," NAACP Part 18.

4. "Address of Rev. Owen H. Whitfield," NAACP Part 18.

5. Ellison, "A Congress Jim Crow Didn't Attend," 5–8.

6. "2500 at Missouri Meeting," *UCAPAWA News,* May–June 1940 (quotes); "Cotton Council Sets Up New Headquarters," *UCAPAWA News,* July–August, 1940; William Tanner to Butler, August 2, 1940, Reel 14, STFU Papers; Honey, *Southern Labor and Black Civil Rights,* 124–28.

Chapter 4: Religion Applied

1. Belfrage, *South of God,* 319 (first quote); Williams to Donald Henderson, July 28, 1940 (second quote), Folder 15, Box 2, Williams Papers, Wayne State University.

2. "No Enemy to Face at Present," *New York Times,* May 12, 1905 (quotes); Honey, *Southern Labor and Black Civil Rights,* 13–43; Carney "The Contested Image of Nathan Bedford Forrest," 601–30.

3. Honey, *Southern Labor and Black Civil Rights,* 44–92; "Memphis Negroes Elect Mayor," *New York Amsterdam News,* November 16, 1927; Egerton, *Speak Now against the Day,* 224–25.

4. Honey, *Southern Labor and Black Civil Rights,* 94–114, 125, 132.

5. "Cotton Workers School," Memphis, [August] 1940, Folder 28, Box 17, Williams Papers (all quotes); Honey, *Southern Labor and Black Civil Rights,* 132.

6. Williams to Rev. Majority, n.d. [1947], Folder 11, Box 18, Williams Papers.

7. "Cotton Workers School," program, Memphis, 1940, Folder 28, Box 17, Williams Papers.

8. Charles R. Joy, "Claude Williams: 'A Fool by Calling and Preference,'" *Christian Register* December [194?], Folder 10, Box 4, Williams Papers.

9. Honey, *Southern Labor and Black Civil Rights,* 132.

10. Williams to Harry Koger, n.d. [1970s], Folder 6, Box 14, Williams Papers.

11. "The People's Institute of Applied Religion," n.d. [1941], Little Rock, Folder 17, Box 2, Williams Papers.

12. Ward quoted in "People's Institute of Applied Religion: A Program," n.d. [1941] (quote), Folder 18, Box 2, Williams Papers; "Reverend Claude Clossie Williams," FBI report made at Memphis, Tenn., September 25, 1941, pp. 4–9, FBI Records—1083802.

13. James Martin to Williams, December 10, 1940, Folder 16, Box 2, and Williams to Donald Grubbs, n.d. [1960s] (quotes), Folder 8, Box 12, both in Williams Papers; Willens, *Lonesome Traveler,* 62, 96.

14. Dunaway, *How Can I Keep from Singing?* 80–90, 478; Klein, *Woody Guthrie,* 188–93; "Commonwealth Labor Songs," Spring Quarter 1938, Folder "Clippings: Commonwealth College and Claude Williams," Box 3, Hays Papers, Smithsonian Institution; Woody Guthrie to Dear Cathy, Dear Me, n.d. [1941] (Guthrie quote), Folder "Correspondence: Arlo, Joady and Marjorie Guthrie," Box 1, Hays Papers.

15. "'In Defense of Democracy': Proceedings of the Annual Civil Rights Institute," Detroit, Michigan, January 31–February 1, 1941 (quotes), Folder 1, Box 19, Williams Papers; Belfrage, *A Faith to Free the People,* 235–36; "Who's Who of Discussion, Leaders of St. Louis Institute," Kester Papers, Reel 60, STFU Papers.

16. PIAR newsletter, Evansville, Indiana, n.d. [1941], Organizational File "PIAR," Tamiment Library (first and last quotes), New York University; "Claude Williams," FBI report made at Little Rock, Ark., September 20, 1941, p. 5 (middle quotes), and FBI report made at Birmingham, Ala., August 29, 1947, p. 7, FBI Records—1083802.

17. "La. Farmers to Observe Anniversary," *Chicago Defender,* May 24, 1941.

18. Harold Preece, "The South Stirs: Brothers in the Union," *The Crisis,* October 1941, 318 (first two quotes); Preece, "The South Stirs: The Pulpit and the New South," *The Crisis,* December 1941, 388–89 (final three quotes).

19. Claude Williams to Reverend Majority, c/o Owen Whitfield, n.d. [1941], Folder 10, Box 18, Williams Papers.

20. PIAR newsletter, Evansville, Indiana, n.d. [1941], Organizational File "PIAR," Tamiment Library (all quotes); William Henderson, "Annual Report: Progress of the CIO in Memphis (October 1, 1940–October 1, 1941)," Folder 12, Box 58, Highlander Records; Honey, *Southern Labor and Black Civil Rights,* 44–52, 133, 180.

21. Williams quoted in Belfrage, *South of God,* 327.

22. "10 Memphis Plants Now in IWA Fold," *The Timber Worker,* August 28, 1941, Folder 29, Box 17, Williams Papers; Henderson, "Annual Report: Progress of the CIO in Memphis," Folder 12, Box 58, Highlander Records, Wisconsin Historical Society Archives; Honey, *Southern Labor and Black Civil Rights,* 133, 180; Will Jones, *The Tribe of Black Ulysses,* 150.

23. "Needs Close Examination," *Memphis Commercial Appeal,* n.d. [1941], Folder 28, Box 17, Williams Papers; Alva Taylor, "Rev. Claude," *The Protestant,* January 1942, 4–11,

Organizational File "PIAR," Tamiment Library; Belfrage, *A Faith to Free the People,* 4–5, 237–39 (other quotes, p. 259); "Claude Williams," FBI report made at Little Rock, Ark., September 20, 1941, p. 2, File 100-507, FBI report made at Memphis, Tenn., September 25, 1941, pp. 5–18 (first quote), and FBI report made at Birmingham, Ala., August 29, 1947, pp. 1–5, FBI Records—1083802.

24. "CIO to Organize South," *Chicago Defender,* November 29, 1941.

25. Honey, *Southern Labor and Black Civil Rights,* 183–86 (quote p. 183).

26. Harry Lasker, reports on "Extension Program" from November 1941 to January 1942, Folder 12, Box 58, Highlander Records; Honey, *Southern Labor and Black Civil Rights,* 183–84.

27. "Rev. Owen Whitfield," FBI report made at St. Louis, Mo., January 9, 1942, p. 3, File 100-1194, FBI Records—1083786.

28. "Union Doubles Cotton Picking Pay," *UCAPAWA News,* October 27, 1941 (first two quotes); "Cotton Pickers Get Double Pay," *New York Amsterdam News,* November 22, 1941 (final quote).

29. Owen Whitfield to Julia Katz, Director of Auxiliaries, Washington, DC, December 16, 1941, Frames 679–81, Reel 7, Series 3, NNC Papers.

30. "Sharecropper Leader Wins Government Help," *UCAPAWA News,* December 22, 1941.

31. Owen Whitfield to Claude Williams, March 2, 1942, Folder 15, Box 24, Williams Papers.

32. "Historic Meet Held in Memphis," *UCAPAWA News,* March 11, 1942.

33. "Institute of Applied Religion," St. Louis, April 30–May 3, 1942, Kester Papers, Reel 60, STFU Papers.

34. "Fight for 30c Wage Floor Gains Momentum," *UCAPAWA News,* May 27, 1942 (quotes). For more on the strike, see Roll, *Sprit of Rebellion,* 166–70.

35. Whitfield to "THE SOUTH'S MOST HATED PREACHER" (Claude Williams), November 3, 1942, Folder 24, Box 15, Williams Papers.

36. Whitfield to Williams, December 3, 1942, Folder 24, Box 15, Williams Papers.

37. Whitfield to "THE SOUTH'S MOST HATED PREACHER," November 3, 1942, Folder 24, Box 15, Williams Papers.

38. Whitfield to Fannie Cook, November, 4, 1942 (first, second, and fifth quotes), and Cook to Whitfield, November 8, 1942 (sixth and seventh quotes), both in Folder 4, Box 6, Cook Papers, Missouri History Museum Library and Research Center; Owen Whitfield to Claude Williams, December 3, 1942 (fourth quote), and Whitfield to "THE SOUTH"S MOST HATED PREACHER," November 3, 1942 (third quote), both in Folder 24, Box 15, Williams Papers.

39. Honey, *Southern Labor and Black Civil Rights,* 186.

40. "'Git Thar Fustest': Forrest Probably Said It Differently," *Memphis Commercial Appeal,* July 13, 1940; "Crump Thinks Negroes Given Fair Treatment," *Chicago Defender,* April 8, 1944 (quote).

41. Williams to Henry Jones, April 3, 1942, and Henry Jones to Jacob Long, April 30, 1943, Folder 12, Box 19, Williams Papers; Belfrage, *A Faith to Free the People,* 258–60.

42. "Troops Restore Calm in Detroit," *Chicago Tribune,* June 23, 1943 (quote); Sugrue, *The Origins of the Urban Crisis,* 17–27; Meier and Rudwick, *Black Detroit and the Rise of the UAW,* 109–10.

43. Williams to Henry Jones, April 3, 1942, Folder 12, Box 19, Williams Papers.

44. Wilbur Caswell, "Educating the Bible Christian," *The Churchman,* February 15, 1944, Folder 8, Box 3, Williams Papers (all quotes); "Institute Moves Headquarters to Detroit," *Detroit News,* July 10, 1943, Folder 1, Box 18, Williams Papers.

45. Caswell, "Educating the Bible Christian" (first quote), Folder 8, Box 3, "The People's Institute of Applied Religion, New York Sponsoring Committee," February 1943 (fourth quote), Folder 17, Box 18, "The Man Who Has An Answer . . . Claude Williams," 1943 (fifth and sixth quotes), Folder 1, Box 19, and "People's Institute of Applied Religion, Inc.: A Report of ACTION and for ACTION," n.d. [1943] (second, third, and seventh quotes), Folder 4, Box 19, all in Williams Papers.

46. Williams to Reverend Henry D. Jones, April 3, 1942, Folder 12, Box 19, Williams Papers.

47. Williams quoted in "Institute Moves Headquarters to Detroit," *Detroit News,* July 10, 1943 (first quote), Williams, "About the People's Institute of Applied Religion," both in Folder 1, and Williams, "The Hell-Brewers of Detroit" (all other quotes), Folder 13, all in Box 18, Williams Papers.

48. "The Man Who Has an Answer . . . Claude Williams," [1943] (quote), Folder 1, Box 19, and Williams to Harry Koger, n.d. [1970s], Folder 6, Box 14, both in Williams Papers.

49. Williams, "Speech before the Church Labor Panel," 1943, Folder 20, Box 23, Williams Papers.

50. Dillard, *Faith in the City,* 64–66, 104–5, 140, 147; Claude Williams to Leslie Bechtel, April 4, 1945, Folder 3, Box 5, and Williams quoted in "Institute Moves Headquarters to Detroit," *Detroit News,* July 10, 1943 (all quotes), Folder 1, Box 18, both in Williams Papers.

51. Williams, "The Hell-Brewers of Detroit," 8, Folder 13, Box 18, "People's Institute of Applied Religion, Inc.: A Report of ACTION and for ACTION," n.d. [1943], Folder 4, Box 19, and Williams to James Wishart, UAW-CIO, November 27, 1944, Folder 9, Box 4, all in Williams Papers.

52. "The People's Institute of Applied Religion, New York Sponsoring Committee," February 1943, Folder 17, Box 18, Williams Papers; Lieberman, *"My Song Is My Weapon,"* 35.

53. "Four Talk on Passive Resistance," *Chicago Defender,* March 13, 1943.

54. Henry Jones to Jacob Long, Board of National Missions, April 30, 1943, Folder 12, Box 19, Williams Papers; Belfrage, *A Faith to Free the People,* 282.

55. Williams, "The Hell-Brewers of Detroit," (first quote p. 11, last quotes p. 10), Folder 13, and Williams to Rev. Majority, n.d. [1947] (middle quotes), Folder 11, both in Box 18, Williams Papers.

56. Campbell to Williams, November 12, 1941, Folder 18, Campbell to Williams, May 17, 1943, Folder 21, and Campbell to Williams, July 10, 1943, Folder 23, all in Box 2, Williams Papers; Belfrage, *A Faith to Free the People,* 235–36, 240, 287.

57. "Detroit is Dynamite," *Life Magazine,* August 17, 1942, 15–23 (last quote).

58. Williams, recorded interview by Buford Posey, September 16, 1966, Posey Papers, Civil Rights Collection, University of Tennessee; Sugrue, *The Origins of the Urban Crisis,* 259–60.

59. Williams, recorded interview by Buford Posey, September 16, 1966, Posey Papers, Civil Rights Collection; "Experts Trace Race Conflicts to Dixie Exodus," *Chicago Tribune,* June 27, 1943 (quotes).

60. "The Babel That Is Detroit," Federated Press Release, July 12, 1943, Folder 17, Box 19 (first and last quote), and Claude Williams, "Lesson I: Religion," n.d. [1940s], pp. 3–4 (all remaining quotes), Folder 15, Box 18, all in Williams Papers.

61. "People's Institute of Applied Religion, Inc.: A Report of ACTION and for ACTION," n.d. [1943], p. 6, Folder 4, Box 19, and Harry Koger to Williams, November 27, 1942, Folder 5, Box 14, both in Williams Papers; Belfrage, *A Faith to Free the People*, 241–42; Korstad, *Civil Rights Unionism*, 151–53, 161–62.

62. "Reverend Owen H. Whitfield," FBI report made at Charlotte, N.C., September 10, 1943, p. 2 (all quotes), File 100-4150, FBI Records—1083786; Korstad, *Civil Rights Unionism*, 177–98.

63. "The Labor Board Reports/Jesus and the People," September 1943, Folder 2, Box 3, Williams Papers.

64. Simpson quoted in "The Living South," *Chicago Defender*, July 31, 1943.

65. William DeBerry to Claude Williams, April 20, 1944, Folder 11, Box 3, "People's Institute of Applied Religion, Inc.: A Report of ACTION and for ACTION," n.d. [1943], p. 6, Folder 4, Box 19, and "The Labor Board Reports/Jesus and the People," September 1943 (quotes), Folder 2, Box 3, all in Williams Papers.

66. "Coast to Coast UCAPAWA Grows," *UCAPAWA News*, December 1, 1943; Korstad, *Civil Rights Unionism*, 200–205; "Reverend Owen H. Whitfield," FBI report made at Charlotte, N.C., September 10, 1943, p. 2 (quote), File 100-4150, FBI Records—1083786.

67. Owen Whitfield to Fannie Cook, March 25, 1943, Folder 5, Box 6, Cook Papers; Case No. R-5568 (July 13, 1943), NLRB, *Decisions and Orders of the National Labor Relations Board*, 51:308–12; "Planters Nuts, Union Agree," *Chicago Bee*, June 23, 1946.

68. Northrup, *Organized Labor and the Negro*, 110–11; "TIWU [*sic*] to Press Tobacco Drive," *Richmond News Leader*, April 16, 1937.

69. Note 128, Folder 11, Box 26, Belfrage Papers; Case No. 5-R-1356 (October 13, 1943), NLRB, *Decisions and Orders of the National Labor Relations Board*, 52:1323; Korstad, *Civil Rights Unionism*, 150–53, 161–63, 188–90, 200–211.

70. Owen Whitfield to Fannie Cook, January 25, 1943 (second quote) and Owen Whitfield to Fannie Cook, March 25, 1943 (first quote), Folder 5, Box 6, Cook Papers.

71. Owen Whitfield to Fannie Cook, January 25, 1943 (quote), Folder 5, Box 6, Cook Papers; Note 128, Folder 11, Box 26, Belfrage Papers.

72. Claude Williams, quoted in Grubbs, *Cry from the Cotton*, 82.

73. Whitfield to Williams, March 2, 1942, Folder 24, Box 15, Williams Papers.

74. "Prophetic Religion in the South," n.d. [1943], p. 48 (quotes), Folder 1, Box 18, Williams Papers; "People's Institute of Applied Religion, Inc.: A Report of ACTION and for ACTION," n.d. [1943], p. 6, Folder 4, Box 19, Williams Papers.

75. Zella Whitfield to Fannie Cook, May 3, 1943 (quote), Folder 5, Box 6, Cook Papers.

76. Whitfield to Williams, October 17, 1943, Folder 3, Box 3, Williams Papers.

77. Williams to Owen and Sister Whitfield, February 10, 1944, Folder 24, Box 15, Williams Papers.

78. Whitfield to Williams, February 15, 1944 (all quotes), Folder 24, Box 15, Williams Papers.

79. Owen Whitfield, "Foreword," 1944, Folder 6, Box 6, Cook Papers.

80. Whitfield to Fannie Cook, February 2, 1944, Folder 6, Box 6, Cook Papers.

81. Whitfield to Williams, March 4, 1944 (first quote), and Whitfield to Williams, March 28, 1944 (second quote), both in Folder 24, Box 15, Williams Papers

82. Williams, *Religion,* [pamphlet], 49–50 (first and second quotes), and Whitfield to Williams, March 4, 1944, both in Folder 24, Box 15, Williams Papers (final two quotes).

83. "Speech by Virgil Vanderburg—Shop Preacher," n.d. [1944] (all quotes), Folder 33, Box 23, and "Minutes of Presbytery Committee to Sponsor the Program of Our Minister of Labor," February 14, 1944, Folder 8, Box 3, both in Williams Papers.

84. Williams, recorded interview by Buford Posey, September 16, 1966, Posey Papers, Civil Rights Collection (quotes); Williams to Leslie Bechtel, April 4, 1945, Folder 3, Box 5, Williams Papers.

85. "Speech by Virgil Vanderburg—Shop Preacher," Folder 33, Box 23, "Minutes of Presbytery Committee to Sponsor the Program of Our Minister of Labor," February 14, 1944, Folder 8, Box 3, Claude Williams to Leslie Bechtel, April 4, 1945, Folder 3, Box 5, and PIAR, "Meeting of the National Council," December 29, 1945, pp. 32–35, Folder 20, Box 18, all in Williams Papers.

86. "Minutes of Presbytery Committee to Sponsor the Program of Our Minister of Labor," February 14, 1944, Folder 8, Box 3, Williams Papers.

87. Kermit Eby to Williams, July 17, 1944, Folder 4, Box 4, Williams Papers.

88. Williams to Whitfield, July 14, 1944 (quotes), Folder 24, Box 15, Williams to Koger, May 17, 1944, Folder 11, Box 3, and "From the Fronts: The Peoples' Congress of Applied Religion," *The Span* (St. Louis), October–November 1944, Folder 8, Box 4, all in Williams Papers.

89. Williams to Reverend Majority c/o Owen Whitfield, n.d. [1947], Folder 11, Box 18, Williams Papers.

90. "PIAR Press Release," July 22, 1944, Frames 824–27, Reel 9, Series 3, NNC Papers; "Rev. Owen Whitfield," FBI report made at Detroit, July 26, 1944 (quotes), FBI Records—1083786.

91. "Rev. Whitfield Will Keynote Conference," *Detroit Free Press,* July 22, 1944, "Church Told to Aid Labor," *Detroit News,* July 25, 1944 (quotes), and "Peoples' Congress of Applied Religion," July 22–24, 1944, all in Folder 4, Box 4, Williams Papers.

92. Henry D. Jones, to Claude Williams, n.d. [April 1944], Folder 10, Box 3, Williams Papers.

93. Belfrage, *A Faith to Free the People,* viii–ix, dust jacket (Levitt quote).

94. "The Story of a Christian Democrat," *New York Times,* October 29, 1944 (quote).

95. Smith to Presbyterian Headquarters (Mr. Buckholz), July 12, 1943, Folder "Claude Williams," Box 11, Smith Papers, University of Michigan.

96. Smith to Presbyterian Headquarters (Mr. Buckholz), September 8, 1943, Folder "Claude Williams," Box 11, Smith Papers.

97. William Molton to Gerald Smith, September 14, 1945 (first quote), Folder "Claude Williams," Box 17, Smith Papers; Cavileer, "Church and Labor Relations," 14 (second quote).

98. Smith to Presbyterian Headquarters, August 1, 1943, and Memorandum from "Matthews" of HUAC to Senator Nye, n.d. (with Nye's handwritten note to Smith, Washington, D.C., July 15, 1943), in Folder "Claude Williams," Box 11, and William Molbon to Smith, September 14, 1945 (first quote), Folder "Claude Williams," Box 17, all in Smith Papers; "Claude Williams," FBI report made at Birmingham, Ala., January 1, 1947, p. 4, and FBI

report made at Birmingham, Ala., August 29, 1947, pp. 38–41, both File 100-1055, FBI Records—1083802.

99. "Claude Williams," FBI report made at Birmingham, Ala., May 23, 1951, pp. 2–3 (first quote), and FBI report made at Birmingham, Ala., December 27, 1949, p. 4 (second quote), both File 100-1055, FBI Records—1083802.

100. Owen Whitfield to Winifred Chappell, n.d. [fall 1944], Folder 11, Box 18, Williams Papers.

101. Whitfield to Williams, September 11, 1944, Folder 24, Box 15, Williams Papers.

102. Zella Whitfield to Claude and Joyce Williams, February 19, 1945, Folder 25, Box 15, Williams Papers.

103. Zella Whitfield to Joyce Williams, October 5, 1944, Folder 24, Box 15, Williams Papers.

104. Zella Whitfield to Mrs. Claude Williams, August 1944, Folder 24, Box 15, Williams Papers.

105. Owen Whitfield to Claude Williams, October 1, 1944, Folder 24, Box 15, Williams Papers.

106. "Mobilization Meeting Draw Over Hundred," *Michigan Chronicle*, October 7, 1944.

107. Koger to Williams, December 31, 1944, Folder 5, Box 14, Williams Papers.

108. Williams to Koger, January 3, 1945, Folder 12, Box 4, and Williams to Whitfield, January 4, 1945 (quote), Folder 25, Box 15, both in Williams Papers.

109. Williams to the Whitfields, Folder 25, Box 15, Williams Papers.

110. Claude Williams, "Meeting of the National Council, PIAR, New York City," December 29, 1945, pp. 6–8 (quotes), Folder 20, Box 18, Williams Papers.

111. Roll, *Spirit of Rebellion,* 173–74.

112. Roll, *Spirit of Rebellion,* 174–75.

113. Roll, *Spirit of Rebellion,* 175–76; Whitfield to Williams, April 15, 1945, and Whitfield to Williams, July 11, 1945 (quote), both in Folder 25, Box 15, Williams Papers.

114. Detroit Council of Applied Religion to "Friend," January 23, 1945, Folder 12, Box 4, Williams Papers; Sugrue, *The Origins of the Urban Crisis,* 27–28.

115. Henry Hoch, "Church Told to Aid Labor," *Detroit News,* July 25, 1944 (first quote); Williams to Henry D. Jones, February 3, 1945 (second quote), Folder 13, Box 4, Williams Papers.

116. Joyce Williams to Zella and Owen Whitfield, July 17, 1945, Folder 25, Box 15, Williams Papers.

117. Whitfield to Williams, July 11, 1945, Folder 25, Box 15, Williams Papers.

118. "R-E-V-I-V-A-L of TRUE RELIGION!" (first quote), and "REVIVAL . . . Hear True Religion Preached," both in Folder 3, Box 18, Williams Papers; "New Teaching for the Masses," *Chicago Defender,* September 29, 1945 (second and third quotes).

119. Owen Whitfield to Williams, September 25, 1945 (quotes), Folder 25, Box 15, and Zella Whitfield to Williams, August 29, 1944, Folder 10, Box 18, both in Williams Papers.

120. Roll, *Spirit of Rebellion,* 175–76; Owen Whitfield, "Anual Report of Years Work P.I.A.R. in Southeast Missouri," November 11, 1945, Folder 25, Box 15, Williams Papers (quote p. 3).

121. Williams to A. L. Campbell, October 5, 1945, Folder 13, Box 5, and Williams to Rose Rose, September 7, 1945 (quote), Folder 11, Box 5, both in Williams Papers.

122. Williams to Mr. and Mrs. Owen H. Whitfield, October 5, 1945, Folder 25, Box 15, Williams Papers.

123. Williams to A. L. Campbell, October 5, 1945, Folder 13 (second quote), and "Some techniques of concern to democracy," n.d. [1945], Folder 12, both in Box 5, "Gerald L. K. Smith Gets Rostrum but Passing the Hat Is OUT," *Detroit News*, September 26, 1945 (first quote), Folder 9, Box 18, and Southern Conference on Human Welfare to Williams, April 12, 1947, Folder 17, Box 6 (last quote), all in Williams Papers.

124. Williams to PIAR members, Autumn 1946, Folder 10, Box 6, Cecil Galey to Dr. Leslie Bechtel, February 26, 1945, Folder 12, Box 4, and "An Open Letter appraising the Religious and Labor Conference held at Pittsburgh, October 9–11, 1944" (quote p. 6), Folder 8, Box 4, all in Williams Papers.

125. Cavileer, "Church and Labor Relations" 4–37 (second quote p. 22); Steve Rosswurm, "The Catholic Church and the Left-Led Unions: Labor Priests, Labor Schools, and the ACTU," in Rosswurm, *The CIO's Left-Led Unions*, 120–37 (first quote p. 129); Williams to Cedric Belfrage, February 21, 1946, Folder 2, Box 6, Williams Papers.

126. Dillard, *Faith in the City*, 160–66; "Reverend Claude Clossie Williams," FBI report made at Detroit, September 25, 1945, p. 13 (first quote), File 100-9103, FBI Records—1083802; Mary Lou Koger to Williams, November 9, 1945 (second quote), Folder 15, Box 5, Williams Papers.

127. Father Coughlin, July 25, 1938, quoted in Tull, *Father Coughlin*, 189–91.

128. Owen Whitfield, "Anual Report of Years Work P.I.A.R. in Southeast Missouri," November 11, 1945 (quotes), Folder 25, Box 15, Williams Papers.

129. "Meeting of the National Council of the People's Institute of Applied Religion," New York, December 29, 1945, pp. 1–2 (Williams quotes), Folder 20, Box 18, Williams Papers.

Conclusion: Clods of Southern Earth

1. "Meeting of the National Council of the People's Institute of Applied Religion," New York, December 29, 1945, pp. 9–11 (quotes), Folder 20, Box 18, Williams Papers, Wayne State University.

2. Alva W. Taylor to Williams, April 19, 1946 (first two quotes), Folder 4, Box 6, Williams Papers; Claude Williams to J. L. O. and Slugger (Raymond and Charlotte Koch), March 7, 1976 (final quote), Folder 40, Box 2, Koch Papers, Wayne State University.

3. Fones-Wolf and Fones-Wolf, "Sanctifying the Southern Organizing Campaign," 5–32; Zieger, *The CIO*, 227–41; William DeBerry to Williams, July 2, 1946 (quote), Folder 7, Box 6, Williams Papers.

4. Whitfield to Williams, January 4, 1946 (first and third quotes), and Williams to Whitfield, January 30, 1946 (second quote), both in Folder 25, Box 15, Williams Papers; "White Pastor's Marriage to Negro Girl Delayed Week," *Chicago Defender*, January 26, 1946 (fourth quote); "Quits Pulpit to Marry Negro Girl," *New York Amsterdam News*, January 19, 1946.

5. "Meeting of the National Council of the People's Institute of Applied Religion," New York, December 29, 1945, Folder 20, Box 18, and "Youth Congress of Applied Religion," New York, December 29, 1945–January 3, 1946 (quote), Folder 22, Box 19, both in Williams Papers.

6. "National Commander Tours South," *UNAVA News*, August–September, 1946.

7. "Reverend Owen Holmes Whitfield," FBI report made at St. Louis, Mo., April 10, 1947, File 100-1194, FBI Records—1083786.

8. Nathan Oser to Revels Cayton, September 3, 1946, Frames 905–7, Reel 32, Series 2, NNC Papers.

9. Nathan Oser to Revels Cayton, September 3, 1946, Frames 905–7, Reel 32, Series 2, NNC Papers; "St. Louis Cop Shooting Case to U.S. Attorney General," *Chicago Bee,* November 10, 1946.

10. "Reverend Owen Holmes Whitfield," FBI report made at St. Louis, Mo., April 10, 1947, File 100-1194, FBI Records—1083786.

11. Edward Strong to Nathan Oser, September 10, 1946, Frame 897, Revels Cayton to Whom It May Concern, September 18, 1946, Frame 887, Owen Whitfield to Revels Cayton, October 12, 1946, Frame 880, "To All Negro Citizens in the Eleventh Legislative District" (quote), Owen Whitfield and Thomas Gates, "Elect William Massingale to the State Legislature," Frames 862–64, all Reel 32, Series 2, NNC Papers; "William A. Massingale," in Bishop, *State Of Missouri Official Manual,* 139.

12. "Reverend Owen Holmes Whitfield," FBI report made at St. Louis, Mo., April 10, 1947, File 100-1194, FBI Records—1083786; Lang, *Grassroots at the Gateway,* 86–89.

13. "THE HOWARD CASE IS *NOT* CLOSED!" (quote), November 7, 1946, Frame 874, H. D. Robinson, State Chairman of the St. Louis NNC, February 5, 1947, Frames 828–29, "CALL TO CONSULTATION ON STATE FEPC BILL," February 11, 1947, Frame 818, all Reel 32, Series 2, NNC Papers.

14. "IF DEMOCRACY is to work in the WORLD, IT MUST WORK IN THE U.S.A. (ST. LOUIS)," August 13, 1947, Frame 793, H. D. Robinson, President, St. Louis NNC to Max Yergan, Edward Strong, and Revels Cayton, August 5, 1947, Frame 32, both Reel 32, Series 2, NNC Papers.

15. Cedric Belfrage to Joyce Williams, n.d. [1947], Folder 7, Box 7, Williams Papers.

16. "Claude Williams," FBI reports made at Birmingham, Ala., January 16, 1947, and August 29, 1947 (quotes p. 11), FBI Records—1083802.

17. Elizabeth Dilling, "Character Assassination, Inc." (all quotes), in "Claude Williams," FBI file, n.d [1947], FBI Records—1083802.

18. West, "Appreciation," in *Clods of Southern Earth,* unpag. (quotes).

19. West, "For Claude Williams," in *Clods of Southern Earth,* 144 (quote); Lorence, *A Hard Journey,* 123–25.

20. Lorence, *A Hard Journey,* 126 (first quote), 129–30; Williams to Rose Rose, June 1947, Folder 1, Box 7, Williams Papers (second quote); Zieger, *The CIO,* 253–93.

21. Seven American Protestant Clergymen, "Religion in Yugoslavia"; PIAR, "With the People," Autumn 1947 newsletter, Folder 4, Box 7, Williams Papers.

22. Seven American Protestant Clergymen, "Religion in Yugoslavia"; Koppelman, *Sing Out, Warning! Sing Out, Love!* 68.

23. Seven American Protestant Clergymen, "Religion in Yugoslavia," pp. 21–22 (quotes), Garrett Evangelical Seminary Library.

24. PIAR, "With the People," Autumn 1947 newsletter (quote), Folder 4, Box 7, Williams Papers.

25. PIAR, "With the People," Autumn 1947 newsletter (all quotes), Folder 4, Box 7, Williams Papers.

26. Harry Koger to U.S. Immigration and Naturalization Service, April 18, 1947, Folder

17, Box 6, Mary Lou Koger to Claude Williams, August 30 and September 5, 1947, Folder 1, Box 7, and Harry Koger to Joyce Williams, October 23, 1947, Folder 5, Box 14, all in Williams papers.

27. "Church Visited by Founder," *Pittsburgh Courier,* January 24, 1948.

28. "To all National Board Members," PIAR newsletter, January 1, 1948, Folder 8, Box 7, and Williams to Louisa Smith, n.d. [1970s], Folder 1, Box 12, both in Williams Papers; Sullivan, *Days of Hope,* 265–67 (quote p. 267).

29. Williams to William F. Hoot, Special Judicial Committee, Presbyterian Church, August 31, 1953, Folder 17, and PIAR bulletin, June 1950, Folder 13, both in Box 7, Williams Papers. Williams never completed or published the "Bible Way of Righteousness." See Boxes 20–22, Williams papers.

30. Williams to Donald Hibbard, Board of Pensions, Presbyterian Church, November 20, 1949, Folder 12, Box 7, Williams Papers.

31. Williams to President Harry S. Truman, n.d. [September 12, 1950], Folder 15, Box 7, Williams Papers (quotes); "Anti-Communist Bill," *The Pittsburgh Press,* September 13, 1950; "The McCarran Bill," *The Hartford Courant,* September 14, 1950.

32. Schrecker, *The Age of McCarthyism,* 55–6.

33. See correspondence between Williams and Marion Davidson in Folder 16, Box 22, Williams Papers.

34. "Cotton Patch Charlie Says," *National Guardian,* October 25, 1948 (second quote); Owen Whitfield to Fannie Cook, March 2 (first quote) and March 17, 1947, Folder 8, Box 6, Cook Papers, Missouri History Museum Library and Research Center; "Reverend Owen H. Whitfield," FBI report made at St. Louis, Mo., April 20, 1949, File 100-1194, FBI Records—1083786 (last two quotes).

35. Cadle, "'Cropperville' from Refuge to Community," 117–31.

36. Internal Revenue Service, Alcohol Tax Unit to FBI, September 4, 1951, File 100-1194, FBI Records—1083786.

37. "Owen H. Whitfield," FBI report made at Springfield, Ill., January 30, 1953, FBI Records—1083786.

38. "Owen H. Whitfield," FBI report made at Springfield, Ill., January 30, 1953 (all quotes except last two), and Memorandum from the Springfield office to FBI Director, March 3, 1953 (last quote), both in FBI Records—1083786; "Reverend Owen H. Whitfield," FBI report made at St. Louis, Mo., April 20, 1949, File 100-1194, FBI Records—1083786 (second to last quote); and on playing the "good darkey," see Whitfield to Belfrage, December 14, 1947, Folder 11, Box 26, Belfrage Papers.

39. "Claude Williams," FBI reports made at Birmingham, Ala., December 27, 1949, March 2, 1950, and September 27, 1950, FBI Records—1083802; France, *My Native Grounds,* 174 (quote).

40. "Claude Williams," FBI report made at Birmingham, Ala., February 16, 1953 (quote), FBI Records—1083802.

41. Ray, *Apostles of Discord,* 261 (first quote), 260 (second and third quotes), 263 (last quotes).

42. France, *My Native Grounds,* 173–76.

43. Presbytery of Detroit, "The Presbyterian Church, U.S.A., Prosecutor, vs. Rev. Claude C. Williams, Accused," transcript of trial beginning January 4, 1954, 74 (first quote), 91 (second quote), and 234 (third quote), Folder 9, Box 2, Williams Papers, Civil Rights Collection, University of Tennessee.

44. France, *My Native Grounds,* 173–76 (quote p. 176).

45. Presbytery of Detroit, "The Presbyterian Church, U.S.A., Prosecutor, vs. Rev. Claude C. Williams, Accused," 141 (first quote), 236 (second quote), 245 (third quote), 206 (fourth, fifth, and sixth quotes), and 279 (last quote), Folder 9, Box 2, Williams Papers, Civil Rights Collection.

46. France, *My Native Grounds,* 176; Eugene Carson Blake, quoted in Schwartz, *Can You Make a Difference?* 89; "Reversal Asked in Heresy Case," *The Baltimore Sun,* May 19, 1954; and "Ex-Pastor Loses Appeal in Heresy," *New York Times,* May 25, 1955.

47. "The Struggle for Full Citizenship," *Baltimore Afro-American,* November 2, 1957; "Claude Clossie Williams," FBI Report made at Birmingham, Ala., February 15, 1962 (quote), FBI Records—1083802; Naison, *White Boy,* 180; Schwartz, *Can You Make a Difference?* 88.

48. "The Struggle for Full Citizenship," *Baltimore Afro-American,* November 2, 1957; Arsenault, *Freedom Riders,* 491–93; Williams to Don West, n.d., [1962?], Folder 23, Box 15, Williams Papers (quotes).

49. "A Tribute to Claude Williams, September 1961" (first two quotes), Folder 7, and Pete Seeger to Williams, January 10, 1963 (final quotes), Folder 13, both in Box 9, Williams Papers.

50. Sally Belfrage, "A Southern Prophet in a New Generation," *The Guardian,* New York, September 26, 1964, Folder 10, Box 4, Claude Williams Committee, "Claude & Joyce Williams," n.d. [early 1970s?], Folder 2, Box 5, and Williams to Cedo (Belfrage) and others, December 18, 1967, Folder 10, Box 4 (quote), all in Belfrage Papers, Tamiment Library, New York University; Kelley, *Hammer and Hoe,* 228–29.

51. Sally Belfrage, "A Southern Prophet in a New Generation" (all quotes except last), Claude Williams Committee to Friend, October 6, 1964, both in Folder 10, Box 4, and Claude Williams Committee, "Claude & Joyce Williams" (last quote), Folder 2, Box 5, all in Belfrage Papers; Schwartz, *Can You Make a Difference?* 89; Naison, *White Boy,* 180–82; "Claude Clossie Williams," FBI report made at Birmingham, Ala., April 7, 1972, FBI Records—1083802. Correspondence between Williams and Naison provides fascinating insight into debates between Old Left and New Left activists. See Folder 11, Box 4, Belfrage Papers, and Folders 16–19, Box 14, Williams Papers.

52. "Unfrocked Pastor Arrives for Rerobing," *Detroit News,* May 9, 1965, "Claude Williams," Biographical File, Tamiment Library, New York University.

53. "Rev. Owen Whitefield, Led Sharecroppers' '39 Protest," *New York Times,* August 13, 1965, 26; Cadle, "'Cropperville' from Refuge to Community," 120–23.

54. Williams to Cedric Belfrage, June 12, 1975, Folder 12, Box 4, Belfrage Papers.

55. "Veteran Demonstrator Memorialized," *The Crisis,* December 1965, 656.

56. "Rev. Owen Whitfield, Led Sharecroppers' '39 Protest," *New York Times,* August 13, 1965.

57. Williams to Louis Cantor, n.d. [1960s], Folder 9, Box 12, Williams Papers (first quote); Williams quoted in Naison, "Claude Williams Talks about Owen Whitfield," 25 (second quote).

58. "Memorial Service: Claude Williams," August 4, 1979, Folder "Claude Williams," Box 2, Hays Papers, Smithsonian Institution.

59. Williams, recording of sermon at a "Freedom Revival," n.d. [late 1960s], Posey Papers, Civil Rights Collection, University of Tennessee.

60. Presbytery of Detroit, "The Presbyterian Church, U.S.A., Prosecutor, vs. Rev. Claude C. Williams, Accused," 304, Folder 9, Box 2, Williams Papers, Civil Rights Collection.

61. Williams quoted in Sally Belfrage, "A Southern Prophet in a New Generation," Folder 10, Box 4, Belfrage Papers.

62. Williams recounted the story of Zella Whitfield in a letter to Cedric Belfrage: Williams to Belfrage, June 12, 1975, Folder 12, Box 4, Belfrage Papers.

63. Williams, *Religion* [pamphlet], 52–55.

64. Williams to Belfrage and others, August 12, 1968, Folder 11, Box 4, Belfrage Papers.

65. Cedric Belfrage quoted in "Memorial Service: Claude Williams," August 4, 1979, pp. 2–3 (quotes), Folder "Claude Williams, Box 2, Hays Papers, Smithsonian Institution.

66. Williams quoted in Naison, "Claude Williams Talks about Owen Whitfield," 24.

Bibliography

Manuscript Collections

Federal Bureau of Investigation, Records Management Division, U.S. Department of Justice, Washington, D.C. (FBI Records)
FOIPA 1083786, "Owen Whitfield"
FOIPA 1083802, "Claude Williams"

Garrett Evangelical Seminary Library, Evanston, Illinois
Seven American Protestant Clergymen, "Religion in Yugoslavia," 1947 report

HBO Archives, New York
"King Cotton's Slaves," March of Time newsreel, volume 2, episode 8, August 7, 1936

Library of Congress, Washington, D.C.
National Association for the Advancement of Colored People Papers, 1842–1999 (NAACP Papers)

Missouri History Museum Library and Research Center, St. Louis
Fannie Frank Cook Papers, 1874–1949 (Cook Papers)

National Archives and Records Administration, College Park and Great Lakes
RG 96, Records of the Farmers Home Administration and Predecessor Agencies (FHA Records, NARA)

New York University, Bobst Library, Tamiment Library and Robert F. Wagner Labor Archives, New York (Tamiment Library)
Cedric Belfrage Papers, 1922–1990, TAM 143 (Belfrage Papers)
Oral History Collections—Unprocessed, TAM 500 (Oral History 500)

Northwestern University, Special Collections and Archives, University Library, Evanston, Illinois
Claude Williams, *Religion: Barrier or Bridge to a People's World? A Handbook for Progressive Leaders,* pamphlet reprinting 1945 speech, Birmingham, 1947

Pennsylvania State University, Historical Collections and Labor Archives, Special Collections Library, University Park
Papers of the United Mine Workers of America, Correspondence between Districts and Presidents (UMW Papers)

Franklin D. Roosevelt Presidential Library and Museum, Hyde Park, New York (FDR Library)
Gardner Jackson Papers
Official Files
Eleanor Roosevelt Papers

Smithsonian Institution, Ralph Rinzler Folklife Archives and Collections, Center for Folklife and Cultural Heritage, Washington, D.C.
Lee Hays Collection (Hays Papers)

Southeast Missouri State University, Kent Library, Special Collections and Archives, Cape Girardeau (KL)
Clippings Collection, 1871–2001

University of Arkansas Libraries, Special Collections, Fayetteville
U.S. Federal Emergency Relief Administration, 1935, MS UN3R (FERA, Arkansas)

University of Michigan, Bentley Historical Library, Ann Arbor
Gerald L. K. Smith Papers (Smith Papers)

University of Missouri, Western Historical Manuscripts Collection, Columbia and St. Louis (WHMC)
Papers of Arthur Mastick Hyde, 1921–1954, C0007 (Hyde Papers)
Lloyd Crow Stark Papers, 1931–1941, C0004 (Stark Papers)
U. S. Works Progress Administration-Historical Records Survey, 1935–1942, C3551
Thad Snow Papers, 1921–1954, SL88 (Snow Papers)

University of North Carolina, Southern Oral History Program Collection, Southern Historical Collection, Wilson Library, Chapel Hill (Southern Oral History Collection)
Don West, oral history interview, January 22, 1975, E-0016, 4007

University of Tennessee, Special Collections Library, Knoxville
Civil Rights Collection, 1913–1970, MS-0334 (Civil Rights Collection)
    Series IV: Rev. Claude Williams Papers, 1934–1954
    Series VIII: Buford W. Posey Papers, 1954–1967

Wayne State University, Walter P. Reuther Library of Labor and Urban Affairs, Detroit
Claude C. Williams Papers, 1929–1979 (Williams Papers)
Papers of Raymond Koch and Charlotte Moskowitz (Koch Papers)
George Clifton Edwards Collection (Edwards Collection)

Wisconsin Historical Society Archives, Madison
Highlander Research and Education Center Records, 1917–1978: Installment 1: Original Collection, 1917–1973, MSS 265 (Highlander Records)

Microfilmed Collections

Files of the Communist Party of the USA in the Comintern Archives. 326 reels. IDC Publishers, 1999–2000. (CP Files)

The General Education Board Archives. 360 reels. Scholarly Resources Inc., 1993
    Okolona Industrial School, 1904–1948, Miss25, Reel 75, Series I: Appropriations, Sub-
    series I: Early Southern Program (Okolona Papers)
The Green Rising, 1910–1977: A Supplement to the Southern Tenant Farmers' Union Papers.
    17 reels. Microfilming Corporation of America, 1978. (*Green Rising*)
H. L. Mitchell Papers (Mitchell Papers)
*Papers of the National Association for the Advancement of Colored People: Part 18: Special
    Subjects, 1940–1955: Series C: General Office Files: Justice Department—White Supremacy.*
    33 reels. University Publications of America, 1995. (NAACP Part 18)
Papers of the National Negro Congress. 94 reels. University Publications of America. (NNC
    Papers)
Papers of the Southern Tenant Farmers Union, 1934–1970. 60 reels. Microfilming Corpora-
    tion of America, 1978. (STFU Papers)
    Selection from the Howard A. Kester Papers, 1934–1949 (Kester Papers)
    Selection from the Socialist Party Papers (Socialist Party Papers)

Newspapers and Magazines

MISSOURI

Charleston Spokesman
Enterprise-Courier (Charleston)
New Madrid Weekly Record
Post-Dispatch (St. Louis)
Sikeston Herald
Sikeston Standard

CITY, NATIONAL, AND INTERNATIONAL

Baltimore Afro-American
The Baltimore Sun
The Chicago Bee
The Chicago Defender (national edition)
The Chicago Tribune
The Crisis
The Detroit Free Press
Detroit News
The Hartford Courant
Life Magazine
Michigan Chronicle
Muskogee Phoenix
The National Guardian
The Negro Star (Wichita, Kansas)
The Negro World
The New York Amsterdam News
The New York Times
Paris Express (Arkansas)

Pittsburgh Courier
The Pittsburgh Press
The Richmond News Leader
The Sharecropper's Voice (Memphis)
Time Magazine
The Times Literary Supplement
UCAPAWA News
UNAVA News

Other Primary Sources

"1912 Presidential Election Results, Arkansas." Available at http://www.uselectionatlas. org/results (accessed March 2010).

"1928 Presidential Election Results, Arkansas." Available at http://www.uselectionatlas. org/results (accessed March 2010).

"1932 Presidential Election Results, Arkansas." Available at http://www.uselectionatlas. org/results (accessed March 2010).

"1936 Presidential Election Results, Arkansas." Available at http://www.uselectionatlas. org/results (accessed March 2010).

Belfrage, Cedric. "Cotton-Patch Moses." *Harper's Magazine* 197 (November 1948): 94–103.

———. *A Faith to Free the People.* New York: Dryden Press, 1944.

———. *Let My People Go.* London: Victor Gollancz, 1940.

———. *South of God.* New York: Modern Age Books, 1941.

Bishop, Esther Downs, ed. *State Of Missouri Official Manual for the Years 1947–1948.* Jefferson City, Mo.: Secretary of State, 1947.

Bright, Margaret L. "Farm Wage Workers in Four Southeast Missouri Cotton-Producing Counties." Master's thesis, University of Missouri–Columbia, 1944.

Cavileer, Jesse. "Church and Labor Relations." *Social Action* 10 (October 15, 1944): 4—37.

Chase, Stuart. "From the Lower Depths: Condensed from Free America." *Reader's Digest* 38 (May 1941): 109–11.

"Claude Clossey Williams, Cumberland Presbyterian Licentiate, 1921–1923." Cumberland Presbyterian Church Archives. Available at http://www.cumberland.org/hfcpc/minister/WilliamsClaudeC.htm (accessed March 2010).

Du Bois, W. E. B. *The Souls of Black Folk: Essays and Sketches.* Chicago: A. C. McClurg & Co., 1903.

Ellison, Ralph. "A Congress Jim Crow Didn't Attend." *New Masses,* May 14, 1940, 5–8.

Federal Bureau of Investigation. *Memorandum for the Attorney General: Investigation Concerning the Sharecropper Situation Existing in Southeast Missouri.* Washington, D.C.: Federal Bureau of Investigation, 1939. (FBI Report)

Fosdick, Harry E. *The Modern Use of the Bible.* New York: MacMillan Company, 1924.

France, Royal W. *My Native Grounds: The Autobiography of Royal W. France.* New York: Cameron Associates, 1957.

Hill, Robert A., and Barbara Bair, eds. *The Marcus Garvey and Universal Negro Improvement Association Papers.* Volume 7, *November 1927–August 1940.* Berkeley: University of California Press, 1990.

Mitchell, H. L. *Mean Things Happening in this Land: The Life and Times of H. L. Mitchell, Cofounder of the Southern Tenant Farmers' Union*. Montclair, N.J.: Allanheld, Osmun, 1979.

Naison, Mark. *White Boy: A Memoir*. Philadelphia: Temple University Press, 2002.

National Labor Relations Board. *Decisions and Orders of the National Labor Relations Board*. Volumes 51–52. Washington, D.C.: Government Printing Office, 1943.

Ray, Ralph Lord. *Apostles of Discord: A Study of Organized Bigotry and Disruption on the Fringes of Protestantism*. Boston: Beacon Press, 1953.

Ridpath, Ben M. "Case of the Missouri Sharecroppers." *The Christian Century* 56 (February 1, 1939): 146–48.

Roosevelt, Eleanor. "My Day." Syndicated newspaper column. Available at http://www.gwu.edu/~erpapers/myday/ (accessed March 2010).

Schwartz, Robert. *Can You Make a Difference? A Memoir of a Life for Change*. New York: Lantern Books, 2002.

"Statistics of the Congressional Election of November 3, 1936." Available at http://clerk.house.gov/member_info/electionInfo/1936election.pdf (accessed March 2010).

Terkel, Studs. *Hard Times: An Oral History of the Great Depression*. New York: Pocket Books, 1970.

Twelve Southerners. *I'll Take My Stand: The South and the Agrarian Tradition*. 1930. Repr., Baton Rouge: Louisiana State University Press, 2006.

Uphaus, Willard. *Commitment*. New York: McGraw-Hill, 1963.

U.S. Bureau of the Census. *Fifteenth Census of the United States: 1930: Population*. Volume 3, Part 1: *Alabama–Missouri*. Washington, D.C.: Government Printing Office, 1932.

———. Manuscript Census Schedules 1870, 1880, 1900, 1930.

———. *Statistical Abstract of the United States: 1919*. Washington, D.C.: Government Printing Office, 1920.

———. *Statistical Abstract of the United States: 1926*. Washington, D.C.: Government Printing Office, 1927.

West, Don. *Clods of Southern Earth*. New York: Boni and Gaer, 1946.

Wintz, Cary D., ed. *African American Political Thought, 1890–1930: Washington, Du Bois, Garvey and Randolph*. New York: M. E. Sharpe, 1996.

Books, Articles, Dissertations

Adams, Frank, with Myles Horton. *Unearthing Seeds of Fire: The Idea of Highlander*. Winston-Salem, N.C.: John F. Blair, 1975.

Alinsky, Saul. *John L. Lewis: An Unauthorized Biography*. 1949. Repr., New York: Vintage, 1970.

Allen, Ernest. "Waiting for Tojo: The Pro-Japan Vigil of Black Missourians, 1932–1943." *Gateway Heritage* 15 (Fall 1994): 16–33.

Arsenault, Raymond. *Freedom Riders: 1961 and the Struggle for Racial Justice*. New York: Oxford University Press, 2006.

Ayers, Edward L. *The Promise of the New South: Life after Reconstruction*. New York: Oxford University Press, 1993.

Baldwin, Sidney. *Poverty and Politics: The Rise and Decline of the Farm Security Administration*. Chapel Hill: University of North Carolina Press, 1968.

Barkun, Michael. *Religion and the Racist Right: The Origins of the Christian Identity Movement.* Chapel Hill: University of North Carolina Press, 1996.

Bauman, Mark, and Berkley Kalin, eds. *The Quiet Voices: Southern Rabbis and Black Civil Rights, 1880s to 1990s.* Tuscaloosa: University of Alabama Press, 1997.

Bevis, Charlie. "Rocky Point: A Lone Outpost of Sunday Baseball in Sabbatarian New England." *NINE: A Journal of Baseball History and Culture* 14 (2005): 78–97.

Boles, John B. *The Great Revival, 1787–1805.* Lexington: University Press of Kentucky, 1972.

Brinkley, Alan. *Voices of Protest: Huey Long, Father Coughlin, and the Great Depression.* New York: Knopf, 1982.

Burkett, Randall K. *Garveyism as a Religious Movement: The Institutionalization of a Black Civil Religion.* Metuchen, N.J.: Scarecrow Press, 1978.

Cadle, Jean. "'Cropperville' from Refuge to Community: A Study of Missouri Sharecroppers Who Found an Alternative to the Sharecropping System." MA thesis, University of Missouri, St. Louis, 1993.

Cantor, Louis. *A Prologue to the Protest Movement: The Missouri Sharecropper Roadside Demonstration of 1939.* Durham: Duke University Press, 1969.

Carney, Court. "The Contested Image of Nathan Bedford Forrest." *Journal of Southern History* 67 (2001): 601–30.

Carpenter, Joel A. *Revive Us Again: The Reawakening of American Fundamentalism.* New York: Oxford University Press, 1997.

Chappell, David L. *A Stone of Hope: Prophetic Religion and the Death of Jim Crow.* Chapel Hill: University of North Carolina Press, 2004.

Cobb, James C. *The Most Southern Place on Earth: The Mississippi Delta and the Roots of Regional Identity.* New York: Oxford University Press, 1992.

Cobb, William H. *Radical Education in the Rural South: Commonwealth College, 1922–1940.* Detroit: Wayne State University Press, 2000.

———. "Southern Tenant Farmers' Union." *The Encyclopedia of Arkansas History and Culture.* Available at http://www.encyclopediaofarkansas.net (accessed January 2010).

Cox, Harvey. *Fire from Heaven: The Rise of Pentecostal Spirituality and the Reshaping of Religion in the Twenty-First Century.* Cambridge, Mass.: Da Capo, 2001.

Craig, Robert H. *Religion and Radical Politics: An Alternative Christian Tradition in the United States.* Philadelphia: Temple University Press, 1992.

Creech, Joe. *Righteous Indignation: Religion and the Populist Revolution.* Urbana: University of Illinois Press, 2006.

Cresswell, Stephen. *Rednecks, Redeemers, and Race: Mississippi after Reconstruction, 1877–1917.* Jackson: University of Mississippi Press, 2006.

Crist, Miriam. "'Everybody on the Left Knew Her': Winifred L. Chappell." MDiv thesis, Union Theological Seminary, 1979.

Cunningham, Agnes "Sis," and Gordon Friesen. *Red Dust and Broadsides: A Joint Autobiography.* Amherst: University of Massachusetts Press, 1999.

Davis, Rebecca L. "'Not Marriage at All, but Simple Harlotry': The Companionate Marriage Controversy." *Journal of American History* 94 (March 2008): 1137–63.

De Jong, Greta. *A Different Day: African American Struggles for Justice in Rural Louisiana, 1900–1970.* Chapel Hill: University of North Carolina Press, 2002.

Dillard, Angela. *Faith in the City: Preaching Radical Social Change in Detroit.* Ann Arbor: University of Michigan Press, 2007.

Dubofsky, Melvyn, and Warren Van Tine. *John L. Lewis: A Biography.* Urbana: University of Illinois Press, 1986.

Dunaway, David. *How Can I Keep from Singing? The Ballad of Pete Seeger.* 1981. Repr., New York: Villard, 2008.

Dunbar, Anthony P. *Against the Grain: Southern Radicals and Prophets, 1929–1959.* Charlottesville: University Press of Virginia, 1981.

Dunbar, Fred. "Coal Mining Strikes." *Encyclopedia of Oklahoma History and Culture.* Available at http://digital.library.okstate.edu/encyclopedia/entries/C/CO005.html (accessed November 2009).

Dyson, Lowell K. "The Southern Tenant Farmers Union and Depression Politics." *Political Science Quarterly* 88 (June 1973): 230–52.

Egerton, John. *Speak Now against the Day: The Generation before the Civil Rights Movement in the South.* Chapel Hill: University of North Carolina Press, 1994.

Emerson, Howard. "Sharecroppers' Strike, 1939." Senior honors thesis, Southeast Missouri State University, 1963.

Evanzz, Karl. *The Messenger: The Rise and Fall of Elijah Muhammad.* New York: Pantheon Books, 1999.

Fairclough, Adam. *To Redeem the Soul of America: The Southern Christian Leadership Conference and Martin Luther King, Jr.* Athens: University of Georgia Press, 1987.

Fannin, Mark. *Labor's Promised Land: Radical Visions of Gender, Race, and Religion in the South.* Knoxville: University of Tennessee Press, 2003.

Feldman, Glenn, ed. *Politics and Religion in the White South.* Lexington: University Press of Kentucky, 2005.

Foner, Eric. *A Short History of Reconstruction, 1863–1877.* New York: Harper & Row, 1990.

Fones-Wolf, Elizabeth, and Ken Fones-Wolf. "Sanctifying the Southern Organizing Campaign: Protestant Activists in the CIO's Operation Dixie." *Labor* 6 (Spring 2009): 5–32.

Gallicchio, Mark. *The African American Encounter with Japan and China: Black Internationalism in Asia, 1895–1945.* Chapel Hill: University of North Carolina Press, 2000.

Gellman, Erik S., and Jarod H. Roll. "Owen Whitfield and the Gospel of the Working Class in New Deal America." *Journal of Southern History* 72 (May 2006): 303–48.

Giggie, John. *After Redemption: Jim Crow and the Transformation of African American Religion in the Delta, 1875–1915.* New York: Oxford University Press, 2008.

Gilmore, Glenda. *Defying Dixie: The Radical Roots of Civil Rights, 1919–1950.* New York: W. W. Norton, 2008.

Glass, William R. *Strangers in Zion: Fundamentalists in the South, 1900–1950.* Macon, Ga.: Mercer University Press, 2001.

Green, James R. *Grass-Roots Socialism: Radical Movements in the Southwest, 1895–1943.* Baton Rouge: Louisiana State University Press, 1978.

Grim, Valerie. "African American Landlords in the Rural South, 1870–1950." *Agricultural History* 72 (Spring 1998): 399–416.

Grubbs, Donald H. *Cry from the Cotton: The Southern Tenant Farmers' Union and the New Deal.* Chapel Hill: University of North Carolina Press, 1971.

Hahn, Steven. *A Nation under Our Feet: Black Political Struggles in the Rural South from Slavery to the Great Migration.* Cambridge, Mass.: Belknap Press of Harvard University Press, 2003.

Hall, Jacquelyn Dowd. "The Long Civil Rights Movement and the Political Uses of the Past." *Journal of American History* 91 (March 2005): 1233–63.

Harvey, Paul. *Freedom's Coming: Religious Culture and the Shaping of the South from the Civil War through the Civil Rights Era.* Chapel Hill: University of North Carolina Press, 2005.

———. *Redeeming the South: Religious Cultures and Racial Identities among Southern Baptists, 1865–1925.* Chapel Hill: University of North Carolina Press, 1997.

Hill, Samuel S., ed. *Encyclopedia of Religion in the South.* Macon, Ga.: Mercer University Press, 1984.

"History of Bethel College." Bethel College. Available at http://www.bethel-college.edu/quick/visitor/menu/history (accessed June 2009).

"History of Moody Bible Institute." The Moody Bible Institute. Available at http://www.moodyministries.net/crp_MainPage.aspx?id=62 (accessed June 2009).

Honey, Michael K. *Southern Labor and Black Civil Rights: Organizing Memphis Workers.* Urbana: University of Illinois Press, 1993.

Jeansonne, Glen. *Gerald L. K. Smith: Minister of Hate.* Baton Rouge: Louisiana State University Press, 1988.

Jones, Jacqueline. *Labor of Love, Labor of Sorrow: Black Women, Work, and the Family, from Slavery to Present.* 1985. Repr., New York: Vintage, 1995.

Jones, Will P. *The Tribe of Black Ulysses: African American Lumber Workers in the Jim Crow South.* Urbana: University of Illinois Press, 2005.

Kelley, Robin D. G. *Hammer and Hoe: Alabama Communists during the Great Depression.* Chapel Hill: University of North Carolina Press, 1990.

Klein, Joe. *Woody Guthrie: A Life.* New York: Knopf, 1980.

Kloppenberg, James T. *Uncertain Victory: Social Democracy and Progressivism in European and American Thought, 1870–1920.* New York: Oxford University Press, 1986.

Koppelman, Robert, ed. *Sing Out, Warning! Sing Out, Love! The Writings of Lee Hays.* Amherst: University of Massachusetts Press, 2003.

Korstad, Robert Rodgers. *Civil Rights Unionism: Tobacco Workers and the Struggle for Democracy in the Mid-Twentieth-Century South.* Chapel Hill: University of North Carolina Press, 2003.

Lang, Clarence. *Grassroots at the Gateway: Class Politics and Black Freedom Struggle in St. Louis, 1936–75.* Ann Arbor: University of Michigan Press, 2009.

Lester, Connie L. *Up from the Mudsills of Hell: The Farmers' Alliance, Populism, and Progressive Agriculture in Tennessee, 1870–1915.* Athens: University Georgia Press, 2006.

Lieberman, Robbie. *"My Song Is My Weapon": People's Songs, American Communism, and the Politics of Culture, 1930–1950.* Urbana: University of Illinois Press. 1989.

Lipsitz, George. *Rainbow at Midnight: Labor and Culture in the 1940s.* Urbana: University of Illinois Press, 1994.

Litwack, Leon F. *Trouble in Mind: Black Southerners in the Age of Jim Crow.* New York: Vintage, 1998.

Lorence, James J. *A Hard Journey: The Life of Don West.* Urbana: University of Illinois Press, 2007.

Martin, Robert F. *Howard Kester and the Struggle for Social Justice in the South, 1904–1977.* Charlottesville: University Press of Virginia, 1991.

McMillen, Neil R. *Dark Journey: Black Mississippians in the Age of Jim Crow.* Urbana: University of Illinois Press, 1990.

Meier, August and Elliott Rudwick. *Black Detroit and the Rise of the UAW.* New York: Oxford University Press, 1979.

Mertz, Paul E. *New Deal Policy and Southern Rural Poverty.* Baton Rouge: Louisiana State University Press, 1978.

Morrow, Hubert W. "Cumberland Presbyterian Theology: A Nineteenth Century Development in American Presbyterianism." *Journal of Presbyterian History* 48 (1970): 203–20.

Naison, Mark. "Black Agrarian Radicalism in the Great Depression: The Threads of a Lost Tradition." *Journal of Ethnic Studies* 1 (Fall 1973): 47–65.

———. "Claude and Joyce Williams: Pilgrims of Justice." *Southern Exposure* 1 (1974): 38–50.

———. "Claude Williams Talks about Owen Whitfield." *Radical Religion* 4 (1978): 24–26.

Northrup, Herbert. *Organized Labor and the Negro.* New York: Harper & Brothers, 1944.

Ogilvie, Leon P. "The Development of the Southeast Missouri Lowlands." PhD diss., University of Missouri–Columbia, 1967.

Payne, Charles M. *I've Got the Light of Freedom: The Organizing Tradition and the Mississippi Freedom Struggle.* Berkeley: University of California Press, 1995.

Phillips, Kimberley L. *AlabamaNorth: African-American Migrants, Community, and Working-Class Activism in Cleveland, 1915–1945.* Urbana: University of Illinois Press, 1999.

Pinn, Anthony B. *Why, Lord? Suffering and Evil in Black Theology.* New York: Continuum, 1995.

Reed, Roy. "Orval E. Faubus: Out of Socialism into Realism." *Arkansas Historical Quarterly* 54 (Spring 1995): 13–29.

Ritterhouse, Jennifer. *Growing Up Jim Crow: How Black and White Southern Children Learned Race.* Chapel Hill: University of North Carolina Press, 2006.

Rolinson, Mary G. *Grassroots Garveyism: The Universal Negro Improvement Association in the Rural South, 1920–1927.* Chapel Hill: University of North Carolina Press, 2007.

Roll, Jarod. *Spirit of Rebellion: Labor and Religion in the New Cotton South.* Urbana: University of Illinois Press, 2010.

Rosengarten, Theodore. *All God's Dangers: The Life of Nate Shaw.* New York: Knopf, 1974.

Rosswurm, Steven, ed. *The CIO's Left-Led Unions.* New Brunswick, N.J.: Rutgers University Press, 1992.

Schrecker, Ellen. *The Age of McCarthyism: A Brief History with Documents.* New York: Bedford/St. Martin's, 2002.

Schultz, Mark. *The Rural Face of White Supremacy: Beyond Jim Crow.* Urbana: University of Illinois Press, 2005.

Schweninger, Loren. *Black Property Owners in the South, 1790–1915.* Urbana: University of Illinois Press, 1990.

Sitton, Thad, and James H. Conrad. *Freedom Colonies: Independent Black Texans in the Time of Jim Crow.* Austin: University of Texas Press, 2005.

Spencer, Robyn. "Contested Terrain: The Mississippi Flood of 1927 and the Struggle to Control Black Labor." *Journal of Negro History* 79 (Spring 1994): 170–81.

Stepenoff, Bonnie. *Thad Snow: A Life of Social Reform in the Missouri Bootheel.* Columbia: University of Missouri Press, 2003.

Stolberg, Mary. *Bridging the River of Hatred: The Pioneering Efforts of Detroit Police Commissioner George Edwards.* Detroit: Wayne State University Press, 1998.

Striffler, Steve, and Mark Moberg, eds. *Banana Wars: Power, Production, and History in the Americas.* Durham: Duke University Press, 2003.

Sugrue, Thomas J. *The Origins of the Urban Crisis: Race and Inequality in Postwar Detroit.* Princeton: Princeton University Press, 1996.

Sullivan, Patricia. *Days of Hope: Race and Democracy in the New Deal Era.* Chapel Hill: University of North Carolina Press, 1996.

Thompson, Heather Ann. *Whose Detroit? Politics, Labor, and Race in a Modern American City.* Ithaca: Cornell University Press, 2001.

Tindall, George Brown. *The Emergence of the New South, 1913–1945.* Baton Rouge: Louisiana State University Press, 1967.

Troy, Bill, with Claude Williams. "People's Institute of Applied Religion." *Southern Exposure* 4 (1976): 49–58.

Tull, C. J. *Father Coughlin and the New Deal.* Syracuse: Syracuse University Press, 1965.

Tyson, Timothy B. "Robert F. Williams and the Promise of Southern Biography." *Southern Cultures* 8 (2002): 38–55.

Vanderwood, Paul. *Night Riders of Reelfoot Lake.* Memphis: Memphis State University Press, 1969.

Waldrep, Christopher. *Night Riders: Defending Community in the Black Patch, 1890–1915.* Durham: Duke University Press, 1993.

Willens, Doris. *Lonesome Traveler: The Life of Lee Hays.* Lincoln: University of Nebraska Press, 1988.

Wilmore, Gayraud S. *Black Religion and Black Radicalism: An Interpretation of the Religious History of African Americans.* 1973. 3rd ed., New York: Orbis Books, 1998.

Wilson, Charles H. *Education for Negroes in Mississippi since 1910.* Boston: Meador, 1947.

Wilson, John B. *Maneuver and Firepower: The Evolution of Divisions and Separate Brigades.* Washington, D.C.: Center of Military History, U.S. Army, 1998.

Woodruff, Nan E. "African American Struggles for Citizenship in the Arkansas and Mississippi Deltas in the Age of Jim Crow." *Radical History Review* 55 (1993): 33–52.

———. *American Congo: The African American Freedom Struggle in the Delta.* Cambridge, Mass.: Harvard University Press, 2003.

Woodward, C. Vann. *Origins of the New South, 1877–1913.* Baton Rouge: Louisiana State University Press, 1951.

Wright, Gavin. *Old South, New South: Revolutions in the Southern Economy since the Civil War.* New York: Basic Books, 1986.

Zieger, Robert H. *The CIO, 1935–1955.* Chapel Hill: University of North Carolina Press, 1995.

Index

ERIK S. GELLMAN is an assistant professor of history at Roosevelt University in Chicago. He is the author of *Death Blow to Jim Crow: The National Negro Congress and Militant Civil Rights*.

JAROD ROLL teaches American history at the University of Sussex, England, where he directs the Marcus Cunliffe Centre for the Study of the American South. He is the author of the award-winning *Spirit of Rebellion: Labor and Religion in the New Cotton South*.

The Working Class in American History

German Workers in Chicago: A Documentary History of Working-Class Culture from 1850 to World War I   *Edited by Hartmut Keil and John B. Jentz*

On the Line: Essays in the History of Auto Work   *Edited by Nelson Lichtenstein and Stephen Meyer III*

Labor's Flaming Youth: Telephone Operators and Worker Militancy, 1878–1923   *Stephen H. Norwood*

Another Civil War: Labor, Capital, and the State in the Anthracite Regions of Pennsylvania, 1840–68   *Grace Palladino*

Coal, Class, and Color: Blacks in Southern West Virginia, 1915–32   *Joe William Trotter Jr.*

For Democracy, Workers, and God: Labor Song-Poems and Labor Protest, 1865–95   *Clark D. Halker*

Dishing It Out: Waitresses and Their Unions in the Twentieth Century   *Dorothy Sue Cobble*

The Spirit of 1848: German Immigrants, Labor Conflict, and the Coming of the Civil War   *Bruce Levine*

Working Women of Collar City: Gender, Class, and Community in Troy, New York, 1864–86   *Carole Turbin*

Southern Labor and Black Civil Rights: Organizing Memphis Workers   *Michael K. Honey*

Radicals of the Worst Sort: Laboring Women in Lawrence, Massachusetts, 1860–1912   *Ardis Cameron*

Producers, Proletarians, and Politicians: Workers and Party Politics in Evansville and New Albany, Indiana, 1850–87   *Lawrence M. Lipin*

The New Left and Labor in the 1960s   *Peter B. Levy*

The Making of Western Labor Radicalism: Denver's Organized Workers, 1878–1905   *David Brundage*

In Search of the Working Class: Essays in American Labor History and Political Culture   *Leon Fink*

Lawyers against Labor: From Individual Rights to Corporate Liberalism   *Daniel R. Ernst*

"We Are All Leaders": The Alternative Unionism of the Early 1930s   *Edited by Staughton Lynd*

The Female Economy: The Millinery and Dressmaking Trades, 1860–1930   *Wendy Gamber*

"Negro and White, Unite and Fight!": A Social History of Industrial Unionism in Meatpacking, 1930–90   *Roger Horowitz*

Power at Odds: The 1922 National Railroad Shopmen's Strike   *Colin J. Davis*

The Common Ground of Womanhood: Class, Gender, and Working Girls' Clubs, 1884–1928   *Priscilla Murolo*

Marching Together: Women of the Brotherhood of Sleeping Car Porters   *Melinda Chateauvert*

Down on the Killing Floor: Black and White Workers in Chicago's Packinghouses, 1904–54   *Rick Halpern*

Labor and Urban Politics: Class Conflict and the Origins of Modern Liberalism in Chicago, 1864–97   *Richard Schneirov*

The University of Illinois Press
is a founding member of the
Association of American University Presses.

Composed in 10.5/13 Adobe Minion Pro
at the University of Illinois Press
Manufactured by Sheridan Books, Inc.

University of Illinois Press
1325 South Oak Street
Champaign, IL 61820-6903
www.press.uillinois.edu